Silent Screams
The History of the Silent Horror Film

Silent Screams

The History
of the
Silent Horror Film

by Steve Haberman

Midnight Marquee Press, Inc.
Baltimore, Maryland

Copyright © 2003 Steve Haberman
Cover Design/Layout Design: Susan Svehla

Without limiting the rights under copyright reserved above, no part of this publication may be reproduced, stored in or introduced into a retrieval system, or transmitted, in any form, or by any means (electronic, mechanical, photocopying, recording or otherwise), without the prior written permission of the copyright owners or the publishers of the book.

ISBN 978-1-936168-15-6
Library of Congress Catalog Card Number 2010939478
Manufactured in the United States of America
Printed by Sheridan Books, Fredericksburg, VA
First Printing by Luminary Press, an imprint of Midnight Marquee Press, Inc., March 2003
Revised Printing by Midnight Marquee Press, Inc., October, 2010

*For my darling
Julia,
who inspired
and then
distracted me*

CONTENTS

8	Introduction: The Conqueror Worm
13	Chapter 1: Seeds of Terror
32	Chapter 2: The Dark German Soul
84	Chapter 3: European Evil
100	Chapter 4: America the Hideous
118	Chapter 5: Genius of the Grotesque
156	Chapter 6: The Weirdest Show on Earth
185	Chapter 7: The Silent Roar
196	Chapter 8: Old Dark Houses
225	Afterword
229	Select Bibliography
232	Index

INTRODUCTION
THE CONQUEROR WORM

Lo! 'tis a gala night
Within the lonesome latter years!
An angel throng, bewinged, bedight
In veils, and drowned in tears,
Sit in a theatre, to see
A play of hopes and fears,
While the orchestra breathes fitfully
The music of the spheres.

Mimes, in the form of God on high,
Mutter and mumble low,
And hither and thither fly;
Mere puppets they, who come and go
At bidding of vast formless things
That shift the scenery to and fro,
Flapping from out their condor wings
Invisible woe!

That motley drama!—oh, be sure
It shall not be forgot!
With its Phantom chased for evermore,
By a crowd that seize it not,
Through a circle that ever returneth in
To the self-same spot;
And much of Madness, and more of Sin
And Horror, the soul of the plot!

But see, amid the mimic rout
A crawling shape intrude!
A blood-red thing that writhes from out
The scenic solitude!
It writhes!—it writhes!—with mortal pangs
The mimes become its food,
And seraphs sob at vermin fangs
In human gore imbued.

Out—out are the lights—out all!
And over each quivering form,
The curtain, a funeral pall,
Comes down with the rush of a storm—
And the angels, all pallid and wan,
Uprising, unveiling, affirm
That the play is the tragedy, "Man,"
And its hero, the conqueror Worm.

This poem, "The Conqueror Worm," was written in 1843 by Edgar Allan Poe and was included in his short story "Ligeia." It concerns the greatest horror facing man; the basis of all other terrors; the one inescapable reality which overshadows every human hope and endeavor: death. All artistic efforts in the horror genre, whether in film, literature, music or the visual arts, are an attempt to come to terms with this frightening inevitability: they are all efforts to put a face on Death.

The creators of horror entertainment encourage their audience to regard death from a perspective of safety and thereby make sense of it. The power of the genre derives from the fact that, no matter how we confront death, we *cannot* make sense of it. The permanent cessation of our existence is irrational and arbitrary in a life that we want to believe is rational and meaningful. The subliminal realization of this in film, whether through the careful creation of a foreboding mood, through the anticipation of the death of a character, or through the brutal depiction of that death, is the basis of the neverending value and fascination of the horror movie.

Through cinema, artists approach the subject of death from many different perspectives. The least comforting, of course, is from that of victim. Forcing the audience to identify or at least sympathize with a character, and then putting that character in impending danger of violent demise has been a strategy for creating fear in films as far back as *The Cabinet of Dr. Caligari* in 1919.

Midway through the movie, the audience watches, helpless, as a homicidal madman silently breaks into the bedroom of an innocently sleeping young woman. Like riders on a roller coaster slowly ascending to the first steep drop, the spectator safely anticipates violent disaster. The killer steps closer and closer to his unsuspecting victim. The audience both identifies and objectifies the young woman. We cannot help but imagine ourselves in her place, soon to be rudely awakened from a repose we all experience. At the same time, her plight is too terrible to share, and we remove ourselves and watch the genre ceremony play itself out as a work of art. This same potent conflict of emotions has effectively moved audiences from *Caligari* to *Frankenstein* and from *The Birds* to *Silence of the Lambs*.

The opposite fascination of the genre is the ability it affords to sympathize with characters who can ruthlessly pursue their goals, however morally reprehensible. Horror movies often encourage the guilty pleasure of identifying with those who attempt to take what they desire and destroy what they hate without conscience. How else to explain the popularity of the horror star—from Lon Chaney to Boris Karloff and from Bela Lugosi to Vincent Price? These actors often allow us to vicariously experience demented aspirations of dizzying heights and murderous hatreds of ugly depths. Chaney in *The Phantom of the Opera*, Karloff in *The Mummy*, Lugosi in *The Raven* and Price in *House of Wax* are insane megalomaniacs whose sufferings we understand even as we thrill to their mad, brave pursuits of love, glory and revenge.

Implicit in much horror fiction is an alternate reality: a world not governed merely by the Darwinian socio-economic paradigms of our society, but by absolutes of Good and

Evil or Sanity and Insanity. Sometimes those worlds take on physical dimensions as in the Expressionistic sets, costumes and makeups of Robert Wiene's *The Cabinet of Dr. Caligari*, in the clean-lined and uncluttered Bauhaus rooms of Edgar G. Ulmer's *The Black Cat*, or in the gray, misty, perpetually dusk-lit fairy tale cottages of Tim Burton's *Sleepy Hollow*.

More often, these alternate realities, while taking place in recognizably naturalistic environments, include laws endowing supernatural powers and weaknesses to various evil creatures. The rules governing the existence of vampires and werewolves have been repeated so often that most viewers know them before the films begin. The laws of Satanic power on earth in movies such as *Curse of the Demon*, *The Devil Rides Out* and *The Craft* are more arcane, but no less imaginative or compelling.

The appeals of these values in art are very similar to their appeals in religion: they allow us to escape from the pressure and repetition of economic, social and sexual struggle to enter a world of direct moral conflict. Values are clear, stakes are high and the problems are resolved in two hours.

The separation of sanity and insanity in horror movies often mirrors the gulf between absolute Good and Evil. The extravagant dementia of the madmen in *The Phantom of the Opera*, *The Mystery of the Wax Museum*, *Halloween* and *Seven*, to name only a few, have but a nodding acquaintance with possible medical case studies. These maniacs bear more resemblance to mythical monsters in that they operate with evil but consistent personal motives, and they have powers and weaknesses unique to their kind. Even madmen based on actual models, such as the characters inspired by real-life lunatic Ed Gein in *Psycho* and *The Texas Chain Saw Massacre*, cannot be mistaken for their real criminal counterpart. Although their touches of humanity often make our responses morally ambiguous, these crazies ultimately represent evil as clearly as the monsters in supernaturally inspired stories.

Much of the power of horror movies derives from the fact that both metaphysical evil and murderous insanity are correlatives for the chaotic disruption of order we all fear in our lives. An added turn of the screw is provided by the implication that we may have brought the chaos on ourselves: Dracula exploits his victims' own sexual lusts to seduce them of their blood; Frankenstein's Monster takes vengeance for his creator's lack of responsibility for his creation; Mr. Hyde is the physical manifestation of hypocrite Dr. Jekyll's secret desires. The deadly giant insects and prehistoric creatures running rampant in the cinema of the 1950s are results of the testing of manmade Atomic weapons. And the murderous lunatics spawned by the success of *Psycho* are homegrown monsters fed on emotional abuse from their dysfunctional parents. The cinema of terror frightens us to wake us from the complacency of our sins. If the ultimate horror is death, then the horror movie is often telling us, in the words of Stephen Sondheim's *Sweeney Todd*: "We all deserve to die!"

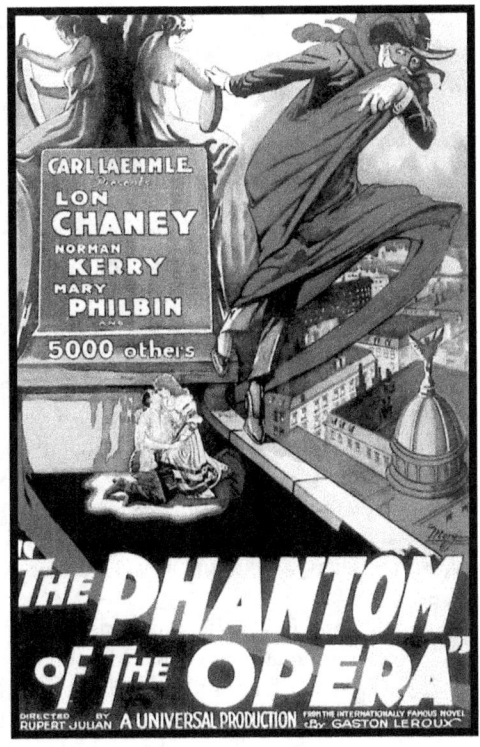

But first, as in life, we must suffer. All sense of security must be stripped away. As in Poe's short story, "The Pit and the Pendulum," the horror movie runs through a full range of phobias so that its protagonists and, by extension, the audience must confront their every fear.

Depending on the philosophy of the filmmaker, this intense terror can be a therapeutic or a disastrous experience for the protagonist. In Roger Corman's darkly pessimistic world view, Guy Correl, played by Ray Milland in *The Premature Burial*, must directly confront his obsessive phobia of the title inconvenience. The experience drives him mad, and he becomes a murdering, vengeful monster. In Steven Spielberg's much more benign vision of life, Sheriff Brody, played by Roy Scheider in *Jaws*, conquers his neurotic fear of the ocean by surviving a one-on-one battle with a giant shark in the open sea.

As the 20th century progresses and death becomes understandable as a bodily malfunction after disease, some filmmakers take the death metaphor to a clinical extreme. Like victims of a lingering illness, their protagonists are stripped of the normal workings of their bodies. The somatic systems of David Cronenberg's heroes in *Shivers*, *Rabid*, *The Brood*, *Scanners*, *Videodrome* and *The Fly* turn on them, manifesting cancers, unnatural appendages and orifices, or simply falling apart. In Ridley Scott's *Alien*, John Hurt's body is a battleground between his own system and an insect-like parasite. The Alien becomes the horror movie equivalent of a growing cancer or virus that eventually erupts from the host and seeks other flesh to devour.

Conversely, the body is the only survivor of vampirism. The spawn of Dracula has become a shell without a soul, "possessed and corrupted" in the words of Dr. Van Helsing in *Horror of Dracula*. When our free thoughts depart, our identity is dead, even if our bodies continue moving. This same terror of loss of personality propels Don Siegel's 1956 science fiction classic, *The Invasion of the Body Snatchers*. The horror is compounded when the victims are aware of the possession and fight for their identities as in *The Wolf Man* or *The Exorcist*.

Less symbolic are the deaths of personality through psychological trauma such as in the cases of Norman Bates in Alfred Hitchcock's *Psycho* and Nicholas Medina in Roger Corman's *Pit and the Pendulum*. These characters also suffer from possession by evil outside forces, not unlike their supernatural and science fiction counterparts. But it is their dead parents who consume their personalities without the trappings of mythology. As in real life, the dead can reach out for the living, even if not literally.

So, does the horror film offer only fear and no hope? Similar to religion, the cinema of terror often conjures the most potent images of destruction and damnation for the purpose of reinforcing our faith in the positive beliefs. For example, the Hammer films of Terence Fisher offer figures of light almost as powerful as the demons of darkness. Dr. Van Helsing in *Horror of Dracula* and *Brides of Dracula* and the Duc de Richelieu in *The Devil Rides Out* combat their evil challengers with encyclopedic knowledge, physical strength and unwavering faith in the Christian God. And despite the supernatural powers of their adversaries, these savants prevail. It is up to the individual viewer to decide whether evil has been defeated through the power of Christ or whether the audience has merely been reassured. There is no doubt as to Fisher's sincerity, however. He states:

> Again, I think it's a truism of experience that we will find, in the end, the ultimate, inevitable triumph of good over evil. Because, of course, we shall find in the end that evil is merely a mistaken concept for the absence of good. You see, there aren't two powers. There's only one. The power of evil is what we give to it.

Likewise, in the majority of films that pit rationality against a destructive force, whether from space, from Atomic mutation or from the twisted thoughts of another human being, the forces of order prevail. Science and the military ultimately defeat *The Thing*, *The Beast From 20,000 Fathoms*, *Them!*, *Godzilla* and *The Invasion of the Body Snatchers* through cooperation, planning and hard work. And in the end, even as hopeless and impenetrable a madness as that experienced by Catherine Deneuve's character, Carol, in Roman Polanski's *Repulsion*, is neutralized for society through its eventual discovery. We are even given a hint as to the cause of her sad and self-destructive mania, rendering it more rational and less shockingly unpredictable.

Since the following history is full of horrors uncountable in their multitude, the last words of the introduction are those of desperate hope. They come from the end of Richard Matheson's screenplay for Jack Arnold's 1957 classic, *The Incredible Shrinking Man*. The plight of the title character is another metaphor for slowly encroaching death. In the face of his eventual non-existence through continual shrinkage, the character of Scott Carey, played by Grant Williams, speaks these lines, more in epiphany than defiance:

> That existence begins and ends is Man's conception, not nature's. And I felt my body dwindling, melting, becoming nothing. My fears melted away, and in their place came acceptance. All this vast majesty of creation, it had to mean something. And then I meant something, too. To God there is no zero. I still exist!

CHAPTER 1
SEEDS OF TERROR

Although bound together by the genre label, horror movies, films that explore the dark side of myth and nature often resist systematic classification. As an artistic medium, film speaks in the voices of its creators, a diverse and disorganized lot. For the most part, great filmmakers, like great writers, follow no formula. More often, they create artistic blueprints that lesser talents attempt to copy to reap the same financial rewards. In a commercial genre like the horror film, this paradigm is repeated constantly. Sometimes, if blessed by the participation of the right talent, the cynically conceived imitations transcend their origins to achieve stature of their own. Thus, the genre inspires itself, growing in surprising directions from the same seeds.

In the case of terror cinema, those seeds were planted by literary writers of the 19th century. The first real horror movies were crude adaptations of Robert Louis Stevenson's *Dr. Jekyll and Mr. Hyde* in 1908, Arthur Conan Doyle's *Hound of the Baskervilles* in 1909, Mary Shelley's *Frankenstein* in 1910 and Edgar Allan Poe's "The System of Dr. Tarr and Professor Feather" in 1912.

Each film lasted about 15 minutes. They were designed in the one-shot-per-scene, stage-bound technique that existed before D.W. Griffith pioneered the use of close-ups and inserts. In other words, each scene was a full shot showing the entire set and the head-to-toe figures of the actors within it. Only when the script required a change of location was there a change of shot. Since the stories had to be told in a short period of time with a small number of sets in the broadest sort of silent pantomime, the limitations for interpretation were profound.

The famous trick films from the French magician Georges Méliès and his imitators preceded *Dr. Jekyll and Mr. Hyde*, but they were designed to amuse and mystify rather than frighten. Despite pioneering crude special effects, the films of Méliès represented a charming dead end in the history of cinema. Born in 1861, Méliès perceived film as an extension and elaboration of his stage illusions. From 1896 to 1912, he produced, directed, designed and occasionally starred in 498 shorts that ran anywhere from two minutes to a half-hour in length. Many featured benign representations of death and evil such as skeletons, witches and the Devil, but these characters served merely as props for simple film illusions. Méliès never allowed them to invade his public's reality or threaten their imaginations. The delightful painted backdrops and exaggerated costumes and makeups insured that the cinemagoers never took Melies' fairy tale grotesques seriously.

On the other hand, the first movie version of Robert Louis Stevenson's 1885 novella, *The Strange Case of Dr. Jekyll and Mr. Hyde*, took itself quite seriously indeed. As an indication of its impact on early filmmakers and audiences, by 1920 the famous story was filmed no less than seven times under its own title as well as under different titles in several unauthorized versions. In fact, only two years after publication of the novel, 30-year-old matinee stage idol Richard Mansfield commissioned Thomas Russell Sullivan to adapt it for the first time for the stage. American audiences gasped and screamed as Mansfield shrank into a hideous dwarf before their eyes. The great actor-manager toured with the play for 20 years.

Sullivan's dramatization first opened in Boston on May 9, 1887 and in New York a week later, then toured the United States to packed houses until June 25, 1888. It arrived in London at Henry Irving's Lyceum Theater on August 4, 1888 just in time to coincide with the actual brutal slayings of prostitutes in Whitechapel by Jack the Ripper. Because of the terrifying ferocity of his portrayal of Mr. Hyde, Mansfied even had the distinction of being briefly suspected of the hideous crimes.

Mansfield was pressured into closing in October 1888 after a 10-week run because newspaper editorials blamed the existence of the Ripper on crime novels and theatrical melodramas. The *Daily Telegraph* reported: "Experience has taught this clever young actor that there is no taste in London just now for horrors on the stage. There is quite sufficient to make us shudder out of doors." Even in the relatively media-light 19th century, moralists and civic authorities found it more convenient to blame criminal behavior on human art rather than the human heart. Perhaps it was because the Victorians, like us, felt that they could control art, and evil was not only beyond their control, but beyond their understanding.

On this trip to England, Sullivan nervously read his adaptation aloud to a skeptical Robert Louis Stevenson. According to Sullivan, Stevenson professed: "I might not have liked it, you know. But I do like it, all through." About the transformation scene that takes place before the eyes of the audience at the end of the third act, he said, "Good. You have done precisely what that scene needed for stage effect. It is very strong." He then added that "Mrs. Stevenson liked it" when she saw it on stage in New York the previous year.

Later, when a review came out calling the adaptation "ugly," Stevenson reconsidered his opinion. "Hyde was the younger of the two," he wrote; not the other way around as it appeared in the play. Jekyll was not a "good-looking" and saintly man. And Mr. Hyde was not "a mere voluptuary" who was jealous of Dr. Jekyll's attractiveness to a female character who did not even appear in the novella. This change gave Mr. Hyde a personal motive for his, in the book, senseless, murder of Sir Danvers Carew. None of this coincided with Stevenson's original intentions. Stevenson angrily wrote to the drama critic:

> The harm was in Jekyll, because he was a hypocrite—not because he was fond of women; he says so himself; but people are so filled full of folly and inverted lust, that they can think of nothing but sexuality. The Hypocrite let out the beast Hyde—who is no more sexual than another, but who is the essence of cruelty and malice and selfishness and cowardice; and these are the diabolic in man—not this great wish to have a woman, that they make such a cry about...

But sex sells. Every major cinematic adaptation of *Dr. Jekyll and Mr. Hyde* since 1908 has included the changes initiated in Sullivan's play. Sullivan interpreted Hyde as the embodiment of Jekyll's repressed desires, especially sexual. Mansfield, the original interpreter of the role, described Mr. Hyde as "unable by reason of his hideous shape to indulge the dreams of his hideous imagination."

A more concentrated, less literary, even more sensational version of the play was written by Luella Forepaugh and George F. Fish in 1897. When it reached Chicago in 1908, a year after Mansfield's death, Colonel William N. Selig, proprietor of the Selig Polyscope Company, sat in the audience. For the rest of the week, the actors spent their daylight hours in Selig's studio enacting a 16-minute reduction of the play. And the American horror film was born. To preserve the "prestige" of a theatrical presentation, the curtain rose and fell at the beginning of each act.

The movie is divided into four parts. The curtain rises on the stage set of a garden behind a small church. Dr. Jekyll's fiancee, Alice Carew, waits for the good Doctor to join her. Just as Dr. Jekyll approaches, however, he transforms into the ferocious Mr. Hyde.

For this first transformation to Hyde in film history, Selig filmed the actor without cuts or dissolves as he followed the instructions in the play by Forepaugh and Fish:

> Dr. Jekyll writhes as though in physical pain; assumes crouching position; during this with one hand he pulls portion of the wig which is brought forward and falls in a tangled mass over his forehead and eyes.

Hyde attacks Alice, obviously with but one thing on his mind. Her father, the Vicar, rushes to defend Alice, but he is no match for this beast. Hyde murders the old man "with fiendish glee and demon strength," as the publicity material puts it. The creature flees, leaving Alice weeping over the broken body of her father. Jekyll soon arrives to comfort her.

Act II takes place in the office of Mr. Utterson, lawyer of Chancery Lane. Dr. Jekyll visits him to tell his secret, but instead suffers a vision of the gallows, a noose around his own neck.

Act III is set in the office of Jekyll's friend, Dr. Lanyon. Mr. Hyde arrives at midnight to procure some drugs Dr. Jekyll requested. The monster mixes a potion, drinks it and turns into Jekyll before the astonished gaze of his friend.

In the final act, Alice visits her remorseful fiance in his laboratory. He promises to see her the next day. But after she leaves, he again takes the drug and turns into Mr. Hyde. As Hyde, he poisons himself to kill the good Jekyll whom he hates. Curtain down.

The reviews of the time were unqualified raves. *The Moving Picture World* said: "The successful reproduction of this well-known drama has surpassed our expectation..." Of Thomas E. Shea, who produced and starred in the 1897 road company as well as starring, unbilled, in Selig's movie, *The Moving Picture World* described his performance as "so convincing that no greater display of ability to fulfill this role could be shown by any actor."

Like most casual observers, Selig confused the play by Forepaugh and Fish with the original novella. He proudly described his film as:

> Presented in strict accordance with the original book, as to scenery, costumes and dramatic cast, involving each detail of pose, gesture and expression. Pictured from the dramatization executed by persons of indisputed dramatic ability.

By filming the stage production instead of adapting Stevenson's work, this first version indicated the direction every subsequent cinematic retelling would take. Despite Stevenson's protests, this was the model for the most notable Mr. Hydes, from John Barrymore in 1920 to Fredric March in 1932 to Spencer Tracy in 1941. As he became for Dr. Jekyll, Mr. Hyde was out of Stevenson's control.

Sometimes, the limitations of pioneer filmmaking forced some interesting decisions in storytelling. For example, in the 1909 Danish company, Nordisk's, interpretation of *Hound of the Baskervilles*, called *Den Graa Dame* or *The Grey Lady*, both the misty moors and the monster hound itself were beyond the capabilities of the production. The story was rewritten by director and star Viggo Larsen to take place in interior sets with the specter of a woman in gray replacing the ghostly canine.

The legend tells that anyone seeing the ghost of the woman, like the hound of the novel, will die. Sherlock Holmes, played by Larsen himself, investigates. He discovers

We'll never know what was happening in this scene from the Sherlock Holmes film *The Grey Lady* starring Viggo Larsen.

that the woman in gray is actually a rich patriarch's nephew who dons the costume of the ghost in order to frighten to death the weak-hearted relatives who stand in the way of his inheritance. In place of the dark moors and mires, the film offers secret rooms and passageways.

This was the sixth and last in a series of Nordisk shorts about Sherlock Holmes starring Viggo Larson. Like thousands of early films printed on flammable and unstable nitrate stock, including Selig's *Dr. Jekyll and Mr. Hyde*, it has been lost. By all accounts, however, the appearances of the ghostly woman were quite frightening to contemporary audiences, making up for the absence of the vicious hound.

No longer lost is James Searle Dawley's 1910 American production of *Frankenstein* for the Edison Kinetoscope Company. Mary Shelley's 1816 novel was considered a classic by 1910 with nine different editions appearing in print since 1890. Obviously knowing what they were attempting, press writers for the Edison version stated, "As a story that reaches the climax of horror and awful suggestion, this work stands alone."

Of course, many plot and character points from the original novel had to be changed or eliminated because of time and production constraints. According to the Edison Company's "DRAMATIC #287 SYNOPSIS," the filmmakers felt their "liberal adaptation of Mrs. Shelley's famous story" caused the effort to "concentrate its endeavors upon the mystic and psychological problems."

The film consists of 25 separate shots, each tinted a color such as blue for night, amber for day or red for fire. Victor Frankenstein is played by Augustus Phillips, a colleague of director Dawley's from their stock company days.

Victor Frankenstein, a young medical student, says goodbye to his sweetheart and father as he goes off to school. At university, Frankenstein becomes obsessed with the idea of creating life, surrounding his study with the skulls and skeletons of animals and humans.

One evening, two years after his arrival, Frankenstein writes a letter to his sweetheart, telling her that tonight he will create "the most perfect human being that the world has yet known," then "return to claim you for my bride." He dashes some chemicals into a cauldron. Smoke instantly rises and Frankenstein retreats from the creation room, slamming massive doors shut and bolting them with a beam of wood. He watches through a small window in the door as a pile of ashes rises from the smoking cauldron.

The creation scene was accomplished, crudely but quite effectively, by burning a *papier mâché* dummy of the monster, then printing the shot in reverse so that the creature seemed to materialize from the burning ashes. The arms of the dummy wave about in the air, frantically, giving it an animated appearance. With the red tint overall and the intercuts of Frankenstein watching, striding about anxiously and gesticulating wildly, this scene was

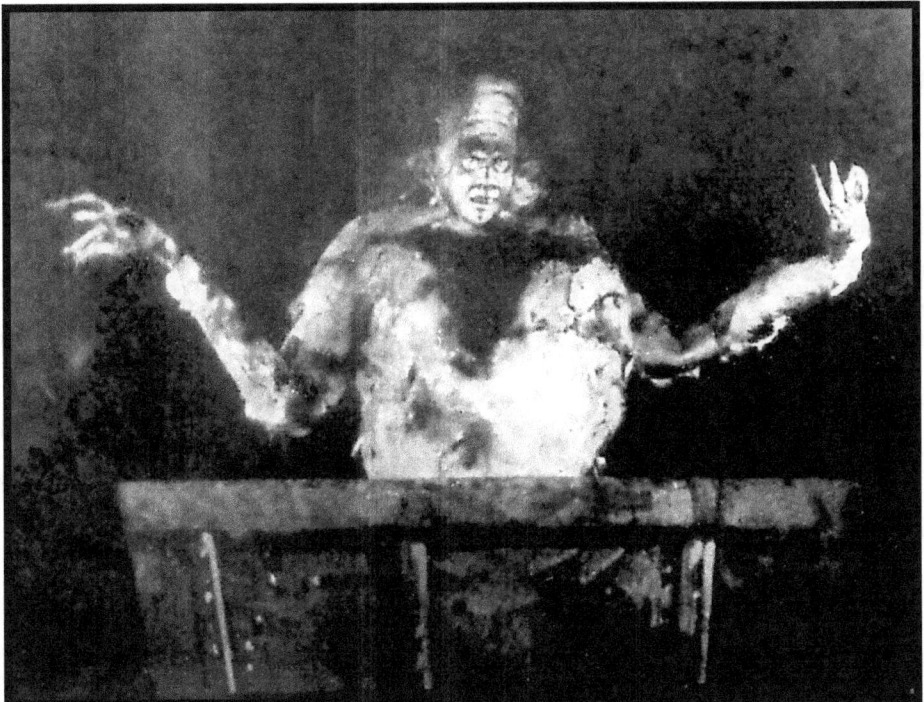

In the 1910 *Frankenstein*, the creation scene was accomplished, crudely but quite effectively, by burning a *papier mâché* dummy of the Monster, then printing the shot in reverse.

undoubtedly awe-inspiring to early filmgoers. Especially disturbing must have been the climax of the scene with the monster's hand bursting forth from between the massive doors, its strength capable of splitting the wooden beam locking it in.

The Monster is played by Charles Ogle, a lawyer turned actor who had entered motion pictures the previous year. His self-created makeup is quite startling with a hunched back, furry chest and hands, a head full of wildly tangled hair, and, anticipating Jack Pierce's famous design for Boris Karloff 21 years later, a high, flat forehead. Ogle's most famous role would be as Long John Silver in Maurice Tourneur's 1920 version of *Treasure Island*, which also featured Lon Chaney as Blind Pew. Ogle died in 1940, without even an obituary in *Variety*.

Frankenstein runs from the lab and throws himself on his bed. The Monster appears at his bedside, smiling hideously at him, and Frankenstein faints.

Frankenstein journeys home to the care of his father and sweetheart. Soon, his strength returns and he prepares for his wedding. But one night, he sees the Monster reflected in the mirror of his bedroom. He convinces his creation to hide behind some curtains so as not to frighten his bride-to-be.

But the creature follows Frankenstein with "the devotion of a dog," as the intertitles put it. When his fiancee gives Frankenstein a rose for his lapel, the Monster jealously snatches it from him. Frankenstein fights with his creature and is thrown to the floor. At that moment, the Monster sees his own reflection in the mirror and runs away in horror.

The Monster jealously seeks out Frankenstein's fiancee. Frankenstein hears her screams and finds her lying on the floor in a faint. The Monster attacks Frankenstein, overpowers

Frankenstein (Augustus Phillips) is threatened by his creature (Charles Ogle) in Edison's *Frankenstein*.

him again and leaves. The creature returns once more to stare at himself in the mirror. This time, he holds out his arms to his reflection and disappears. Frankenstein enters and sees only his own reflection in the glass. His sweetheart joins him for a final embrace.

The writer-director of this first film version of *Frankenstein*, James Searle Dawley, had been working for the Edison Manufacturing Company since May 13, 1907. Previously, he stage managed for the Spooner stock company in Brooklyn and wrote such plays as *Little Miss Sherlock Jr.* and *The Land Beyond the Firelight* in 1900 and *At Old Fort Lookout* in 1902. As part of his stage managing job, he rented and projected films from the Waters' Kinetograph Company between live acts of the stock company. This experience put him in contact with Edwin S. Porter, director of one of the first story films in America, *The Great Train Robbery* in 1903.

Dawley applied for a job with the Edison Company. For $40 a week salary, he assisted Porter for a year, stage managing his films and even keeping payroll. Having learned his craft, Dawley soon directed and co-directed films with collaborator Frederick S. Armitage. Together, they made such early efforts as *The Boston Tea Party* in 1908 and *Where Is My Wandering Boy* in 1909. By 1910, Dawley was an important director with Edison, having earned some good reviews in the *New York Dramatic Mirror* for his primitive efforts. In January of that year, he directed *The Princess and the Peasant* on location in Cuba. Later in the year, of course, he directed *Frankenstein*.

Again, critics of the day were very impressed with Dawley's work. *The Film Index* of March 12, 1910 raved: "The actually repulsive situations in the original version have been carefully eliminated in its visualized form, so that there is no possibility of its shocking any portion of an audience; but the dramatic strength of this gruesome story clings to its

Charles Ogle as Frankenstein

dramatization." This review called the creation scene "probably the most remarkable ever committed to film." It went on to declare: "It is safe to say that no film has ever been released that can surpass it in power to fascinate an audience... (It) will hold an audience spellbound and (will be) certain to excite a great deal of attention and comment."

The *New York Dramatic Mirror* of March 26 agreed: "... the changes make for clarity and the elimination of objectionable details. (However), the spirit of the tale is well preserved... The scene where Frankenstein produces the Monster is particularly well done... The deeply impressive story makes a powerful film subject and the Edison players have handled it with effective expression and skill."

The April 2, 1910 *Moving Picture World* concluded that "Mary Shelley's disturbing story... is here reproduced in a motion picture in a way that will appeal to those who have never read the story as well as those who have. Sometimes the value of the motion picture in reproducing these stories is scarcely realized, yet they do much for literature in that direction. Very many, for example, will see this picture who have never read the story and will acquire a lasting impression of its power." This review called the Monster's birth "a piece of photographic work which will rank with the best of its kind."

Besides the elimination of such "repulsive situations" as Frankenstein's creation of his Monster from dead body parts, the murders of Frankenstein's family and friends by the vengeful creature and the attempted creation of a mate for the Monster, the strangest change

In *Frankenstein*, the only clue that the Monster is supposed to be the evil side of Frankenstein is its exaggerated ugliness.

is the ending. This climax and the curious, repeated use of the mirror in Frankenstein's home point to Dawley's interpretation of Shelley's work.

Even at the time, the March 26, 1910 *New York Dramatic Mirror* noticed that the Monster could be seen as "fashioned in sympathy with the evil in Frankenstein's mind." When Frankenstein watches the Monster's birth through the window of the massive door, his expression is one of demented glee. He seems to be going through some sort of transformation himself, as if he were watching the emergence of his own Mr. Hyde.

The first time Frankenstein sees the Monster after fleeing to his father's home is in the reflection of a mirror. When we gaze into a mirror, we expect to see ourselves. Frankenstein sees the part of himself that he hoped to leave behind: the secret, primitive, ugly shadow of his personality.

Later, the Monster himself recoils at his own reflection. He is becoming both Frankenstein's evil double and an emerging being in his own right. Horrified at his ugliness, he is also responding to his unnatural birth as Frankenstein's dark half.

After Frankenstein fights the Monster for his bride, the Monster looks into the mirror and fades away. Frankenstein has chosen love over his baser impulses, and the symbol for those impulses vanishes. The intertitle spells it out: "The creature of an evil mind is overcome by love and disappears."

The film certainly lives up to its publicity as "psychological" and "mystical." If anything, it is too symbolic, asking the audience to make instant interpretations in order to follow the logic of events. The only clue that the Monster is supposed to be the evil side of Frankenstein is his exaggerated ugliness. His actions and motives are never evil. On the contrary, he behaves like a spurned child, throwing tantrums and running away. He kills no one and seems to be the most needy and vulnerable character. Judging from the contemporary reviews, however, the movie appealed to the audience of its time who may have been repulsed by a more literal version of the novel.

Dawley continued to direct for Edison, filming a version of *Charge of the Light Brigade* in Cheyenne, Colorado two years after *Frankenstein*. He moved to Famous Players Studio in 1913, again collaborating with Porter and directing Mary Pickford, John Barrymore, Billie Burke and Pearl White. He died at age 70 on March 29, 1949 at the Motion Picture Home near Hollywood. Except for his *Frankenstein*, Dawley's films have been completely forgotten, as has the work of so many film pioneers. Even *Frankenstein* was thought to be lost until a tinted print was discovered in the mid-1970s.

In 1912, the Eclair Company of France produced a 15-minute version of the Theatre du Grand Guignol one-act play, *Le Systeme du Docteur Goudron et du Professeur Plume* by Andre de Lorde.

In the spring of 1897, Oscar Metenier opened the 285-seat Theatre du Grand Guignol in Paris after being secretary to the Police Commissioner, a tabloid journalist and a master writer of *rosse* or "crass" one-act plays about the low lives of the lowlifes of Paris. He took the curious name for the theater from "Guignol," a character in the popular "Punch and Judy" puppet shows of Lyons. "Guignol" had become a generic name for all puppet entertainment, so the theater was designated as a "Grand," or large, "Guignol," or puppet show. However, the intended audience was to be decidedly adult and the performers, live people. The insane behavior and extreme violence that excited children in the "Punch and Judy" shows would be intensified and made realistic for the sadistic pleasure of their parents.

A typical Grand Guignol evening consisted of five or six one-act plays alternating between sexy farce and blood-drenched horror. Madness provided the motivation for most of the stabbings, stranglings and mutilations, with unhealthy doses of rape and revenge mixed in. The theater became a major tourist attraction in Paris from its inception until 1962, when its novelty finally wore out.

Andre de Lorde, author of the play and film, *Le Systeme du Docteur Goudron et du Professeur Plume*, was known in France as the "Prince of Terror" due to the over 100 one-acts he wrote for the Theatre du Grand Guignol between 1901 and 1926. The son of a physician, de Lorde developed a fascination with the morbid from his boyhood. Noticing that his son would listen in rapt horror outside his office to the sobs and screams of his patients, his father tried to cure the child of this obsession with pain and suffering. He forced little Andre to keep vigil over the body of his grandmother the night before the funeral to convince him not to be afraid of death. The effort worked in reverse, intensifying the young man's dread. In fact, this incident haunted the future playwright for the rest of his life. His therapist and dramatic collaborator, Dr. Alfred Binet, director of the Psychological–Physiological Laboratories of the Sorbonne, claimed that de Lorde used his macabre playwriting to avoid dealing emotionally with his own phobic and unhappy personality.

Trained as a lawyer, de Lorde was an avid student of abnormal psychology and criminal behavior. In fact, he was one of the first dramatists to set his plays in insane asylums. After serving as secretary to the Minister of Finance, he received an appointment as chief librarian at the Bilbiotheque de l'Arsenal. As a literary enthusiast, he not only wrote plays of horror but also articles analyzing the genre. His idol was Edgar Allan Poe, and he shared with the great writer the dream of writing a play so terrifying that the audience would flee from the theater in panic.

Le Systeme du Docteur Goudron et du Professeur Plume was an adaptation of Poe's short story, "The System of Doctor Tarr and Professor Feather." Poe had treated as a dark farce the situation of a sane man visiting an asylum and being attended by lunatics in the guises of doctors. Ultimately, the fact that raving maniacs were running the asylum and had tarred and feathered the real doctors was meant to be humorous. In 1909, the Edison company made a film version called *Lunatics in Power* which also approached the subject strictly for laughs.

Perhaps something had been lost in its translation to French. Andre de Lorde turned the story into a one-act of mounting paranoia as the visitors realize that their hosts are not only insane but dangerously violent. Unlike Poe's story, in the play, the crazies attack both visitors before the slashed and bloody body of the doctor in charge is dragged in from the next room by the rescuing forces of the police.

The 15-minute movie of de Lorde's play was directed by Maurice Tourneur, who was born Maurice Thomas on February 2, 1876 in Paris. His father sold jewels, and Maurice began his working career as a decorator and a book illustrator. He served in the French artillery in North Africa, then became a student and assistant to the sculptor Auguste Rodin. In 1900, his artistic contacts introduced him to the theater, and he became an actor with Rejane, Andre Antoine and others. After a disagreement with Antoine, Tourneur became an assistant director at the Eclair film company in 1911. The following year, he graduated to directing. *Le Systeme du Docteur Goudron et du Professeur Plume* was his third film in his first year as director. Tourneur's version added sex to the mix by making one of the sane visitors the pretty wife of the other.

A journalist named Brezard is sent to the Berneville Asylum to research an article on Dr. Maillard and his new method of treating psychopaths. Beautiful Madame Brezard accompanies him.

As they approach the ancient castle that houses the asylum, a thunderstorm erupts. Excited by the lightning and thunder, the inmates overpower Dr. Maillard. They hold him down as one of the lunatics raises a knife "to cure him quickly," as the intertitle says.

The Brezards' arrival interrupts the operation. Passing the knife to another inmate, the lunatic rushes into the director's office. "His blanched face, glaring and staring eyes and jerking motions cause the young couple great apprehension," declares the publicity material. The "director" describes for his visitors his revolutionary new cure for insanity:

> To their astonishment the chief step is cutting out an eye, and then, very carefully, the throat is to be sliced with a sharp knife.
>
> Suddenly, a horrible and sickening rattle breaks up the interview. (The lunatic) rushes into the next room and returns a few minutes later, his hands covered with blood. For some little time strange beings have invaded the office. Their attitude is incomprehensible, their gestures wild. The sight of blood slowly oozing under the door awakens their murderous instincts, and they overpower Brezard. They prepare him for the operation. A wilder gust of wind blows the big window wide. The lunatics cower and this gives time for the keepers, now freed, to arrive with straightjackets and master the madmen.

Perhaps inspired by this early movie by his father, Jacques Tourneur would also use the striking shot of blood oozing under a door to depict a violent death in his own horror film of 1943, *The Leopard Man*.

Of *Le Systeme du Docteur Goudron et du Professeur Plume*, British trade critic George Blaisdell wrote: "It is a powerful story and a horrible one, yet fascinating in spite of its horror. Don't show it to your patrons without looking at it for yourself, for it is no food for infants or weaklings." In fact, the film was such a *tour de force* of sadism that when it reached America as *The Lunatics* in 1913, one reviewer judged it "too grim for Sunday showings."

In Germany, by 1913, intellectuals and theorists were beginning to write about the artistic possibilities of film. Paul Wegener agreed with many of his contemporaries that the movies offered the ability of blending the real and the unreal in new and exciting ways. Wegener was born on December 11, 1874 in Bischdorf, East Prussia. Although he initially studied law, he became a stage actor in 1895. Wegener joined Max Reinhardt's Deutsches Theater in Berlin in 1906 and became one of the great actors of German drama, playing many classical roles such as Oedipus Rex and Macbeth. Despite his theater training, he felt that the cinema should communicate with the image alone, using its own grammar, completely independent from literature and the stage.

"The real creator of the film must be the camera," he said. "Getting the spectator to change his point of view, using special effects to double the actor on the divided screen, superimposing other images—all this, technique, form, gives the content its real meaning."

A series of comic photographs showing a man fencing and playing cards with himself made Wegener realize that cinema was the ideal form to portray the Romantic and supernatural world of E.T.A. Hoffmann, the great German writer of short fantasy stories of the early 19th century. Hoffmann was a master of *Serapionism*, the technique of presenting the supernatural convincingly. He could arouse the momentary suspension of disbelief for the most outrageous fantasies by setting his stories in the real, prosaic world, then injecting metaphysical concepts into it. Often, as in Hoffmann's masterpiece, "The Golden Flower Pot," he presented his wildest wonderlands as the mental visions of the protagonist. Dostoyevsky frankly admitted his debt to Hoffmann in the depiction of psychological states. For his first film, Wegener chose an original story inspired by Hoffmann.

"*The Student of Prague* with its strange mixture of the natural and the artificial, in theme as in setting, interested me enormously," he said. The story was written by German novelist Hanns Heinz Ewers, one of the proponents for *Autorenfilm*, the idea of a movie being judged as the work of an author. This concept, similar to the French *auteurist* theory of the 1950s, was quite revolutionary in 1913, when film was rarely thought of as an art, much less as the product of an artist.

Ewers was one of the most accomplished practitioners of the second wave of the German literary movement, *schauerromane*, or "shudder novels." The first wave occurred at the end of the 18th century when writers such as Spiess, Cramer, Schlenkert and I.F. Arnold created works designed to terrify their readers. Unlike the early English gothic novelists who invariably offered some natural reason for their supernatural events, the Germans, influenced by dark Romanticism, presented the irrational without explanation. These writers directly inspired Mary Shelley to create *Frankenstein* and caused Edgar Allan Poe to assert in his preface to *Tales of the Grotesque and Arabesque* that the terror at which he aimed was "not of Germany, but of the soul."

During the second wave, in the first two decades of the 20th century, Ewers joined Meyrink, Panizza and Przybyszewski in lacing their horror with social comment, black humor and sadistic eroticism. Ewers was born in Dusseldorf in 1872, the son of an important portrait artist. Like Wegener, he was educated in the law but turned to the arts early. Insatiable for adventure and danger, Ewers traveled extensively while writing poetry, essays and his famous *schauerromane*. In this vein, Ewers penned *Das Grauen* in 1907, *The Student of Prague* in 1913 and later *Vampir* in 1920. His greatest success was his lurid supernatural novel, *Alaune*, written in 1911 and adapted to films many times between 1918 and 1952. Like Wegener, Ewers championed the new art of cinema almost from its inception, even opening his own movie theater. He also lectured on Nietzschean philosophy and Satanism, dressed in the flamboyant manner of a 19th-century dandy.

For *The Student of Prague*, Ewers was inspired by Hoffmann's story of 1814, "A New Year's Eve Adventure:"

In Hoffmann's tale, a husband and father named Erasmus Spikher falls passionately in love with Giuletta, a demon from Hell in the form of a bewitchingly beautiful woman. Erasmus jealously murders an Italian who is flirting with her and must flee Italy for his native Germany. The seductress insists that he leave his reflection with her by which to remember him. When he returns to his wife and son, Erasmus tries to conceal the loss of his reflection. His family discovers that he has no image in a mirror, and they reject him as unnatural and cursed by God. The devil, in the form of a Dr. Dapertutto, tries to tempt Erasmus to poison them and return to Giuletta, but he refuses. Erasmus ends up wandering the earth, without family or reflection.

Ewers combined the concept of a man giving his reflection to the devil with the idea of the *doppelganger*, or double, as presented in Edgar Allan Poe's short story of 1839, "William Wilson." Inspired by the first wave of German *schauerromane* writers, Poe tells the tale of a cruel, selfish man named William Wilson who is plagued by his exact double. This metaphysical twin ruins Wilson's reputation by destroying his evil plans. In fury, Wilson stabs his double to death in a duel. But as the *doppelganger* dies, he tells Wilson: "...henceforth art thou also dead—dead to the World, to Heaven, and to Hope! In me didst thou exist—and, in my death, see by this image, which is thine own, how utterly thou hast murdered thyself."

Blending the two stories, Ewers crafted, in *The Student of Prague*, the narrative of Baldwin, a poor student and fencing expert of the early 19th century, who exchanges his mirror reflection for money from a little old man named Scapanelli, actually the devil.

As Baldwin uses his new fortune to woo an engaged Countess, he is followed by his reflection, an exact double of himself. This *doppelganger* frightens the Countess away from Baldwin. Later, the reflection kills her noble fiance in a duel after Baldwin has promised the Countess' father to spare the suitor. In spiritual terror, the Countess rejects Baldwin forever. The student desperately shoots his double. But the *doppelganger* disappears, and it is Baldwin who sustains the mortal gunshot wound. After Baldwin dies, Scapanelli gleefully tears up his contract with the student and scatters the pieces over the body before prancing away.

The hour-long movie, credited by some historians as the first feature-length motion picture, was directed by the Danish Stellan Rye who was assigned by the producing company, Paul Davidsohn's Union Film, to collaborate with Wegener. They filmed on actual locations in the medieval quarter of Prague. Ewers chose Prague as a setting because of its historical reputation as Europe's occult capital. Golden Lane, where some of the action was shot, was still known as the "Street of the Alchemists" because such distinguished practitioners of the black arts as Cornelius Agrippa, Paracelsis and even, it was believed, Dr. Faustus himself, had resided there. Since Ewers' story was a paraphrase of Faustus' pact with the devil, the location was ideal.

The film differs from many of the later German horror films produced after World War I in that the supernatural occurs in a recognizably naturalistic world. Every effort was made to stage the story on actual locations. For example, when the Jewish community refused to

Paul Wegener (as *The Golem*, 1914, shown with Lyda Salmonova) became the first real horror film star.

allow the company to film in their medieval cemetery, facsimiles of the headstones were erected in a Prague forest instead of in the studio. This is an accurate translation of Hoffmann's literary style in which the uncanny erupts without warning amid the realistically presented taverns, streets and homes of his time.

Stellan Rye's cinematic technique is still pre-Griffith, with one shot per scene, but the characters are often blocked in depth, stepping toward the camera from the background or arranged with foreground and background action occurring simultaneously. Despite the lack of editing within scenes, the film has a somewhat cinematic feel. This is mainly due to the realistic action on location such as the Countess' fox hunt featuring horses and dogs kicking up clouds of dust through the paths of the forest.

The most filmic device, and one possible only in the movies, is the use of split screen to show Baldwin and his double interacting. When the picture premiered on August 22, 1913 in Berlin, the audience actually screamed as they beheld Wegener's image step out of the mirror while, in the same shot, the real Wegener watched. This may seem like a gross over-reaction when judged from the perspective of a century of movies, but audiences of the time had never seen such effects combined with a serious and sinister atmosphere.

However, seen in retrospect, Ewers' story, while effective as a supernatural shocker, lacks the depth and poetry of his inspirations. In Hoffmann's "A New Year's Eve Adventure," the author tells us that Erasmus' reflection represents his "dream ego": the emotional, romantic aspect of his personality. In Poe's, "William Wilson," the narrator's double clearly symbolizes his moral conscience. It foils his perverse plans while holding up a mirror to Wilson, showing him his own evil.

But the meaning of Baldwin's double in *The Student of Prague* is less clear. His main purpose seems to be to thwart Baldwin's quite sincere romance with the unhappily engaged Countess. As such, he does not seem to represent Baldwin's other self or his "dream-ego."

Rather, he is merely an emissary from Scapanelli who is bent on seducing and destroying Baldwin just for the evil fun of it. Nothing in Baldwin's character, save his poverty, draws the devil to him. Perhaps this is the main source of horror: the arbitrary nature of the devil's attraction to his victim. Baldwin's vulnerability through lack of funds allows Scapanelli to tempt him, trick him and ruin him. It could happen to any of us. "There but for the grace of God..."

With *The Student of Prague*, Wegener became the first real "horror star" in cinema history. Drawn to the dark and terrifying, he would specialize in such roles in European-made productions until the end of the silent era. Most of his sinister characters resulted from his own fascination with myths and legends. He would go on to star as a manmade monster in *The Golem*, appear in the first horror sequel in *The Golem and the Dancing Girl* and the first prequel in *The Golem, How He Came Into the World*. He also created Satanic villains in frightening films for other producers such as Rex Ingram's *The Magician* and Henrik Galeen's *Alraune*. With his massive bulk, his unusually sharp features and his often subtle shadings of evil, he introduced audiences and artists to the joys of contemplating the wicked and the occult.

In 1914, just before embarking on his epic, *The Birth of a Nation*, the greatest film director of his day, D.W. Griffith, made a tribute to Edgar Allan Poe called *The Avenging Conscience*. Ultimately more Griffith than Poe, the hour-long movie is a fascinating mosaic of the author's verse and perversity and the director's Victorian morality and cinematic technique. The works of Poe may have been the starting point, but his obsessive, gothic sensibilities are overshadowed by Griffith's preference for sentimentality, sympathetic characters, Christian redemption and suspenseful spectacle.

The story loosely paraphrases Poe's "The Telltale Heart," reset in 1914 rural America:

When a baby's mother dies in childbirth, the boy's one-eyed uncle raises him like a son. The infant grows to be a young man, played by Griffith favorite Henry B. Walthall, who would next play the Little Colonel in *Birth of a Nation*.

The aging uncle becomes jealous of the young man's love for a girl named Annabelle, played by another Griffith regular, Blanche Sweet. He fears that the boy will leave him for her. When he rudely forbids the boy from going to a garden party with Annabelle, the couple breaks up.

But the boy murders his uncle for his inheritance and his freedom. After strangling the old man, the boy walls his body up in the back of a brick chimney.

Unfortunately, the murder is observed by a passing Italian worker who blackmails the boy. The young man has a nervous breakdown and sees visions of Christ on the cross and the tablet containing the commandment, "Thou Shalt Not Kill." He is also haunted by the ghost of his uncle who reenacts the strangulation.

The uncle's old friend becomes suspicious and sends a detective to investigate. When the policeman questions the boy, the killer has visions of "ghouls" from Hell coming to get him. He breaks down, runs to his cabin retreat, is defended in a gun battle from the approaching posse by the Italian and his small gang, and ultimately hangs himself when the posse defeats the defenders. Annabelle witnesses the suicide and jumps off a cliff to the rocky seashore and her death.

At this point, the boy wakes up and realizes the whole thing is a dream brought on by reading the works of Poe. After gratefully making up with his uncle, the young man marries Annabelle.

Naive in its narrative but sophisticated in its presentation, the film highlights the best and worst of Griffith at this time in his career. The unnamed boy is hardly the hypersensitive lunatic of Poe's story. He behaves like a perfectly ordinary young man until the contrivances of the plot force him to observe that "life is one long series of murders." He witnesses a spider devouring a fly and an army of ants attacking a beetle. As visually effective as these details may be, they are not strong enough to replace the detailed description of a madman's mind in Poe's story.

Likewise, the uncle's discreetly patched eye never serves the same function as the hideous webbed orb of the old man in "The Telltale Heart." In fact, in Griffith's movie, the boy does not notice it at all, robbing it of any symbolic or psychological meaning.

The scenes of the uncle's ghost are eerie and effective for their time, and they perfectly dramatize the young man's guilty conscience. However, the heavy-handed religious images of Christ on the cross and the glowing tablets of the 10 commandments veer the movie in another direction, a path Poe never takes. Griffith cannot resist injecting his own Southern Presbyterian morality into what should be a purely psychological drama.

Griffith constantly opens up the story, robbing it of the claustrophobic intensity of Poe's interior monologues. The director introduces a comedy relief couple as "contrast" to the serious lovers at the garden party, then abruptly drops the light characters when the drama becomes intense. The garden party itself seems unnecessary, contributing only some scenery, extras and a strange Roman dance.

Griffith maneuvers the story to one of his shoot-outs between a small number of defenders and an invading army. Aside from completely removing the piece from its intimate origins, the scene does not work as movie suspense because the outnumbered defenders of the little cabin are the bad guys and the invading army are the forces of law and order. The sole fascination of the episode, aside from the expert filming of the action, is the depth of madness and depravity to which the young man has sunk.

The final and most glaring miscalculation is the visualization of the young man's puerile poetry. In an epilogue, Griffith shows the lovers sitting together under a double-exposed clouded sky as the boy begins to recite. The director then actually fades to a scene of Pan playing his pipes beside a meadow. Little girls dressed in school-play fairy costumes emerge from the trunk of a tree and scamper happily to Pan. This is the final image of a film that is, for most of its running time, a tragic depiction of hatred, murder, guilt and punishment. Like the dream framing device, the scene patronizes the audience by completely dispelling the mood of impending doom so effectively built up throughout the film.

Henry B. Walthall as the tortured lead in D.W. Griffith's *The Avenging Conscience*

The most impressive aspect of the work is Griffith's early mastery of shooting and editing for maximum emotional impact. His use of insert shots, close-ups, double exposures and cross-cutting make even a self-consciously artistic effort like *The Student of Prague* appear extremely primitive by comparison.

Griffith intercuts scenes constantly, comparing and contrasting the characters' feelings and relationships. For example, as the boy reads Poe, Griffith cuts back and forth to a scene of Annabelle excitedly preparing to visit him. The boy reads of madness, murder and obsession at the same time as his girlfriend thinks only of him.

Griffith carefully shows the uncle's jealousy of youth by cutting to his views of happy couples enjoying the garden party and pampering their newborns. This not only motivates the Uncle's actions visually, but it renders his attitude both understandable and sympathetic. We experience his longing to engage in the excitement of life as we comprehend his bitterness.

The scene in which the detective questions the boy is a *tour de force* of cinematic ideas and editing. Griffith forces the audience to experience the boy's mounting hysteria by cutting together close-ups of the calm detective, close-ups of the guilty young man, inserts of the detective tapping his pencil on the table, inserts of the detective's foot tapping the floor, inserts of the pendulum of the clock ticking back and forth and shots of an owl hooting rhythmically outside. As Alfred Hitchcock would do many times years later, Griffith makes a scene with no outward action feel dynamic and compelling by emphasizing the small details within the consciousness of one anxious character. Griffith's early understanding and mastery of the subjective possibilities of cinema reaches its climax here. In this scene alone, he displays his simultaneous invention and expert manipulation of modern film language.

The boy leaps to his feet as he hallucinates abstract visions of grotesque, animal-headed men crawling out of the darkness. He opens the door, beckoning them, then imagines himself bound in a chair and watched over by a living skeleton. All of this is presented in flashcuts alternating with close-ups of the young man's terrified face. The camera constantly pushes in on the visions through the blinding white sparks of a Roman candle as if trying to see them clearly before they vanish again. The intertitle quotes lines from Poe's "The Bells" about creatures "neither beast nor human," but "ghouls." This is as close as the film gets to capturing the subjective, phantasmagoric insanity of Poe's verse and prose. Here, Griffith mixes with Poe in equal measures, and the results are stunning.

A year after Griffith's Poe film, another adaptation of a horror classic was also presented as a dream so as not to unduly disturb its viewers. A second American version of Mary Shelley's *Frankenstein* was endowed with life from the Ocean Film Corporation, a new company formed to produce and market "unusual features of themes never heretofore touched, largely adaptations from literary masterpieces," according to *Moving Picture World*. During the second week of November 1915, the company was formed with a capitalization of $200,000 with Jesse J. Goldburg as General Manager. Unfortunately for the future of the endeavor, Mr. Goldburg also chose to write the script for their initial offering. His many mis-steps began when he retitled the famous story, from *Frankenstein* to *Life Without Soul*.

Goldburg's Monster was not the horrifyingly ugly living corpse envisioned by Shelley but a menacing brute of average appearance. This, of course, removed much of the creature's motivation for his feelings of rage and isolation from mankind. Goldburg further confused matters by telling the tale without benefit of its most notable character's name. *Life Without Soul* was not about Victor Frankenstein, but rather, Victor Frawley:

Young Dr. Victor Frawley tells his fiancée, Elizabeth, that he has created a potion that restores life to the dead. After being warned of the dangers of his experiments by his family and friends, Victor falls asleep while reading Mary Shelley's novel, *Frankenstein*. He dreams the story with himself in the same situations as the title character. With his potion, Frawley brings to life a normal-looking man who is immensely strong and brutal. The creature forces Frawley to create a mate for him, but Victor destroys the female to spare the world from two such horrors. In revenge, the artificial man murders Victor's sister, Claudia and his friend, Clerval. He even kills Elizabeth on her wedding night. Victor wakes up from his terrible dream and destroys his life-giving fluid.

Why Goldburg chose to tell this "literary masterpiece" one step removed, as the dream of another similar protagonist, and use that character's name while retaining the names of the supporting characters from the original work, is only one of the mysteries of this now lost production. Perhaps Goldburg felt that he could not set the story in the contemporary America of 1915 without changing the famous hero's name. The original novel was already in the public domain in 1915, so there was no question of having to buy rights. Maybe Goldburg was inspired by Griffith's Poe pastiche, but *The Avenging Conscience* was at least presented as an "original" story "inspired" by the works of Poe rather than as a straight adaptation like *Life Without Soul*.

Production on the film under the direction of Joseph W. Smiley actually began three to four weeks before Ocean's incorporation in November. According to their publicity, Ocean

wanted as "varied atmosphere as was possible to procure" for *Life Without Soul*. Therefore, Smiley filmed for five days at Dahlonega, Georgia, three days in St. Augustine, Florida, two weeks at Jacksonville, Florida and then the crew returned by steamer to New York. The finished production featured scenes of deserts, semi-tropics, mountains, the ocean, a passenger liner and the big city. Among the 463 scenes filmed was one in which the crew exploded the side of a mountain to create a landslide.

Thirty-four years old when he directed *Life Without Soul*, Joseph W. Smiley started his theatrical career as an actor in the 1893 stage production, *Fantasma*. He toured in repertory with Fanny Davenport and appeared for several seasons in vaudeville. Early motion picture companies such as Imp and Lubin employed Smiley to both act and direct.

On November 21, 1915, Ocean invited exchange men, states right buyers and exhibitors to a private, afternoon screening of the five-reel *Life Without Soul* at the Chandler Theatre in New York. The reviews were surprisingly good. *Motion Picture News* called *Life Without Soul* "impressionistic in character... at times the picture refuses to convince, but its interest is always averagely high because of the theme's unusualness." In terms of the acting, the reviewer praised Percy Darrell Standing as the "brute man" creation. More than anything else, this critic admired the cinematography and location work as "pronouncedly strong features." Appreciating screenwriter Goldburg's efforts to minimize the tragedy and gruesome aspects of the story by turning it into a dream, the paper wrote, "it is pleasant to see that all the characters are alive in the epilogue."

The November 26 *Variety* was also impressed: "... adapted from Mary Shelley's novel *Frankenstein*... it is the familiar story of a physician who discovers a life-giving fluid and creates a superman of enormous physique but without a conscience... here is a subject worth the effort of a Griffith. The Ocean folks have done well with it, despite numerous inconsistencies... their scenario is at times rather vague, but the novelty of the idea for filming will be sure to create a healthy demand for the picture."

How wrong they were. Ocean was only able to secure *Life Without Soul* a very limited release. During February 1916, the Raver Film Corporation took over ownership of the

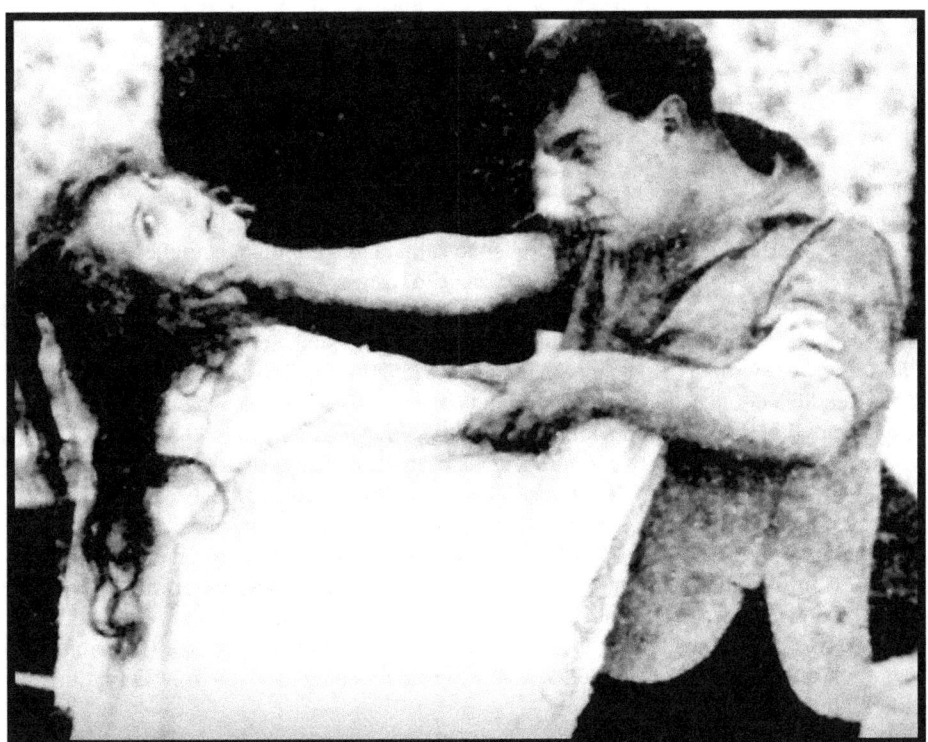

The Monster (Percy Darrell Standing) kills Elizabeth (Lucy Cotton) on her wedding night in *Life Without Soul*.

picture along with two others that Ocean managed to start before disbanding: *The Fortunate Youth*, written and directed by Smiley and based on W.J. Locke's novel, and a "photo-revival" of the play *Driftwood*. Immediately after acquiring Ocean, Harry Raver, the man who brought Pastrone's classic 1914 Italian epic *Cabiria* to America, altered *Life Without Soul* for re-release. In addition to adding color tinting, Raver shot supplementary footage to "clarify" the story. According to the May 6, 1916 *Moving Picture World*, the revised film featured scenes of "blood coursing through veins and arteries, the conjugation of cells and the reproduction of life in the fish world." Raver felt that these new additions were not only educational, but made the laboratory scenes more convincing. Apparently, they were not enough to save the film because its re-release did little better than its original presentation, and *Life Without Soul* was lost and forgotten.

CHAPTER 2
THE DARK GERMAN SOUL

By the time World War I erupted in 1914, Hollywood already dominated international cinema. During the war, the American film industry perfected the comsumability of its product. The "star system" created celebrity for popular actors and actresses by developing stories for their individual strengths. Invisible camera and editing techniques emphasized the smooth transition from shot to shot and scene to scene and de-emphasized the storyteller in favor of the story. With Europe in turmoil, America only strengthened its hold on the world's screens. Millions of people in every country attended Hollywood movies weekly. Narratives were written to appeal to mass tastes without offending or challenging the huge, diverse audience. In such a climate, stories that emphasized horror, which was somewhat offensive by its very nature, practically disappeared from American motion pictures.

In Germany, Paul Wegener continued his fascination with the dark myths of the continent. While filming *The Student of Prague*, Wegener, who was a Gentile, became acquainted with the Jewish legend of the Golem. "I got the idea for my *Golem* from the mysterious clay figure brought to life by the Rabbi Loew, according to a legend of the Prague ghetto, and with this film I went further into the domain of pure cinema," Wegener said. "Everything depends on the image, on a certain vagueness of outline where the fantastic world of the past meets the world of today. I realized that photographic technique was going to determine the destiny of the cinema. Light and darkness in the cinema play the same role as rhythm and cadence in music."

According to legend, the life-size clay statue was created by Rabbi Judah Loew ben Bezalel in the 1580s to save the Jews of Prague from a pogrom threatened by Rudolph II of Hapsburg after false rumors of ritual child murders. While filming *The Student of Prague*, Wegener undoubtedly saw the twin statues of Rabbi Loew and the Golem, which means "shapeless mass," in the medieval quarter of the city. He was intrigued by rumors that the actual legendary statue of old was hidden in the dark and dusty attic of the synagogue in Altneau.

For his first of three films about the Golem, Wegener and his director and co-screenwriter, Henrik Galeen, who had been personal secretary to Hanns Heinz Ewers, set the story in modern times circa 1914:

The Golem, played by Wegener himself with a huge sculpted wig, giant boots and gray, clay-like makeup, is uncovered in the ruins of an old synagogue by workers. An antiquarian buys it and brings it to life with words from an ancient Cabalistic text. The soulless creature works as the antiquarian's servant until it discovers human feelings and falls in love with his daughter, played by Wegener's then wife, Lyda Salmanova. According to law, if the Golem is brought to life for other than noble tasks, its strength and power will become uncontrollable. The daughter turns from the monster in horror, and it goes on a murderous rampage. Finally, it falls to its destruction from a tower.

After enjoying great success in Europe, *The Golem* opened in New York under the title, *The Monster of Fate*, the same week that the United States broke off diplomatic relations with Germany. Unfortunately, the film vanished, the victim of the destruction of its native country through two wars.

Also lost is Wegener's 1917 parody, *The Golem and the Dancing Girl*, in which Wegener dons the costume of the Golem to frighten a beautiful ballerina he wishes to seduce.

Fortunately, Wegener himself would write, direct and star in one more Golem film after the war, and that movie, his masterpiece, exists.

According to stills from the productions, Wegener's appearances as the Golem were remarkably consistent. The costume was designed by the sculptor Rudolf Belling, whose figurative style fused Cubist and Futurist principles. The creature had the classic look of later movie monsters such as Jack Pierce's Frankenstein creation. Already a big man, Wegener's bulk was increased with padded shoulders and chest and a huge belted doublet with a Star of David. The lifted boots and distinctive sculpted wig increased his height so that he towered ominously over the other players.

The climate for Wegener's third, most expensive and artistically ambitious Golem film was created by another post-war German movie that would change the destiny of that country's film industry for a decade.

Between Wegener's first two Golem movies, from 1914 to 1918, Germany was engaged in the most devastating war up until that time. Although the physical destruction in no way matched the almost complete obliteration following its second defeat in 1945, Germany was still in physical, emotional and financial chaos.

The young Czech poet, Hans Janowitz, served as officer of a German infantry regiment but re-entered civilian life convinced of the immorality of war and with an intense hatred of the power that could send millions to their deaths. In Berlin, he met Carl Mayer, a penniless young sketch artist who had been compelled to undergo traumatic psychiatric examinations by a high-ranking military doctor to determine his fitness for service. The repeated interrogations left Mayer, like Janowitz, embittered against all authority.

Directly inspired by Paul Wegener's dark fantasy films, Janowitz asked Mayer, who had never written a word, to collaborate on a screenplay. They would vent their frustration metaphorically in a disturbing tale of the uncanny.

Janowitz told Mayer a true story about what happened to him one October evening in Hamburg a year before the war. He was searching a crowded fair on the Reeperbahn for a beautiful girl he glimpsed. From the darkness of a park bordering the Holstenwall, he thought he heard the girl's laughter from some bushes. Then, the giggling stopped. Janowitz spied a young man emerging from the shrubbery, and, for a fleeting moment, the poet caught sight of the shadow's face. He appeared to be an ordinary middle-class gentleman.

The next day, the local newspaper headlines screamed, "Horrible Sex Crime on the Holstenwall." A young woman had been murdered in the park. Janowitz was compelled to find out: was it the girl he had followed? He attended the victim's funeral. There, he recognized one of the mourners: he was the shadow in the park. The man seemed to realize that Janowitz had seen him that night. The incident haunted Janowitz for years, even after all he had experienced in war. He wondered how many other murderers were roaming free on the streets of the city.

Mayer responded with his own personal histories. He shared with his new friend, not only his mental duels with the military psychiatrist, but stories of his father who had been obsessed with finding a foolproof method of winning at gambling. Mayer's father sold all his property to put his theories to the test at the gaming tables of Monte Carlo. After losing everything, he turned the 16-year-old Carl and his three younger brothers out of the house and committed suicide. Like Janowitz, Mayer was a victim of irresponsible authority early in life.

After his father's death, Carl supported himself and his brothers by wandering Austria, working in local theaters and doing odd jobs. As he sang in peasant choirs and played extras in small productions, he became enamored with the theater.

After struggling all day to find a story, the two collaborators would make a nightly visit to a loud and colorful fair on Kantstrasse. Mayer pulled Janowitz into a sideshow tent called "Man or Machine." Inside, an apparently hypnotized man performed feats of strength while uttering strange, dark predictions of the future.

This was the experience that wove all the strands together. That night, the excited young men began to structure their tale. Janowitz worked in his personal story of nocturnal murder, Mayer patterned the main villain consciously after the hated army psychiatrist and unconsciously after his obsessed and selfish father, and both men included the character of the hypnotized sideshow performer who made dire forebodings. Janowitz later called himself "the father who planted the seed, and Mayer the mother who conceived and ripened it." The young men took six weeks to finish their project.

Even by the end of this time, they had not found their villain's name. Janowitz was skimming through a rare volume called *Unknown Letter of Stendhal* when a strange name caught his attention. It belonged to an officer whom Stendhal met at La Scala in Milan right after returning from war. Janowitz showed it to his writing partner. Both men agreed: the evil doctor in their story must be called Caligari.

In their original draft, the story of *The Cabinet of Dr. Caligari* is told 20 years after the events by the prosperous Dr. Francis and his wife, Jane, to a group of friends drinking punch on the terrace of their country home. Dr. Francis sees a band of roving Gypsies. He and Jane become pensive and quiet, and, at the urging of his friends, he begins to tell the tale:

It takes place in Northern Germany in a fictitious village, significantly called Holstenwall. A fair comes to town and with it, a sideshow entertainer named Dr. Caligari. He is a strange old man who advertises an exhibit built around a somnambulist named Cesare.

Cesare (Conrad Veidt) kidnaps Jane (Lil Dagover) in *The Cabinet of Dr. Caligari*. [Photofest]

When Caligari applies for a permit for his show, a bureaucratic clerk treats him disdainfully. The next morning, the clerk is found murdered in his room.

The following day, Francis and his friend Alan (in the script, tutor and pupil, but in the film, both are young students) take their mutual love, Jane, to the fair. They go into Caligari's tent show and witness the strange doctor rousing his sleeping creature who lives in a coffin-like "cabinet." Caligari tells the crowd that Cesare will answer questions about the future. When Alan asks how long he will live, Cesare answers, "Until dawn."

That night, a shadow slinks into Alan's bedroom and stabs him to death in his bed. Francis suspects Caligari and his somnambulist and sets out to convince the authorities.

As Francis watches Caligari and what he thinks is the sleeping Cesare in their wagon, the real Cesare silently breaks into Jane's bedroom and raises his dagger over her sleeping form. But he is unable to kill her beauty. He abducts her, struggling and screaming, from her bed. Her father and several townspeople chase him over the rooftops and roads until he collapses, dead from exhaustion.

The confused Francis and the police find only a dummy of Cesare in Caligari's wagon. Dr. Caligari manages to run away, pursued by Francis. He sees Caligari duck into an insane asylum. Francis approaches the director of the institution. He is Dr. Caligari.

That night, Francis and the attendants discover a diary that belongs to the Doctor. In it, he writes about his obsession with a medieval sorcerer named Caligari who journeyed through Europe with a somnambulist completely under his control. He wanted to know whether the sleeper could be commanded to perform acts such as murder that he would never do while

awake. When a somnambulist was brought into the asylum, the Doctor decided to repeat Caligari's experiments and even took his name.

Francis confronts the Doctor with Cesare's dead body, and the old man attacks him. He is put into a straightjacket by his own attendants and thrown into his own padded cell.

Unconsciously, Janowitz and Mayer created the character of Dr. Caligari as a symbol of the insane authority that had victimized them. Caligari does not mind sacrificing human lives to test his selfish theories of domination over Cesare and to revenge himself for petty slights against his dignity. This was how the authors saw the German government during war-time—with its omnipotent power to draft the youth of the country and send them to their deaths. The somnambulist Cesare represents the common man hypnotized by this dominating authority and willed to commit murders against his conscious morality. In the end, when the psychiatrist is exposed as Caligari, reason finally overcomes unreasonable power, and insane authority is metaphorically abolished.

But even the authors did not detect their message at the time. Janowitz wrote, "It was years after the completion of the screenplay that I realized our subconscious intention, and this explanation of our characters, Doctor Caligari and Cesare, his medium, that is: The corresponding connection between Doctor Caligari, and the great authoritative power of a Government that we hated, and which had subdued us into an oath, forcing conscription on those in opposition to its official war aims, compelling us to murder and to be murdered."

Early in 1919, Janowitz and Mayer offered the scenario to Erich Pommer, the shrewd chief executive of Decla Bioscope. A natural promoter born in Hildesheim on July 20, 1889, Pommer understood both the business and artistic aspects of motion pictures. To the authors' surprise, he accepted their strange project for production. Pommer later explained his decision to George A. Huaco:

The German film industry made 'stylized film' to make money. Let me explain. At the end of World War I the Hollywood industry moved toward world supremacy. The Danes had a film industry. The French had a very active film industry, which suffered an eclipse at the end of the war. Germany was defeated: how could she make films that would compete with the others? It would have been impossible to try and imitate Hollywood or the French. So we tried something new: the Expressionist or stylized films. This was possible because Germany had an overflow of good artists and writers, a strong literary tradition and a great tradition of theater. This provided a basis of good, trained actors. World War I finished the French film industry; the problem for Germany was to compete with Hollywood.

Janowitz and Mayer informed Pommer of their desire to have the sets supervised by the visionary designer and engraver, Alfred Kubin, whose hallucinatory work was a forerunner of the surrealists and featured strong contrasts of swirling light and shadow. Kubin's *Caligari* would have been gloomy and Goyaesque without being necessarily abstract. But Pommer had other priorities. "They wanted to experiment," he wrote in 1947, "and I wanted to keep costs down."

Rudolf Meinert, the production supervisor assigned by Pommer, tried to satisfy both parties. He gave the scenario to the designer Herman Warm whose credo was, "Films must be drawings brought to life." The artist studied it with two studio painters, Walter Rohrig and Walter Reimann.

"We spent the whole day and part of the night reading through this very curious script," wrote Warm. "We realized that a subject like this needed something out of the ordinary in the way of sets. Reimann, whose paintings in those days had Expressionist tendencies, suggested doing the sets Expressionistically. We immediately set to work roughing up designs in that style."

Expressionism was an art movement begun in Germany around 1910. It started in painting and poetry, progressed to literature and the theater and finally, entered the more expensive arts like opera and, in *The Cabinet of Dr. Caligari*, the motion picture. As part of the Modernist movements such as Cubism in France, Futurism in Italy and Constructivism in the Soviet Union, it sought to assault the established practices of the realistic novel, representative painting and the well-made play. Expressionism emphasized disunity over unity, collage over the realistic, and was guided by the subjectivity of 19th-century German Romanticism. As such, it embraced depictions of the uncanny and the insane. In fact, it celebrated a retreat from the realities of the world into a human perception of that world: the more distorted the better. Its anti-authoritarian political position was thus a contradiction: while Expressionism was a reaction against the madness of modern life, it appeared as a vision of insanity and distortion.

The next day, Dr. Robert Wiene, the director assigned to the project, gave his agreement. Rudolf Meinert cautiously thought about it for a day, then told Warm, "Do these sets as eccentrically as you can."

Director Robert Wiene, born in Breslau, Silesia on April 27, 1873, was the son of Carl Wiene, a famous Dresden actor. Wiene originally studied law at the University of Vienna, earned his doctorate, and became an attorney. While practicing law, Wiene made contact with the theater world through the continuing career of his father. In 1908 and 1909, Wiene managed theater in Vienna with a partner, but the collaboration ended quickly. Wiene became a scriptwriter in 1912 with the two-reeler, *The Arms of Youth*. He wrote or directed over 30 films before *The Cabinet of Dr. Caligari*, including five writing collaborations with Walter Turszinsky and 14 very successful scripts directed by Rudolf Biebrach in which Henny Porten, the most popular actress on the German screen, starred. Wiene's father suffered a nervous breakdown and loss of memory toward the end of his life, so the subject matter of insanity in *The Cabinet of Dr. Caligari* was not unfamiliar for the son.

The beauty of designer Herman Warm's approach, as far as Pommer was concerned, was that the sets could be economically created by painting canvas flats instead of constructing actual distorted buildings and rooms. Also, since the elaborate schemes of light and shadow were also to be painted instead of created through time-consuming lighting, the process of filming would be simplified and accelerated. Even the cost of electricity for the lights would be kept down in the economically uncertain post-war economy.

Warm constructed not only the interior rooms, but the exterior buildings and roads on stage so that their forms could be twisted and distorted. Most of the patterns emphasized sharp, pointing, dagger-like shapes that echoed Cesare's weapon. Only in Jane's rooms were the shapes round and soft.

Since Warm's credo was that "films should be drawings brought to life," the set design determined where Wiene's camera was to be placed. Like a two-dimensional painting, the sets were created to be seen from only one angle. Editing within a scene consisted of punched-in closer shots from that same perspective. Camera moves were practically unknown in films at the time, but Wiene's method for *The Cabinet of Dr. Caligari* severely restricted the use of editing which had been pioneered and perfected by Griffith.

Many later filmmakers, such as the Russian montage proponent Sergei Eisenstein, argued that *The Cabinet of Dr. Caligari* was a film that betrayed the art of cinema by ignoring its most fundamental technique: editing. Others have argued that the movie's Expressionism did not extend to unusual and expressive camera angles. These criticisms betray a restrictive

In *The Cabinet of Dr. Caligari*, **Caligari (Werner Krauss) and Cesare wore costumes and makeup in the exaggerated style.**

and dogmatic attitude toward what can be considered "cinematic" and ignore the unique look and the powerfully foreboding mood successfully conveyed in this one-of-a-kind experimental film.

The actors, who wore period costumes, became graphic elements in the scenes. As Pommer noted, Berlin enjoyed wonderful theater at the time, especially from the legendary director and producer, Max Reinhardt. Reinhardt's troupe provided the German cinema with not only Paul Wegener but Werner Krauss, who played Dr. Caligari, and Conrad Veidt, who interpreted Cesare. Veidt was born in Potsdam, near Berlin, on January 22, 1893. He made his stage debut at Reinhardt's Deutches Theater in Berlin in 1913. Krauss was born in Gestunghausen, Germany, on July 23, 1884 and became a distinguished performer of the German and Austrian stage before entering films in 1914. Both were accomplished mimes who created eccentric movements for their characters. In Krauss' case, he provided Dr. Caligari with a halting, jerky, arthritic walk and eyes glowing with hatred behind his sometimes insincere, sometimes mocking smile. Veidt's Cesare glided slowly through the Expressionist sets as if he were a part of them. The close-up of Cesare almost imperceptibly opening his eyes when summoned by Caligari was as chilling as the similar scene 13 years later when Boris Karloff awakened as *The Mummy*.

Only Caligari and Cesare wore costumes and makeup in the exaggerated style. Cesare's stark white face contrasted with his black tights, hair, lips and eye makeup. On his tights, more dagger-like shapes were roughly drawn with chalk. Caligari's white hair was streaked with black stripes, as were the backs of his white gloves. His black-rimmed round glasses and tall black hat also stood out against his pale face.

Like Paul Wegener, Conrad Veidt spent the rest of the silent era specializing in films of terror. His tall, thin body and gaunt, haunted face became familiar to audiences as the demented Ivan the Terrible in *Waxworks*, the good doctor and the evil criminal in a German adaptation of *Dr. Jekyll and Mr. Hyde*, the paranoid pianist in *Hands of Orlac* and Balduin and his enigmatic reflection in a remake of *The Student of Prague*. He lacked the dark humor and warmth of Wegener, but to each role, Veidt brought a frantic commitment and an almost balletic use of his body to convey character.

The brilliant and autocratic young writer and director Fritz Lang was originally slated to helm *Caligari*, but he could not complete his epic adventure, *The Spiders*, in time. Before recommending Wiene, Lang contributed a framing story different from the one envisioned by Janowitz and Mayer. According to Lang's 1967 interview with Peter Bogdanovich, Lang told Pommer, "Look, if the Expressionistic sets stand for the world of the insane, and you use them from the beginning, it doesn't mean anything. Why don't you, instead, make the Prologue and Epilogue of the picture normal?"

According to Lang's plan, in the beginning, Francis would be discovered sitting on a bench with another man. Upon seeing an apparently hypnotized Jane, Francis would tell the man his story. At the end of the tale, Francis would be revealed to be insane himself, and the characters in his story would be harmless inmates in the asylum in which he and his listener are imprisoned. The Director of the asylum would be the same actor portraying Dr. Caligari, but without the bizarre makeup and costume. Francis attacks him, and is himself put into a straightjacket and padded cell. The Director, upon hearing Francis accuse him of being Caligari, would now know how to restore him to sanity.

Lang convinced Pommer that the framing story, showing the distorted sets as the vision of a mad narrator, would help the public accept them. The garden in the framing story is less stylized in that the walls do not have painted shadows, and the bare branches of a tree hanging over the bench appear to be real. But the set is stark enough not to give away the twist. In the end of the framing story, the courtyard of the asylum appears exactly as it does in Francis' tale with painted shadows and strange architecture. The cell in which Francis is ultimately imprisoned is the same one that held the straight-jacketed Caligari. The Expressionistic design is identical in the story and in the frame, but the strange patterns on the walls have been painted over. The paint strokes can clearly be seen because visible technique is one of the tenants of Expressionism.

Of course, the framing story muddled the anti-authoritarian subtext envisioned by the two authors. Authority, in the form of the benign Director of the asylum, was now shown to be paternal, kind and helpful. Janowitz and Mayer violently protested, but the powers-that-be overruled them. Janowitz wrote, "Dr. Wiene, a man in his early 50s, of an older generation than ours, was afraid to venture in this new form of Expressionist art. Therefore, to excuse the story, the oblique angles of the roofs and rooms of the scenery, the stylized masks of the actors, the askew painted world, the 'Caligaric world,' the 'crazy world of 1919,' he intended to change our script on a very important point: at the end of the film our symbolic story was to be explained as being a tale told by a mentally deranged person, thus dishonoring our drama—the tragedy of a man gone mad by the misuse of his mental powers—into a cliché, in which every incident was to be explained in a cheap manner, in which the symbolism was to be lost."

Actually, the new ending, with its grand theatrical twist, increases the emotional impact of the film by undermining all sense of security. Even the narrator, our sympathetic protagonist, is mad. And because we witness the story before we know it is the ravings of a lunatic, we still experience its symbolic truth. The framing device distances the story, but it

Not only the interior rooms, but the exterior buildings and roads on stage were constructed so that their forms could be twisted and distorted in *The Cabinet of Dr. Caligari*. [Photofest]

also encourages the audience to ponder it. How much is true and how much fantasy? Why would Francis imagine such a disturbing tale? Thus, the authors' intentions are preserved. The writers, in effect, are Francis, driven mad by persecution from authority of all kinds, and communicating their frustration symbolically in this fantastic, twisted and emotionally heightened movie.

Even Janowitz begrudgingly concedes: "This dramaturgic somersault, hazardous as it was, did not interfere with the gripping fascination, aroused in the audience by the story of our invention, the tragedy of a psychiatrist gone mad by misuse of his mental powers; nothing could interfere with that fascination, because once the mood of an audience has reached such a state of tenseness, no blunder is foolish enough to break this fascination. At any rate Dr. Wiene's 'box within a box' framework was not foolish enough to do so. Actually it was clever enough to explain the unknown Expressionism (the Expressionism of writing, of painting and of acting) in such a way as to bring it within the grasp of the audience. Nevertheless, it was the nucleus of the tragedy of a psychiatrist who had lost his mind, the gripping story of a man whose *idee fixe* compelled him to 'become Caligari' in order to learn, whether murder through commanding a hypnotized medium was possible..."

The last image in the extant copy of Janowitz and Mayer's script shows Francis and Jane standing in front of a plaque with the following inscription:

> Here stood the Cabinet of Dr. Caligari
> Peace to his victims—Peace to him!
> The City of Holstenwall

This conventional happy ending distances the protagonists and the audience from the unease of the story.

By contrast, the last shot of Wiene's film is an ambiguous close-up of the kindly asylum Director. As he announces his plan for a cure for Francis, the camera irises in on his face. He puts on his spectacles and stares sternly at us. We hold on him for an extended beat before finally fading out. Since it is the same actor who portrays the evil Dr. Caligari, and since this is exactly the same type of iris-in that introduced us to the sinister character, we cannot help but be reminded of the mad showman. So, is this Director another example of dominating, irresponsible authority? Will his cure for Francis be worse than the disease? The final fade-out is anything but happy or triumphant. With the masterfully cinematic touch of holding the close-up a beat too long, Wiene undermines any sense of hopefulness the narrative has created. Like everything else in the movie, the ending of the frame story is dark and disturbing.

The movie premiered at the Berlin Marmorhaus for a four-week run on February 27, 1920. This initial showing was so popular that it was extended an extra week to accommodate the crowds. As Pommer predicted, the film opened markets that had been closed to Germany since the war. In America, Samuel Goldwyn released the film on April 3, 1921, not as a German product, but as a "European" movie. Promoting the mystery and novelty of the piece, Goldwyn lavished an extensive ad campaign and opened the film at the Capitol Theater in New York, the largest movie theater in the world with 5,300 seats.

The New York critic Kenneth MacGowan called it "the most extraordinary production yet seen... its narrative far more exciting and gripping than any but a very few of our native products." He saw the film as a "danger signal" to the American film industry: "American producers have got to shake themselves out of the ruts of machine production and mere money-squandering and try to see the full possibilities of their art." The author and art critic

Willard Huntington Wright agreed: *"The Cabinet of Dr. Caligari* represents the inevitable line along which the cinema must evolve," Wright told *Variety*, "and the first American producer who has the insight and intelligence and courage to turn in that direction... will not only succeed financially, but will go down in the moving picture history of America as the truly great man of the industry." Wright felt that motion pictures "have reached an impasse — every producer who is honest with himself will admit this. A change is necessary, and the only possible change lies along the lines of the *Caligari* picture."

Variety was impressed but skeptical. "It may catch the popular fancy," it admitted. "But it is morbid. Continental creations usually are." *Moving Picture World* called it a "degenerate German invention," adding that what the post-war world really needed was "sane and helpful fiction, not allopathic doses of the morbid and grotesque." The paper advised exhibitors to "Play on the novelty of the picture and keep quiet about the German origin of the work."

When Goldwyn attempted to open the movie in Los Angeles at Miller's Theatre on May 15, 1921, around 2,000 angry protesters demonstrated from noon until 8:30 p.m. The mob consisted of members of the Hollywood post of the American Legion, hundreds of sailors from the Pacific fleet, local members of the Motion Picture Directors Association, wounded veterans and outraged citizens. The crippled World War I soldiers carried signs that read, "Why Pay War Tax to See German-Made Pictures?" The Hearst-owned *Los Angeles Examiner*, which boasted the slogan "America First" on its masthead, had printed editorials stating that with all of its critical acceptance, *The Cabinet of Dr. Caligari* presented an economic and cultural threat to the pre-eminence of the American film industry. They further added that all German pictures should be banned.

By nightfall, the demonstration escalated into rioting. Police reserves and the naval provost guard arrived to subdue the protesters, but their efforts were unsuccessful. They and the theater were pelted with rotten eggs. Finally, Roy H. Marshall, adjutant of the Hollywood Post of the American Legion, climbed to the top of a ladder and announced to the crowd that Fred Miller, owner of the theater, would immediately remove the film from his program. The replacement attraction would be the American made drama, *The Money Changers*, based on a novel by Upton Sinclair. The crowd quickly calmed down and, to show their support of American movies, swarmed into the theater to see the new offering.

The Cabinet of Dr. Caligari was given only one screening in Paris in November 1921. This showing was such a sensation with the artists, writers and taste shapers who attended that the film was given a two-month run in Paris in the spring of 1922.

Building slowly, country by country, *The Cabinet of Dr. Caligari* was ultimately an international sensation. No other movie since D.W. Griffith's *Birth of a Nation* in 1915 caused such excitement and controversy. The intertitle, "Until dawn," spoken by Cesare in answer to Alan's question of how long he will live, became as famous as Griffith's, "War's peace," in *Birth of a Nation* when Griffith showed a gruesome pile of dead soldiers in a ditch. *The Cabinet of Dr. Caligari* helped legitimize film as an art form among the intelligensia. Because of constant revivals in the 1920s, it fostered the creation of cinema clubs and art theaters for the showing and discussion of aesthetically ambitious films around the world.

Clever showman that he was, Pommer accurately saw the potential of combining the invisible methods of storytelling and editing already perfected by Hollywood with the obvious technique of a modern art movement like Expressionism. Thus, he appealed both to mass audiences seeking entertainment and sophisticated patrons intrigued by an aesthetic display. Actually, of course, the Expressionism was merely window dressing for a compelling and original thriller full of suspense, twists and strange characters. Because of the subject matter, it worked beautifully, unlike other forays into abstract set design like Wiene's subsequent

Expressionist movie, *Genuine*. *The Cabinet of Dr. Caligari* remained the summit of the silent German horror film in story, theme and conception, a peak attempted but never really reached again.

For his 1920 version of *The Golem*, subtitled *How He Came Into the World*, Paul Wegener told the original story of the Golem's creation in medieval times, which he had heard in 1913 while filming *The Student of Prague*:

The Emperor plans to banish the Jews from their Prague ghetto. The elderly Rabbi Loew and his young alchemist assistant endow life into the clay Golem by means of a magic word spoken by the demon Astaroth, written on a piece of parchment and placed in the Star of David on the Golem's chest. The statue saves the Emperor's life when his palace collapses as a result of his court's disrespect toward the Rabbi. In gratitude, the Emperor pardons the Jews.

But the longer the Golem lives, the more willful and destructive he becomes. The Rabbi is forced to snatch the Star of David from his chest, immobilizing him. In a jealous rage, the holy man's assistant restores the Star so that he can command the Golem to punish a knight from the Emperor's court who has taken liberties with the Rabbi's flirtatious daughter. The Golem throws the knight from a tower and will not let the assistant remove the Star from his chest. The monster kidnaps the Rabbi's daughter and sets fire to the laboratory. After sending the entire ghetto into a panic, the Golem drops the daughter when he sees small children playing outside of the ghetto's gates. The creature picks up one of the little girls, fascinated by her innocent beauty. The child curiously takes the Star of David from the Golem's chest, and the statue falls to the ground, once again a lifeless piece of clay.

Even in the wake of the success of *The Cabinet of Dr. Caligari*, Wegener denied that he envisioned an Expressionist film. In fact, Wegener's greatest influence was his former employer, the experimental German stage director, Max Reinhardt.

From 1907 to 1919, Reinhardt was the foremost interpreter of theater in Berlin and Vienna. Fans often attended his Deutsches Theater more than once a week because his program changed daily. He pioneered the use of chiaroscuro lighting with harsh contrasts between light and shadow, illuminating characters and objects of importance while leaving others in vague darkness. In addition, he created fantastic effects such as twinkling stars in a black night sky while dark, magic lantern clouds moved across them.

During the war, when material for theatrical productions was in short supply, Reinhardt further experimented with the extremes of lighting and staging. Shifting lighting effects disguised the bare sets and signaled the change of one location to another on a largely empty stage. In addition, they varied the mood and atmosphere in non-realistic but highly emotional ways. Reinhardt evolved a new method of grouping actors and giving the tableaus depth by means of light. Crowds could be made to appear larger by having them recede into darkness.

His techniques sought to supplant the stifling realism of the previous generation of theatrical presentations. Unlike the Expressionists, his intention was not to shock or outrage, but to seduce. Reinhardt appealed to his audience's imaginations by dazzling them with visual stimulation.

In *The Golem* of 1920, Wegener adapted Reinhardt's magical effects to the needs of the cinema. To do this, he required talented collaborators. Primarily an actor, he preferred to have a technician such as Stellan Rye on *The Student of Prague* with whom to work. Carl Boese directed Wegener's wife, Lyda Salmanova, in *Die Tanzerin Barberina* in 1919,

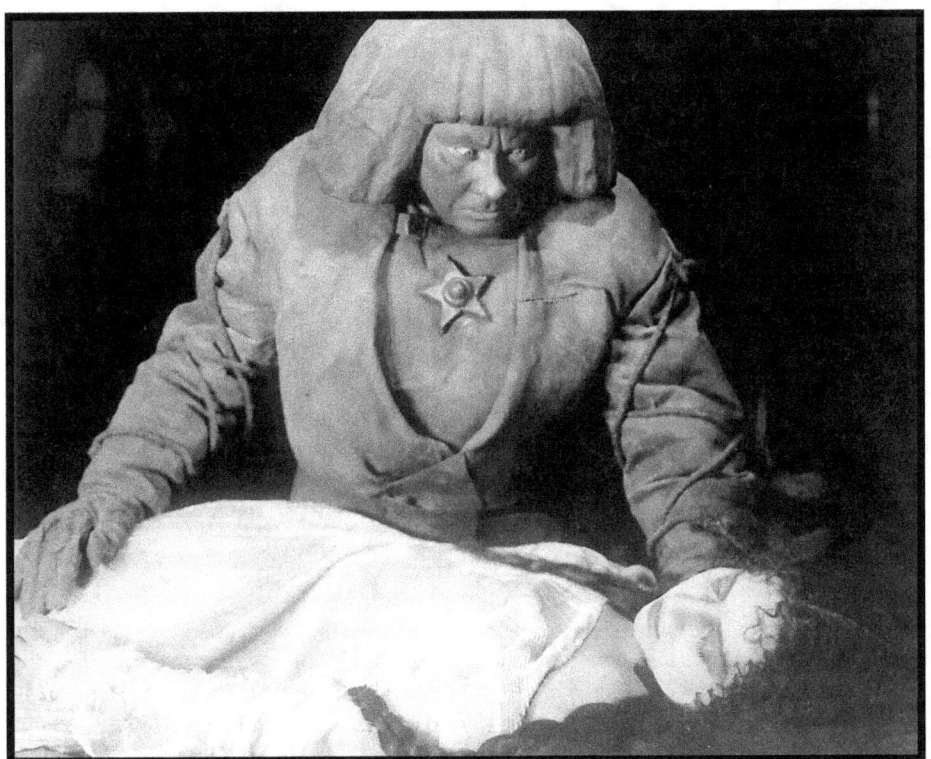
Paul Wegener as The Golem with Lyda Salmonova [Photofest]

and Wegener asked him to co-direct the new *Golem* for Union Films. Boese proposed the extraordinary architect Hans Poelzig to sketch the production. Wegener had known Poelzig before the war when the artist had designed the reconstruction of a Berlin circus into a theater for Reinhardt: the Grosses Schauspielhaus. The interior resembled a mysterious cavern with stalactites and stalagmites. The foyer and corridors were Egyptian. The exterior featured narrow arcades as in the Coliseum but with gothic touches.

Born in 1869, Poelzig designed according to his own private aesthetic unrelated to any artistic movement. "The effect of architecture is magical," he declared in his lectures. Fusing the concrete reality of building with mysticism, Poelzig filled his library with books on the occult and astrology. His daughter acted as a medium at seances that he organized at his home. He felt that a hidden power existed behind reality, a power which he called *Andere* or "Other," and he sought to find this force in his work. Like Wegener and Ewers, he also searched for the mystical in cinema by expressing the metaphysical with the real. He wrote in his notebook, "Film... the magic of form... the form of magic... Devil's Mass." Wegener described Poelzig in his 1936 eulogy of the architect as a "gothic mystic."

After the defeat of Germany in World War I, perhaps partly because of his abrasively dictatorial personality, Poelzig found it difficult to secure work. He eagerly accepted the offer to sketch settings for Wegener's new, studio-bound *Golem*. Poelzig's wife, Marlene, who had sculpted the eccentric columns for the Grosses Schauspielhaus, formed clay models of Poelzig's designs for *The Golem* sets. The brilliant builder, Kurt Richter, supervised the massive constructions, including the streets of the medieval Jewish ghetto with steep, angular, teetering dwellings that seemed about to collapse. Wegener told an interviewer from *Film-Kurier*, "It is not Prague that my friend, the architect Poelzig, has built. Not Prague and not any other city. Rather, it is a city-poem, a dream, an architectural paraphrase on the theme 'Golem.' These alleys and plazas are not intended to resemble reality; they create an atmosphere in which the Golem breathes."

When Boese's director of photography, Guido Seeber, fell ill, Boese chose Karl Freund. After brilliantly lighting and composing the images for *The Golem*, Freund went on to film the subjective and moving camera masterpieces, *The Last Laugh* and *Variety*, such influential genre classics as Fritz Lang's *Metropolis*, Tod Browning's *Dracula* and Robert Florey's *Murders in the Rue Morgue*, as well as directing *The Mummy* with Boris Karloff and *Mad Love* with Peter Lorre.

Freund was able to adapt much of Reinhardt's atmospheric lighting to film for Wegener: the stars glowing unnaturally against the inky sky, the blinding glare of the flames from the alchemist's furnace, a servant's face slowly emerging in a dark doorway as he approaches with a lantern, the row of crackling torches illuminating the night, and, in the synagogue, the light dancing over the huddled Rabbis wrapped in cloaks with their Menorah's seven candles haloed against the darkness. A directional Rembrandt glow suffuses the interiors, detailing the old Rabbi's wrinkled face and casting his young assistant and daughter into glowing relief against the dark background. The only obviously Expressionistic lighting and set design involves the twisting, shell-like staircase that shines brightly against the darkness of the Rabbi's laboratory. Other than that, the effects are too subtle to be called Expressionism, never intending to shock or call attention to themselves.

The fact that the results were subtle did not mean that they were not difficult to achieve. The orthochromatic black and white film stock was not sufficiently sensitive to capture fine shades of gray between black and white. The emulsion required intense light to register any details. Carl Boese wrote that at the time, "...Karl Freund... was splendid at composing images, but unwilling to risk his hand at executing trick shots. So I had to take care of them myself, while Freund helped me with the lighting.

"The whole was, moreover, filmed with a normal Debrie [Parvo] camera. We used diaphragms for shutter dissolves, iris diaphragm dissolves and superimpositions, which in those days were prepared and executed in the camera itself during the actual shooting."

With the primitive film emulsion, even capturing sunbeams falling from a window into the Rabbi's darkened laboratory, as called for in one of Poelzig's sketches, required elaborate preparation and execution. Because filmmakers still worked in glass studios, Boese decided to use the sun itself for the powerfully bright light source required. The laboratory set had to be constructed in such a way that sunlight would fall into it through the high window for a few hours a day. Even then, the fine particles of dust would not register brightly enough to make the sunbeams seem luminous. A special dust composed principally of ground, highly reflective mica was scattered in the air. It filled the set long enough, but it caught the light so well that Freund had to mask the lamps illuminating the area around the sunbeams, creating a dark zone bordering them so that they would stand out.

In the scene in which the Rabbi and his assistant draw a magic circle on the floor and invoke the demon Astaroth, the laboratory had to be built on scaffolding so that technicians could crawl underneath wearing gas masks to control the flames and smoke that burst from the circle. Freund tilted spotlights down onto the smoke to make the billowing clouds appear to glow from within.

To present fireballs flying outside of the magic circle, frames were counted on the original negative of the Rabbi and his assistant, and the fireballs were superimposed over the scene. Boese wrote: "Scraps of the magic word that the Rabbi sought had to come out of the mouth of a demoniac mask. This effect was... executed by a mobile camera in front of black velvet, using dissolves and lap dissolves, and the whole was superimposed on the negative in the camera itself... by counting frames. The letters of the words were cut out in yellowish cardboard, they were harshly lit... while using two negative emulsions from time to time in order to light some more than others and to make them dip and sway."

After the demon Astaroth tells Rabbi Loew the magic word, the old man writes it on a small piece of parchment and slips it into the Star of David affixed to the Golem's chest. The Golem opens his eyes and comes to life. Boese wrote: "We were unwilling to cut this shot, which would have simplified the replacement of the clay statue by Wegener himself....This time the effect was neither technical, chemical or physical. I appealed quite simply to the illusion and imagination of the spectator himself."

With the Golem statue in the background, Boese directed the Rabbi to approach the stationary camera until his hands holding the Star of David filled the screen. While the Rabbi blocked the background and folded the parchment into the back of the Star of David, four stagehands removed the immobile statue of the Golem, and Wegener quickly stood in its place. Then, the Rabbi walked into the background, unblocking the camera's view of the Golem. He replaced the Star of David onto Wegener's chest, and the actor opened his eyes. Boese thus achieved the effect without a cut as he required.

The influence of *The Golem* can be seen in many horror films including 1931's *Frankenstein*.

When the film arrived in America in June 1921, *The New York Times* was impressed: "The black magic of the Middle Ages, sorcery, astrology and all of the superstitious realities of people so legendary in appearance and manners that the unnatural seems natural among them have been brought to the screen... in *The Golem*, the latest motion picture to come from the explorative innovators of Germany. The photoplay gives the impression of some fabulous old tale of strange people in a strange world, fascinating, exciting to the imagination and yet so unfamiliar in all of its aspects that it almost seems remote, elusive even, when one would like to get closer to its meaning....This power is derived mainly from a combination of exceptional acting and the most expressive settings yet seen in this country."

Silent Screams

***The Golem*'s massive sets, period costumes and unusual makeups contribute to the haunting remoteness of the tale. [Photofest]**

Unlike *The Cabinet of Dr. Caligari*, this film marks the path that German cinema would take until the advent of sound. Actually, very few German horror films of the 1920s can be called Expressionistic. This common misconception derives from the popularity and striking look of *The Cabinet of Dr. Caligari* as well as ignorance about what actually constitutes Expressionism. Touches of Expressionistic exaggeration inform certain moments of German silents, but their overall styles are usually closer to a Romantic theatricality. *The Golem* influences and anticipates the genre by creating its own stylized but believable world using every resource of the studio of its time: set design, photography, acting and special effects. And it does so in the service of a dark, fantastic tale that would be the paradigm for several to follow.

More than Edison's *Frankenstein*, Wegener's *The Golem* serves as the model for the monster-on-the-loose films of the sound era. Director James Whale certainly recalled it when making his classic version of *Frankenstein* in 1931. The pattern is firmly set in Wegener's film: the creator endows the inanimate monster with life, attempts to control it, loses control when the monster finds its own will, and must destroy it or be destroyed by it when the creature goes on an angry rampage. Even the monster's weakness for beauty and the innocence of children is anticipated in this seminal masterpiece. In both *The Golem* and *Frankenstein*, the monster develops a personality or "soul" beyond the workings of its human creator.

Like the steady, inexorable movement of the Golem itself, the film strides forward in stately but unpredictable fashion. The film's slow pace, especially in the first half, creates an atmosphere of classical dignity at odds with later styles of rapid storytelling. But the deliberate movement, like the massive sets, period costumes and unusual makeups, contribute to the haunting remoteness of the tale. Even in 1920, Wegener required audiences to surrender to his unusual style in order to experience the world of faith, sorcery, passion and violence that he created.

German designer, painter and architect Albin Grau founded Prana-Film with businessman Enrico Dieckmann on a capitalization of 20,000 marks in January 1921 for the express purpose of producing movies of the occult, the Romantic and the bizarre. Grau stated that his films would be created according to "new principles." He derived the name from the Buddhist concept of *prana,* which referred to the sacred breath that endowed life.

Grau, whose magical designation among the occult community was Frater Pacitus, was a Master of the Pansophical Lodge, which introduced Tantric sexual magic to Europe, and an initiate of the Order of the Oriental Templars who believed themselves to be the heirs to the forbidden rituals of the original Knights Templar of the Middle Ages. Grau's Order worshipped the infernal god Baphomet, linked through the ages of occult studies with Lucifer. In Christianity, Lucifer was considered a sin-punishing demon, but in the Order of the Oriental Templars, Lucifer was hailed as the deity who enlightened man in the form of the serpent of Eden.

Although neither Grau nor Dieckmann had any direct experience in motion pictures, they accurately saw the cinematic potential of Bram Stoker's 24-year-old novel, *Dracula.* However, with the impracticality of artists, they did not bother to secure the rights to the book from Stoker's 64-year-old widow, Florence, before embarking on their project.

Dracula fascinated Grau because of a personal experience six years earlier. In a 1922 issue of *Buhne Und Film,* he told of being billeted in a Serbian peasant home during World War I and of the host's story of his father returning from the grave as a vampire in 1884 to prey on the village. The host called his father *nosferatu,* or "undead." Finally, the host's father was laid to rest with a wooden stake driven through his heart.

Henrik Galeen, the Reinhardt alumnus who had co-written and co-directed the first version of *The Golem* with Wegener, was hired to adapt *Dracula* into a screenplay. Obviously pirating the work deliberately, Galeen changed all the characters' names from the book: Count Dracula became Count Orlok; Jonathan Harker became Thomas Hutter; Mina was renamed Ellen; Renfield became Knock and Professor Van Helsing was called Professor Bulwer.

While Stoker set his story in his own time of Victorian England so that the supernatural would erupt in a recognizably modern world, Galeen placed the action in the distant period of the Wisborg plague of 1843.

Galeen streamlined the sprawling novel, eliminating Dracula's brides from his castle, the transformation of Dracula's victims into vampires, many of Dracula's powers and weaknesses, and the hunt for Dracula from England to Transylvania by the brave troop of Victorian vampire fighters. In place of the creation of new vampires through Dracula's bite, Galeen substituted the monster's spread of the plague. All Christian iconography was removed from the story, including Dracula's fear of crosses. Galeen emphasized science over religion, especially when the Van Helsing character, a follower of the 16th-century alchemist and physician Paracelsus, compared vampires to Venus fly traps and transparent, "phantom" polyps. In addition, Galeen initiated a piece of vampire lore not included in the novel but accepted in almost every other cinematic version of it: the destruction of the vampire by exposure to the rays of the sun. In his novel, Stoker had written of Count Dracula walking about Picadilly Circus in broad daylight.

F.W. Murnau

However, Galeen retained enough of the basic structure of the book to expose the new work as a recognizable adaptation: the young solicitor's journey to Transylvania to sell Dracula a house in a modern city; the vampire's sea voyage to his new home and attack on the young man's wife; the psychic connection between Dracula and an incarcerated lunatic; and the revelation of vampire lore by a patriarchal savant. Galeen renamed the adaptation after the word learned by Grau, *Nosferatu*, which also echoed Stoker's working title for his novel: *The Undead*.

Grau himself rendered pre-production sketches of amazing detail and atmosphere. Later, he even painted the striking and imaginative posters for the film's release. His design for the vampire owed little to Stoker, but was, nevertheless, inspired and effective. Count Orlok's face looks like the skull of a rat with a bald, bony head, sunken cheeks, long, pointed nose, two sharp front fangs and pointed ears. His overcoat covers hunched shoulders and long arms ending in talon-like hands. Grau's designs for the interiors of Hutter's room in the castle, Ellen's bedroom with its picture window overlooking Orlok's new house and the hold of the ship carrying Orlok's casket were followed almost exactly in the film. As a believer in the occult, Grau even designed the prop letter from Orlok to Knock which is covered in astrological and Cabalistic characters. The fact that Knock could read this coded letter from the Count revealed his early link with the evil vampire.

To direct their first venture, Prana Film hired 32-year-old Friedrich Wilhelm Murnau, another pre-war pupil, actor and assistant director of Max Reinhardt. Born Friedrich Wilhelm Plumpe in Bielefield, Germany on December 28, 1888, Murnau was the son of a textile merchant of Swedish descent. Theatrical even as a child, he would often play make-believe stories with his siblings and friends. He studied art and the history of literature at the University of Heidelberg, then went to Berlin where he worked for Reinhardt. He took the name "Murnau" from a town in Germany.

During World War I, he was a German combat pilot. He crashed his plane twice and damaged one of his kidneys so badly that he was never able to drink alcohol. On one mission, he strayed off course in a heavy fog and landed in Switzerland where he stayed until the end of the war, directing a play and compiling propaganda footage for the German embassy in Berne. After the war, he began his career as a film director in 1919 in Germany.

In 1920, Murnau directed an unauthorized film adaptation of Stevenson's *The Strange Case of Dr. Jekyll and Mr. Hyde* for Lipow Film, entitled *Der Januskopf*, or in English, *The Head of Janus*. Writer Hans Janowitz had chosen to follow up his triumphant *The Cabinet of Dr. Caligari* with this version of Stevenson's classic and had even retained the original names of Stevenson's characters in his script, which was subtitled *A Tragedy on the Border of Reality*. But Lipow Film changed the names in order to camouflage the source, thereby avoiding the costly copyright question.

In Murnau's film of Janowitz's script, Conrad Veidt played the dual role of Dr. Warren and Mr. O'Connor. Unfortunately, the negative and all prints were reportedly confiscated and

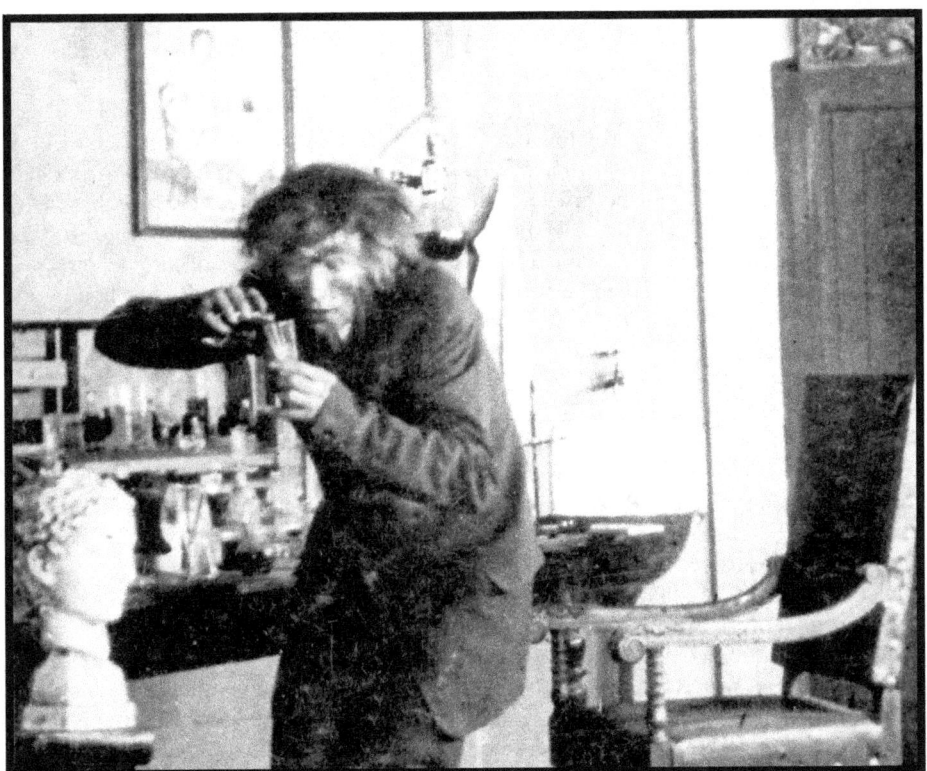

Conrad Veidt as Dr. Warren/Mr. O'Connor in *The Head of Janus* [Photofest]

destroyed by the courts due to copyright infringement, and only the screenplay and a few photographs remained. According to the script, Janowitz changed the story considerably:

The good Dr. Warren is obsessed with a bust of Janus, the two-faced Roman god, that he purchases from an antique store. One face reveals his nobler aspects while the other is that of a leering, hideous satyr. Under the influence of this sculpture, Dr. Warren transforms into the evil Mr. O'Connor, a lusting, murderous monster. Mr. O'Connor drags Dr. Warren's fiancee to a Whitechapel brothel and kills a little girl in the street. Finally, Dr. Warren takes poison and dies rather than let Mr. O'Connor completely possess him. His body is found clutching the bust of Janus.

When the film opened at the same theater that had housed *Caligari* four months previously, none of the German critics recognized Stevenson as the source, even with a credit that said the film was based on "an English original." Exhibitors later screened the film under the title *Schrecken* or *Terror*, as well as *Love's Mockery*. In Austria, the title was closer to the source: *Dr. Warren and Mr. O'Connor*.

Since Murnau had deliberately pirated a famous literary work before, Grau and Dieckmann must have thought he was just the man to helm their unauthorized version of *Dracula*. Murnau, with cameraman Fritz Arno Wagner, began shooting *Nosferatu* in the two northern German towns of Wismar and Lubeck on the Baltic Sea in August 1921.

Most of these locations for *Nosferatu* still exist because Murnau chose historically important sites that looked at least 80 years old. For example, the first shot establishing

Hutter's hometown was shot from the tower of St. Marian's Church looking down on the famous marketplace of Wismar. Unfortunately, part of the tower was later damaged in a World War II bombing raid. However, the streets through which Hutter walked have been perfectly preserved in the nearby town of Lubeck. The deserted house purchased by Nosferatu, with its rows of dark, inscrutable windows, was in reality a warehouse for salt built in the late 1500s. Restored and protected, it would actually be one of the most expensive pieces of property on the Baltic coast. Edvard Munch sketched its haunting facade in 1902, and this may have influenced Murnau's selection of it as the home of the vampire. The Wismar hospital, now a museum, served as the yard and fountain of the Harding house from which Hutter began his journey to Transylvania. The beautiful scenes of Ellen waiting for Hutter and the ship slowly sailing into town with its horrible cargo were done at the Wismar beach and harbor. The famous Wismar gate, one of the most striking examples of Gothic architecture, framed Count Orlok as he crept into the city carrying his coffin under his arm. A large Lubeck mansion represented the front of Hutter's home.

In October, Murnau and his crew traveled south to the Western Tatras Mountains which formed the border between Poland and Slovakia to shoot in and around Orava Castle. The inn at which Hutter stopped on his journey actually existed next to a country road. Likewise, the shrine Hutter passed as he walked to the castle was not a prop but a real monument to Christianity on the mountainside. Orava Castle itself, which represented Count Orlok's Transylvanian home, was built in the 13th century on rocks high above the rushing Orava River. An authentic medieval fortress complete with a torture chamber, it had been renovated over the centuries with Roman, Gothic, Renaissance and even Neo-Gothic architecture. The filagoria, or outlook house, in which Hutter wrote his letter to Ellen while being attacked by mosquitoes, was built on the castle grounds in the 1800s and had a spectacular view of the river and mountainside. Murnau even used some of the castle interiors, such as one for the scene in which Hutter discovered Orlok's body resting in his crypt during the day. Thus, the highly controlled and designed studio settings of *Caligari* and *The Golem* were absent, replaced by carefully composed location shots with a static camera.

Murnau did not follow the script slavishly, but improvised a great deal, which is apparent when comparing his personally annotated screenplay with the finished film. For example, the script does not indicate the final shot of the film, the exterior of a ruined castle filmed 20 miles from Orava Castle in Slovakia. When location shooting was completed, Murnau and his crew filmed the remaining interiors on sets built at Jofa Studios in Berlin-Johannistal.

Murnau directs *Nosferatu* in the Expressionistic shadow of *Caligari*, yet his style appears more influenced by German Romanticism of the 19th century. Expressionism and Romanticism have much in common. Both emphasize emotion over intellect, and both conjure dreamscapes of the mind over objective reality. But Expressionism responds with despair over the lust, violence and hate of society, especially following the horrors of World War I. In cinema, this results, of course, in distorted sets and sharp, tortured camera angles, all lit with chiaroscuro shadows.

But Murnau was at heart a Romantic, much influenced by Scandinavian filmmakers like Victor Sjostrom. As in such Sjostrom works as *The Outlaw and His Wife*, the natural settings in Murnau almost become characters in the narrative. The words of the German philosopher Schelling could be Murnau's artistic credo. He wrote, "The plastic arts provide an active bond between the soul and nature." The artist must work "at the core of things and speak through signs and shapes as by symbols only."

The images in *Nosferatu* reveal Murnau's love of outdoor settings as both emotional landscapes and psychological metaphors. Murnau manipulates nature by camera placement

Most of the locations for *Nosferatu* still exist. Max Schreck as Count Orlak

and the movement of characters and objects through it. His use of Gothic arches, seascapes at sunset, twisted tree branches against the sky and small, dark figures in vast landscapes recall Romantic painters of the 1800s such as Caspar David Friedrich.

Because Murnau emphasizes the natural world in Hutter's journey to Orlok's castle, the viewer is better able to suspend disbelief when the precepts of that world are altered by

The images in *Nosferatu* reveal Murnau's love of outdoor settings as both emotional landscapes and psychological metaphors.

the supernatural. Unlike the fantasy genre which changes physical laws from the beginning, horror often works best when those principles are superseded gradually. The viewer then feels uncertain, wondering what might happen if the rules of the game have indeed been amended to include metaphysical evil. Murnau achieves this sense of uncertainty when Hutter is confronted by the superstitious peasants warning him not to continue his journey.

The Book of Vampires that Hutter finds by his bedside at the inn puts the story firmly in the world of the supernatural, but the transition to our acceptance of that world takes place slowly during Hutter's coach ride to Orlok's castle. Murnau alters the natural order by undercranking the film, giving the carriage and horses a quick, jerky movement. Also, one shot is printed on negative stock so that the branches of the trees appear white and thorny against the black sky. Interestingly, Murnau changes Orlok's costume and the drapery around the coach from black to white in the negative shot so that they appear black in both positive and negative.

Despite his homosexuality, Murnau idealizes women in true Romantic fashion, especially pure Madonna-like figures such as Ellen in *Nosferatu*. She becomes an icon to be adored by Hutter and desired by Count Orlok more than an actual, living, breathing woman. Virtuous Madonna figures will turn up in later Murnau movies such as *Faust* and *Sunrise*.

In fact, all of the characters in *Nosferatu* are types rather than complex people. Each has one strong trait so that they seem to represent different facets of a single personality. Thomas Hutter is shown as childlike, active but ineffectual and uncomprehending. His first reaction to the tales of vampires in Transylvania is denial, even when he finds puncture marks on his own throat. When he can no longer ignore the horror around him, he literally hides his face in his bedcovers and eventually runs away. Professor Bulwer is his opposite: a complete and mature man, secure and self aware.

Even Hutter's relationship with his wife seems immature. On a literal level, none of the characters in *Nosferatu* are sexual, but, as in Stoker's novel, symbolically, the entire story is about sex and desire. Murnau, the Romantic, reveals Ellen's sexual frustration with Thomas through her actions: she teases a cat with a ball of thread as she waits for him to come home and pulls a needle through cloth as she embroiders. She is constantly framed through windows, a common symbol of female sexuality and receptivity. Thomas characteristically behaves like an overgrown, asexual child around her. He runs away to Transylvania like a boy off on an adventure rather than staying in Wisborg to satisfy his wife. Even toward the climax of the film, he sleeps in a chair as she reclines in bed.

If the characters represent different facets of one personality, then Count Orlok, with his unchecked animal desires, is definitely the id to Hutter's ego. Max Schreck, whose last name, coincidentally, means "terror" in German, plays Count Orlok wearing the disturbing makeup and costume of Grau's production sketches. Schreck was born in Berlin in 1879 and began his stage training at the Staatstheatre in Berlin. He debuted there in *Messeritz* before touring Germany for two years. Eventually, he joined Reinhardt's company in Berlin and the Kammerspiele of Munich. He appeared in 20 films before his death from a heart attack in 1936 at age 57. But he will forever be remembered for his appearance and performance as cinema's first Dracula in *Nosferatu*.

As the film progresses, Schreck's appearance seems to become more hideous. The first time Hutter meets him, Orlok discreetly wears a leather hat. When the Count is finally revealed as a predatory vampire to Hutter, he sees Orlok's bony, white head fully exposed for the first time, and the vision is startlingly horrific. Suddenly, all of his rat-like features coalesce without the humanizing hat to distract from them. Each time Orlok reappears, his fingernails have lengthened until they become sharp talons that move like the spindly legs of an albino spider.

Murnau often places Orlok at the center of the screen, emerging from darkness. On board the ship taking him to Wisborg, Orlok is surrounded by web-like ship rigging as the Captain awaits death, bound to the wheel like a fly. Later, Orlok is surrounded by the frames of small windows like an arachnid in his snare as he watches his new fly, Ellen, in the house across the street.

The horror genre often explores taboo subjects such as homosexuality, incest and necrophilia symbolically without having to confront them directly. Hutter inadvertently attracts Orlok when he cuts his thumb at dinner. Orlok's unwanted attention is intense and personal as he backs Thomas into a chair by the fire.

Only when Orlok sees the miniature portrait of Ellen is his lust transferred from Thomas to her. In fact, when Orlok approaches Hutter's bed in Transylvania, Murnau cross-cuts to Ellen's bedroom in Wisborg. She cries out, and Orlok turns from Thomas and leaves. The intertitle says that Hutter psychically hears Ellen's call of warning. But Murnau's visual of Orlok turning from Thomas to look screen right in response to Ellen's gesture toward screen left makes it clear that it is Nosferatu who hears her call, not of warning, but of desire.

From this point on, Orlok ignores Hutter and concentrates all his efforts in coming to Ellen. As the ship carrying Orlok speeds to Wisborg, Ellen waits on the beach. Again, the intertitle contradicts Murnau's images. The words tells us that Ellen stares across the ocean, pining for Thomas, but it is Orlok who comes by sea, not Hutter. As Thomas struggles home by land, Orlok sails to Ellen, fueled by her frustrated lust.

Nosferatu has truly become Hutter's id, hurrying to fulfill Thomas' duties as a husband in his own uniquely perverted way. In the hold of the ship, Orlok rises stiffly from his coffin, like an erection. The long bow of the ship, emphasized in Murnau's camera angles, points straight through the waves toward Ellen, serving as another phallic symbol. When Nosferatu disembarks, he carries his coffin under his arm, its long form jutting before him. As he enters his new home, the coffin penetrates the walls first, and he and the coffin fade away as they disappear inside.

In Murnau's later films, *Faust* and *Sunrise*, good and evil struggle within the soul of an incomplete man. In both cases, this inner turmoil is instigated by the power of a sexually demanding female. Also in both cases, the man finds spiritual salvation through the love of a pure-hearted woman. In *Nosferatu*, the good and evil are split between the two characters of Hutter and Orlok. Their struggle takes place in the physical world and is initiated through the desire of a woman who craves sexual attention. This woman also becomes the virtuous martyr who destroys the evil character through her sacrifice.

In the end, Ellen opens her bedroom window, a clearly sexual symbol, inviting Orlok to enter. She plans to seduce him with her blood to stay until morning, at which time the rising sun will destroy him. Just as she plans, Nosferatu feeds at her throat too long and vanishes in the first rays of dawn. Ellen is no longer the pure Madonna, and she dies after her violation by the evil undead.

Hutter, ineffectual as always, arrives too late to help. Actually, many young male characters in German films of this time were equally passive and useless. The frustration and anger of the German people after their defeat in World War I may be responsible for this self portrayal as powerless pawns in a hostile, overwhelming world.

Of all the masterpieces of silent German horror, *Nosferatu* demands the most tolerance of then-experimental cinematic techniques. Filmed on locations on a relatively low budget, it lacks much of the studio perfection of *The Golem* or even *The Cabinet of Dr. Caligari*. But its atmosphere of Romantic reality enhances its sense of a distant time and place in which the horrible impossible could occur. Murnau's attempts to disrupt his naturalistic style with radical techniques such as fast motion and printed negative are not as effective as the simple introduction of the monstrously ugly vampire into authentic locations or the grim spread of rats and disease into the quiet community of Wisborg. But unlike *The Golem*, this film moves rapidly through its story, piling up so many haunting cinematic moments that any brief miscalculation of effect or lack of production resources are quickly forgiven.

Prana Film held a lavish premiere with printed programs and full orchestral accompaniment at the Marble Hall of the Berlin Zoological Gardens on Saturday, March 4, 1922. The reviews were mostly good, with the vampire seen as a metaphor for dark aspects of the human soul after the trauma of war. However, Prana Film's fiscal irresponsibility soon overshadowed their artistic accomplishment. Following the premiere, the press reported that Prana Film had already spent more on publicity than on the actual cost of production. Bills went unpaid.

Meanwhile, at her Williams Street address in Knightsbridge, England, Florence Stoker received the program and advertising for the Berlin premiere of *Nosferatu, Eine Symphonie des Grauens*, "freely adapted" from Bram Stoker's *Dracula*. Stoker's widow was livid. Of all of her late husband's books, only *Dracula* remained constantly in print, providing her with a small but steady income. Her financial situation was uncertain. She would never sell her art collection, and her accountant son, Noel, maintained a rather distant relationship with her.

Upon hearing of this unauthorized version, she joined the British Incorporated Society of Authors for the express purpose of utilizing their lawyers to protect her rights. Their German attorney, Dr. Wronker-Flatow of Berlin, contacted Prana Film in May. According to

In *Nosferatu* Murnau often places Orlok at the center of the screen, emerging from darkness. [Photofest]

the Society's correspondence with Mrs. Stoker, "the film company had put up some foolish points as defense." But by June, Prana Film's lack of funds had driven it into receivership.

The Society now attempted to pursue the receiver of Prana's assets rather than Grau and Dieckmann. That proved a complicated business because the Society would have to chase the film all over the globe, trying to prevent sales and unauthorized screenings. The German receivers attempted to make a participation deal with Mrs. Stoker, provided the film could be called *Dracula* in Great Britain and the United States. She refused because no advance was offered, and she would have to be paid in marks, an extremely unstable currency at the time.

The German court ruled against the receivers, the Deutsch-Amerikanisch Film Union, and Mrs. Stoker asked for £5,000 to let them have title to the film. They appealed, and in February 1925, again lost to Mrs. Stoker in the appellate court. Realizing that she would probably never see money from the receivers, Mrs. Stoker decided to have all negatives and prints of the film destroyed. Finally, on July 20, 1925, three years after she had begun the legal maneuvers, Mrs. Stoker received word that Prana's liquidator had given up. The Society's German lawyer was paid by the receiver, and all prints and negatives of *Nosferatu* were ordered obliterated. Mrs. Stoker had just sold the stage rights of *Dracula* for a small amount of money to Hamilton Deane, an actor-manager who toured the provinces of England, so she was doubly victorious.

Although the original negative of *Nosferatu* never resurfaced, Mrs. Stoker occasionally heard of showings of a print. In every case, she insisted on preventing the screening and having the print burned. Producer and film historian Ivor Montagu battled Mrs. Stoker for the right to show F.W. Murnau's *Dracula*, as it was called, to members of the British Film Society for free, but she refused. Like the vampire hunters of the novel, Mrs. Stoker and

***Nosferatu* added to the vampire legend by having sunlight destroy vampires.**

her legal representatives attempted to find the print of *Nosferatu* in London. They finally traced it to an importer, Sargent's Trust Ltd. of Chancery Lane. But the film canisters, like the Count's last coffin, could not be located. By January, the Society of Authors wrote Mrs. Stoker, "I beg to inform you with great regret we must drop the case of the film *Dracula*.... The Sargent's Trust have already done everything to help us trace the man who actually held the film, but we find this person has disappeared entirely." Thus, *Nosferatu*, like the creature that inspired it, had invaded London and escaped.

F.W. Murnau survived the *Nosferatu* scandal to become one of the greatest film artists of the silent era. His next masterpiece was *The Last Laugh* from a script by Carl Mayer which used moving camera, studio sets and subjective angles to plunge the audience into the experiences of an aging hotel doorman, all without resorting to title cards to help tell the story. Following that, Murnau filmed the awe-inspiring fantasy of *Faust*, utilizing all of the resources of the German silent studio to create unforgettable scenes of Mephistopheles' temptation and destruction of the good Doctor. Hollywood took notice, and in 1926, Murnau came to Los Angeles with a five-picture deal at Fox. His first American movie, *Sunrise*, was another cinematic masterpiece, a suspenseful and ultimately romantic story of a simple farmer and his wife coming to the big city, again based on a scenario by Carl Mayer. The picture was a huge commercial and critical hit, but Murnau's next two Fox productions, *Four Devils* and *City Girl*, did not match this success.

Murnau left Fox after the three pictures and teamed with documentary film director Robert Flaherty to film the South Sea island drama, *Tabu*. Murnau ultimately disagreed with Flaherty about the picture and bought him out, completing it himself. After finishing *Tabu*, he signed a contract to work at Paramount like other directors who had made their marks in Germany such as Josef von Sternberg and Ernst Lubitsch.

But a week before *Tabu* premiered, on March 11, 1931, en route from Los Angeles to Monterey, Murnau's car swerved off the road. The director had hired a handsome 14-year-old Filipino boy named Garcia Stevenson as valet, and it was this boy who was at the wheel of the Packard. Though the driver and another passenger were not injured, Murnau was thrown from the car and cracked his head open on a pole. Gossip spread that Murnau was having sex with Stevenson when the car went off. Because of the scandal, only 11 people, including Greta Garbo, attended Murnau's funeral. The Swedish movie star commissioned a death mask of the great director and kept it on her desk during all of her years in Hollywood.

Screenwriter Henrik Galeen's next exercise in the macabre for the German cinema was *Das Wachsfiguren Kabinett*, released in November 1924 and known in English as *Waxworks*. Taking his cue from Fritz Lang's 1921 three-story omnibus fantasy, *Der Mude Tod*, Galeen presented a trio of original tales, two grim and one darkly amusing, based around wax figures at a carnival.

A young writer, played by future director William Dieterle, answers an advertisement asking for an artist to create startling stories around the wax figures at a sideshow. With the owner's pretty young daughter looking enthusiastically over his shoulder, the writer begins to create a tale of cruelty and fear about the figure of Ivan the Terrible:

Ivan is a paranoid sadist who gleefully watches the dying gasp of one of his victims in the Kremlin torture chamber. The Poison Mixer shows the victim a huge hour glass with the poor man's name on it. When the last grain of sand slips to the bottom of the glass, the victim dies from the poison.

The Astrologer warns Ivan to beware of his Poison Mixer, and Ivan orders his assassins to murder the man. Sensing his fate, the Poison Mixer has time to write Ivan's name on the largest hour glass before the killers invade his cellar to strangle him.

A nobleman arrives at the palace to remind Ivan that he promised to attend his daughter's wedding. Ivan orders the nobleman to change clothes with him. Ivan will drive the coach, and the nobleman, dressed as the Czar, will ride in the back.

As they travel through the streets, an assassin fires an arrow at what he thinks is Ivan. The arrow kills the nobleman, and Ivan keeps whipping the horses to the wedding.

The carriage pulls up to the ceremony. Secretly, Ivan commands one of his minions to abduct the bride back to the Kremlin. The groom realizes his bride is gone, and the Czar condemns him to the torture chamber.

At the palace, Ivan attempts to rape the bride. She witnesses her husband-to-be hanging by his wrists, stripped to the waist and tortured. Ivan gloats at her horror.

The Astronomer finds Ivan and shows the Czar the hour glass with his name on it that was found in the Poison Mixer's cellar. Convinced that he has been poisoned, Ivan turns the glass over so that the sand cannot run out, laughing maniacally, thinking he can cheat death. The titles tell us that he goes mad, obsessively turning the hour glass until the end of his days.

The first story over, the wax museum owner tells the writer that the arm of the figure of Haroun Al-Raschid has broken off. The writer promises to explain the missing arm in his next tale.

This second story takes place in the Baghdad of old and begins with the fat Caliph Haroun Al-Raschid losing in chess to his Grand Vizier. The Caliph blames his defeat on the smoke from the nearby bakery. He orders the Vizier to send the baker to Allah.

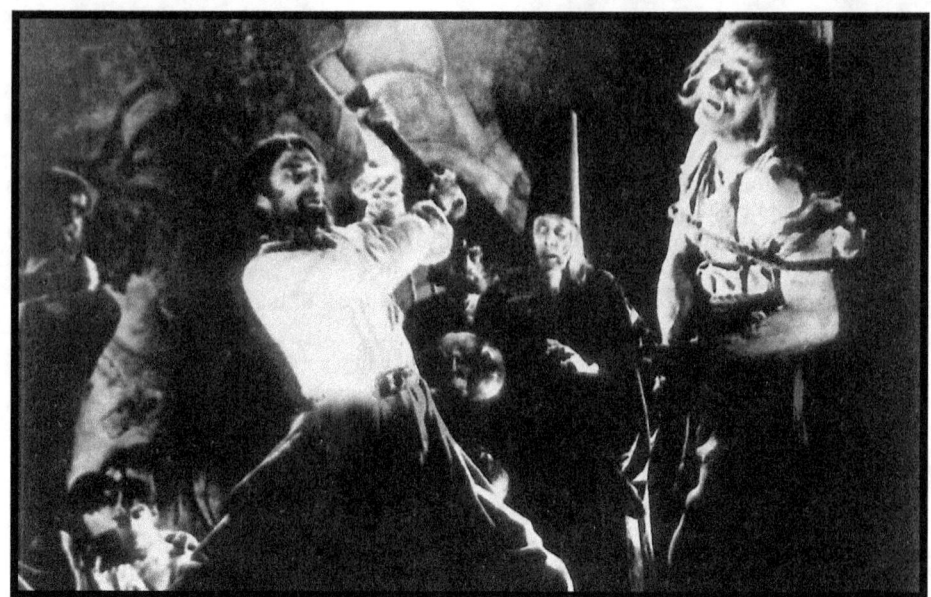
Conrad Veidt tortures a victim in the Ivan the Terrible segment of *Waxworks*. [Photofest]

When the Caliph asks to see the Baker's head, the Vizier tells him that he forgot about arresting the man when he saw his gorgeous wife. Intrigued, the Caliph goes straight to the bakery.

Meanwhile, the Baker's Wife complains that her husband never takes her anywhere or gives her anything. To prove his love, he vows to steal the Caliph's wishing ring and bring it back to her.

As soon as the Baker has left for the palace, the Caliph creeps into the bedroom of the Wife. She immediately sits up in bed and begins flirting with the rotund ruler.

The Baker enters the Caliph's bedroom. A figure that looks exactly like the Caliph sleeps in the enormous, ornate bed. Thinking that be cannot slip the ring off without awakening the ruler, the Baker cuts the figure's arm off and runs away with it. The noise arouses the guards, who chase the Baker.

Hearing the Baker approach, the Caliph desperately hides in the bakery oven, and the wife shuts the door on him. The Baker enters with the arm and ring. Suddenly, guards break in and seize the Baker. The Caliph opens the door to the oven and whispers to the confused Wife that he always puts a wax figure of himself in bed when he sneaks out at night.

As the guards drag her husband out, the Wife grabs the wax arm. She threatens to make a wish on the ring. The guards shrink back in terror, releasing the Baker.

The Wife wishes that the Caliph would come to life again. Hearing this, the Caliph, covered in soot, crawls out of the oven. The Wife also wishes that the Caliph would appoint her husband as the Royal Baker. Happily, the Caliph grants her wish, presumably to keep her close to him in the palace.

The writer tries to come up with a story for the Jack the Ripper figure, but he falls asleep at his desk. He dreams that Springheeled Jack steps off his stand and stalks the writer and the owner's daughter through the fairground. The writer thinks that he has lost the Ripper, but the figure suddenly appears and stabs him. He awakens with a start, comforted by the owner's daughter. Safe and alone, the writer and the daughter kiss passionately.

As in *The Cabinet of Dr. Caligari*, the horror in *Waxworks* results not from the supernatural but from the twisted psyches and deepest fears of the stories' protagonists. Writing in a German film magazine in 1929, Galeen explained his approach:

> What does the old 'fantastic' fairytale world of the Brothers Grimm and Wilhelm Hauff, or E.T.A. Hoffmann and even, perhaps, of Edgar Allan Poe, mean to us and our children today? Let us look at it through today's spectacles. It is stimulus to us, a stimulus of genius, but no more than that; for what we see around us today is more fantastic than anything even a Jules Verne could conceive. Today's reality has become the equivalent of yesterday's fantasy. In our films, therefore, we had to look for new problems in this field.
>
> What can we still call "fantastic" today? Everything that seems possible in our unconscious, although it is not to be found in our common, everyday reality.

Galeen uses his characters' mental aberrations to create worlds of obsession within realistic contexts. The horror of the Ivan the Terrible episode results from the Czar's unpredictable paranoia and his mad compulsion of turning the hour glass to prolong his evil life. Even the Baghdad story keeps threatening to turn grim because of the selfish, immoral desires of the Caliph for the Baker's Wife, the Wife for riches and the attention of other men and the Baker for the Caliph's wishing ring. And the Jack the Ripper story is a visual realization of the writer's unconscious fears erupting in a nightmare.

Galeen's screenplay was interpreted by a director in perfect accord with his theory. Paul Leni was born in Stuttgart, Germany, on July 8, 1885. He lived in Berlin from age 15 and was a struggling *avant garde* painter before becoming a set designer for the stage productions of Max Reinhardt and others. He started in German films in 1914 as an art director. In 1916, he directed his first movie, *Das Tagebuch des Dr. Hart*. By the time he made *Waxworks* in 1924, he had directed 10 films. Leni's great strength was as a designer, and he knew what could be done for a film by variations in costume and setting. In *Waxworks*, each of the stories has a distinct look derived from its period and country.

Leni explained his technique in the 1924 edition of the German film magazine *Kinematograph*:

> If the designer merely imitated photography to construct his sets, the film would remain faceless and impersonal. There has to be the possibility of bringing out an object's essential attributes so as to give the image style and colour...
>
> This is particularly necessary for films set wholly in a world of unreality. For my film *Waxworks* I have tried to create sets so stylized that they evince no idea of reality. My fairground is sketched in with an utter renunciation of detail. All it seeks to engender is an indescribable fluidity of light, moving shapes, shadows, lines and curves. It is not extreme reality that the camera perceives, but the reality of the inner events, which is more profound, effective and moving than what we see through everyday eyes, and I equally believe that the cinema can reproduce this truth, heightened effectively.
>
> I may perhaps cite the example of *Caligari* and *The Golem*, in which Hans Poelzig created a town's image. I cannot stress too strongly how

important it is for a designer to shun the world seen every day and to attain its true sinews ...

It will be seen that a designer must not construct 'fine' sets. He must penetrate the surface of things and reach their heart. He must create mood (*Stimmung*) even though he has to safeguard his independence with regard to the object seen merely through everyday eyes. It is this which makes him an artist. Otherwise I can see no reason why he should not be replaced by an adroit apprentice carpenter.

In the United States, Leni would become an early master of the moving camera, but in *Waxworks*, he still photographs his extraordinary sets and costumes in mostly static shots. However, the images themselves teem with movement because of the imaginative decor.

The Ivan the Terrible episode is set in a hazy chiaroscuro. Out of the darkness emerge isolated pieces of setting such as an ornamental beam, a carved door, an icon and the large, glowing globes of the hour glass. The ceilings and arches in the palace, the torture chamber and the bridal party are oppressively low, and Conrad Veidt as Ivan must crouch and bend his body in unnatural angles to accommodate the spaces. Already the most Expressionistic of actors, Veidt uses the cramped sets to further exaggerate his movements and gestures.

Despite his character's cruelty, Veidt is able to find the human vulnerability in Ivan's constant fear of death. Veidt explained his intentions in 1929 in a Berlin film magazine: "Characters called 'evil' are not as bad as they appear on the surface; if I enjoy playing them, it is not because their destructiveness attracts me, but rather because I want to show the remnants of humanity which is hidden in even the most evil evildoer."

This Veidt definitely accomplishes in his portrayal of Ivan. The part could have been played as merely a leering sadist, but Veidt constantly emphasizes the almost childlike fear Ivan suffers of those around him, even in his own palace. Though he is the Czar, he seems like a wicked little boy among grown-ups, staring at them with wide, guilty eyes, waiting for one of them to punish him. And when he believes himself to be poisoned, his glee at thwarting the poisoner by constantly turning the hour glass seems like the exaggerated delight of a child getting away with something.

Sergei Eisenstein's sound masterpiece, *Ivan the Terrible* of 1946, was heavily influenced by Leni's film. Even though Eisenstein approaches Ivan with more serious intentions, he mirrors Leni's use of the character as a crooked figure in an oppressively abstract setting full of low arches, dark corridors and angular shadows.

In the Hauron Al-Raschid story, Leni creates an entirely different look for the sets and costumes to match the period, country and lightened mood. The buildings are full of flowing, round shapes for the doors, windows and even the roofs. These sets appear to be stylized renderings of an Arabian Nights tale as well as light, airy buns hot out of the Baker's oven.

The constructions also match the soft, round shape of Emil Jannings as the Caliph. Wearing a white turban and padded, jeweled robe, he looks like a Christmas tree ornament come to life. Like Veidt, Janning exaggerates his performance, but unlike Veidt, he plays his tyrant as a winking, smiling lech with a heart of gold.

As they did in the Ivan the Terrible episode, William Dieterle and Olga Belajeff, who play the writer and the owner's daughter in the framing story, here portray the young couple threatened by the selfish ruler. In one extraordinary shot, Dieterle's face is multiplied dozens of times as he sees himself in each cut of the Caliph's diamond wishing ring. In both stories, the young couples' parts are completely overshadowed by Leni's concentration on the two human monsters and the look of the world in which they live.

The most abstractly Expressionistic episode depicts the young writer's nightmare of being pursued by Jack the Ripper, played by Dr. Caligari himself, Werner Krauss. Unlike the opening of the film in which the fairground is quickly established with a few realistic shots, the Jack the Ripper sequence uses the spinning lights and moving shapes of the carnival in superimpositions over the characters to create a frightening world of confusing chaos.

The sets through which the murderer stalks are painted flats reminiscent of the look of *Caligari*. Large triangles and rhomboids pierce black space, and sudden flashes of light collide with impenetrable darkness. Jack the Ripper glides slowly, inexorably through this visual disorder, never deviating from his victims' path. The physical world is too hostile and unpredictable to offer shelter from this killer's threatening advance.

Finally, Springheeled Jack becomes lost in the jumble of lights and shapes. And then the killer strikes, emerging from the cinematic chaos to stab the writer. In this brief sequence, Leni created the closest equivalent to a nightmare that the cinema had yet presented.

Because of its exaggerated look and extreme characters, *Waxworks* largely avoids many of the problems symptomatic of anthology movies. Instead of offering the rising arc of a single narrative and the deepening understanding of characters, *Waxworks* presents the viewer with a kaleidoscope of surface fascination. The atmosphere of the movie changes with each story, signaled by a shift in set design, lighting, costumes and narrative. Because the looks are so uniquely appropriate to each episode, viewers do not feel that the filmmaker is demanding a new emotional commitment from them, but that they are being presented with another opportunity to savor a complete stylistic world. This enjoyment is enhanced by the introduction of a new star villain in each story, portrayed by masters of Expressionistic acting: Conrad Veidt, Emil Janning and Werner Krauss. Like most omnibus films, this one leaves its audience unmoved in the conventional sense of experiencing a single powerful emotional reaction, but it compensates by offering the more superficial joys of inspired design and execution.

Les Mains d'Orlac, the 1920 French novel by Maurice Renard, is an example of the type of mystery perfected in English by John Dickson Carr and later in French by the team of Pierre Boilieau and Thomas Narcejac: a story which details a series of apparently supernatural occurrences that turn out to have a rational explanation. This structure derives from the English Gothic novels of the late 18th century in which the light of reason ultimately dispels the shadow of otherworldly terrors. The first of many film versions of *Les Mains d'Orlac* was directed in 1924 by Robert Wiene, the director of *The Cabinet of Dr. Caligari*, for the Austrian company Pan Film and starred Conrad Veidt, by then specializing in such parts, as the tortured hero.

The hands of the famous pianist Paul Orlac are crushed in a train wreck. By torchlight, Mrs. Orlac searches the wreckag until she finds Paul and rushes him to a clinic.

Paul sees a head staring at him through the window in the door of his darkened hospital room. The face is brutish, and Orlac thinks the man is laughing at his bandaged hands.

Later, the doctor unwraps the hands to reveal that they have healed. Paul asks if he will ever be able to play the piano again. The doctor tells him that his "spirit" must be willing, and he must persevere.

That night, Paul sees the face again in his dreams, a giant head filling his hospital room. The head becomes a fist which descends from the darkness. Orlac wakes up in a panic and finds a note on his bed. It tells him that his hands are not his own.

The doctor gently tells him that his own hands were "smashed beyond hope... Dr. Sorel replaced them with those of an executed murderer. His name was Vasseur." Paul tries to put

Fritz Kortner as Nero torments Paul Orlac (Conrad Veidt) in *The Hands of Orlac*. **[Photofest]**

his wedding ring on. He finds that his finger is too big. He begs the doctor to "liberate" him from the hands.

At the same time, a row of bill collectors demand payment from Mrs. Orlac. She asks them to wait a month, but they refuse. She decides to go to Paul's wealthy father for help. Despite Mrs. Orlac's pleas, her father-in-law refuses to help because he hates his son.

Paul goes to his father's dark house himself. But he finds the old man murdered, a knife in his chest with a distinctive handle containing an X.

Orlac runs to the police station. The inspector identifies the knife as belonging to the dead murderer Vasseur. He also finds Vasseur's fingerprints in the father's room.

Orlac finds another knife with an X in the handle sticking to his front door. Feeling guilty, he hides it in a desk.

That night, Mrs. Orlac's maid, distraught, writes a letter to an unknown person. In it, she claims that she does not want to live any longer. "But never again will I submit to your demands—never," she writes.

Paul walks through the darkened house, repeatedly stabbing the air with Vasseur's knife. He screams at his wife, "Don't come near me!" After she reluctantly backs away, Paul holds the knife over one of his hands as if to stab it, but he stops himself.

As Paul wanders the streets at night, he is confronted by a large man, every part of him covered by a cloak except his face. And the face is that of the man in Paul's hospital visions.

The stranger tells him that he knows Paul is his father's heir. The man wants a million marks the next night in payment for his hands. He pulls his cloak back to reveal shining metal hands and forearms.

The man claims to be the executed murderer Vasseur. When Orlac laughs at him, the stranger rips open his collar to reveal the scar of the guillotine all the way around his neck. The man says that if Orlac refuses to pay, he will let the police know that Paul is his father's killer. After all, Paul now has Vasseur's fingerprints, and the maid will testify that she saw the knife in Paul's house.

Orlac rushes home and finds the knife missing from the desk. He breaks down and tells his wife the whole story while the maid listens from behind the door. Mrs. Orlac convinces him to take his story to the District Attorney. The D.A. instructs him to give the money to Vasseur that night.

Orlac hands the money to the blackmailer. At that moment, the police arrive. The inspector recognizes the man as Mr. Nero, a crook who once worked as Dr. Sorel's assistant. The inspector pulls the silver gloves from Nero's hands and the fake scar from his neck. But Mr. Nero insists that only Orlac has the hands that could make Vasseur's fingerprints.

Just as the inspector is arresting Orlac, the maid reveals that she was working with Mr. Nero. Vasseur and Nero were friends, and Nero had rubber gloves made with Vasseur's fingerprints. Mr. Nero is the real murderer.

After *The Cabinet of Dr. Caligari*, this is Wiene's best film. Unlike the former work, the style of decor and costumes in *The Hands of Orlac* is realistic and contemporary. On a cinematic level, the film is competently directed with no flourishes, very much in the American studio manner. The camera never moves within a shot, but there is a conservative use of close-ups and inserts. In one scene, Orlac walks toward the camera with his arms stretched before him until a single clutching hand fills the screen.

The cinematography by Hans Androschin and Guenther Krampf illuminates the characters against relentlessly dark backgrounds, even in the hospitals and living rooms. The scenes of the wrecked train have a nightmarish quality. The crowds of scurrying rescuers and survivors are lit against the black sky by torches, their glow dancing across the confusion of train cars lying on their sides and piled up against each other.

Except for the dream scene, the presentation remains objective, with Veidt's powerful performance the only element allowing the audience to participate in Orlac's torment. Even the dream scene is somewhat objective, being shown as a long shot with Orlac in bed on the left side of the frame while his visions appear in the darkness above him on the right. A director such as Griffith, Murnau or Hitchcock, who understands the presentation of a character's mental states through point of view shots, inserts, moving camera and emotionally charged angles, undoubtedly could have rendered Orlac's experiences more powerfully. Wiene's detached approach does not allow much audience identification except in terms of responding to the mysteries and surprises of the narrative.

Conrad Veidt uses his whole body to portray a man convinced that another's spirit is fighting for control of his actions. He holds the alien hands before him and follows their dictates, moving like a sleepwalker as they lead him to the murderer's knife. Later, he wields the weapon in a sort of ballet of attack, his legs following as his hand thrusts the blade up and down in imaginary deathblows.

Veidt achieved the physical intensity of his portrayal by the technique of becoming possessed himself, at least in his imagination. In an attempt to explain the ferocious energy of his performances, he told journalist Paul Ickes in 1927:

For days or even weeks before filming I withdraw into myself, contemplate my navel, as it were, concentrating on a kind of infection of the soul. And soon I discover how the character I have to portray grows in me, how I am transformed into it. The intensity of the process almost frightens me. Before long I find, even before the cameras begin to turn, that in my daily life I move, talk, look and behave differently. The inner Conrad Veidt has become the other person whom I have to portray, or rather into whom my self has changed by autosuggestion. This state could best be described as one of being "possessed."

Orlac's Handes previewed in Berlin on September 24, 1924 at the Haydn-Kino and premiered to the public on January 31, 1925 in Berlin at the *Theater am Nollendorfplatz*. Actually an Austrian film, it did not open in its country of origin until March 6, 1925 in Vienna.

Unlike later film criticism which compared the film's objective realism unfavorably to Wiene's Expressionistic masterpiece, *The Cabinet of Dr. Caligari*, contemporary reviews were laudatory. The critic for *Die Filmwelt* wrote: "Director Robert Wiene has created a unique atmosphere in this film. He has succeeded in uniting two film principles: suspense-packed action and subtle psychology. The train disaster is just as brilliant an achievement as, for instance, the scenes of Orlac's delusion. Incidentally, those who have ever seen this director at work—concentrated, highly tense, extracting from every actor everything he can give and supervising the scene to minutest detail—know that every Wiene film has to become a masterpiece."

The *LichtBildBuhne* discussed the film's successful presentation of the supernatural in an otherwise realistic environment. The reviewer for the *Film-Kurier* noted that "one has found the right director for the rendering of the mysterious psychology and the suspense-laden story of this film. The enigma of man's fate is a subject that Robert Wiene knows how to deal with." The *Deutsche Allgemeine Zeitung* went so far as to state, "Wiene matches [Ernst] Lubitsch, Murnau, Lang and [Karl] Grune, surpasses them in consistent scene sequencing, and forces Veidt, [Alexandra] Sorina and Fritz Kortner to play together in a way that seems to have been last achieved with [Emil] Jannings and [Elisabeth] Bergner in *Nju*." Even the novel's author, Maurice Renard, was impressed: "The cinematographic adaptation of *Orlac's Hands* gratifies all my wishes. I was never understood so passionately nor interpreted with such power."

Along with Veidt's haunting performance, the fascination of the movie lies in screenwriter Ludwig Nerz's accumulation of inexplicable evidence convincing Orlac and the audience that his hands have an evil life of their own. The strongest scene is the culmination of this in which Orlac stabs the air with the murderer's knife and warns his wife to stay away from him. By then, the events and Orlac's reactions to them persuade us that he could become a killer, even without the supernatural domination of his hands.

This powerful psychological suspense is carefully built only to be quickly dispelled. Unfortunately, when Orlac goes to the police in the third act, the story becomes prosaic. The final revelation leaves no room for doubt, and no unease about the hands' remains. The final impression is of a long shaggy dog story, the conclusion of which does not justify the build-up.

By 1925, Fritz Lang had become the most powerful and demanding director in the German film industry. Born in Vienna on December 5, 1890, he was expected to become an architect like his wealthy father. He attended a technical high school and studied at the College of Technical Sciences of Vienna's Academy of Graphic Arts. Unhappy with the career his father had chosen for him, he ran away from home at the age of 21 to study art in Munich and Paris.

At the outbreak of World War I, he returned to Vienna and distinguished himself in battle, rising through his bravery and skill from the rank of private to lieutenant. He was wounded four times, the last incident in 1916 resulting in temporary blindness that necessitated hospitalization for a year. During his convalescence in Vienna, he began to write stories and screenplays. A friend acting as Lang's agent sold several of these to Joe May and other German directors.

Lil Dagover and Bernhard Goetzke in Lang's *Der Mude Tod*

After leaving the hospital, Lang joined Erich Pommer's Decla-Bioscope company in Berlin as a reader and story editor. Soon, he became a staff screenwriter and in 1919, a director. His third film, the two-part adventure melodrama, *The Spiders*, scored a tremendous hit with the public. It was the completion of this elaborate epic that prevented Lang from directing *The Cabinet of Dr. Caligari*.

In 1920, Lang began collaborating with a female screenwriter, Thea von Harbou. Their first critical hit was *Der Mude Tod*, produced by Pommer. It was an allegory about a girl attempting to persuade Death to spare her lover and revealed Lang's early mastery of design and composition as well as his obsession with fate.

Late in the same year, Lang's wife, Lisa Rosenthal, caught the director making love to his screenwriter on their couch. That night, the police were summoned to the Lang residence where Frau Lang's body was found in the bathtub with a bullet hole between her breasts from the director's Browning revolver. Producer Erich Pommer and cameramen Karl Freund, who filmed *The Golem* and Fritz Arno Wagner, who filmed *Nosferatu*, were summoned to the apartment by Lang for support. Lang was an important director, and Pommer used his considerable power and persuasive skills to have all mention of Lisa Rosenthal's "suicide" expunged from the official records of the Berlin police. On August 26, 1922, the director and his screenwriter were married.

Together, Lang and von Harbou created an unprecedented string of artistically impressive films. Before their nuptials, they completed *Dr. Mabuse, The Gambler*, a two-part thriller about an archcriminal, played by von Harbou's first husband, Rudolf Klein-Rogge. Dr. Mabuse changes identities through makeup and hypnotizes wealthy card players to manipulate events for his own megalomaniacal interests before going mad when caught by a grimly determined police inspector. The film's dark, brooding atmosphere reflected the decadence and demoralization of Germany at the time.

When Pommer's Decla-Bioscope was absorbed by Universum Film Aktien Gesellschaft, known as UFA, the largest, most modern studio in Germany, Pommer became head

Lang and Thea von Harbou worked together on *Dr. Mabuse*

of production. Pommer entrusted Lang and von Harbou with another two-part epic, this time inspired by the 13th century Siegfried legend that also formed the basis of Richard Wagner's opera cycle, "Der Ring des Nibelungen." Lang's spectacular and moody *Die Nibelungen* was released in 1924 and was an attempt to counteract the pessimistic spirit of the time by depicting Germany's legendary heritage and epic past.

The first half, entitled *Siegfried*, revealed Lang the painter and architect with its huge, brilliantly designed sets, artistic deployment of extras, studio-built forest and impressive, mechanical dragon. The second half, called *Kriemheld's Revenge*, was clearly the product of Lang the filmmaker and was one of the most ferociously brilliant movies of his career. Lang tells Kriemheld's tragic story of betrayal, murder and revenge with an awe-inspiring lack of sentiment.

After the premiere of *Die Nibelungen* in October 1924, Lang and Pommer visited New York en route to Hollywood to study American motion picture production techniques. Lang later liked to tell the story that the idea of *Metropolis* was inspired by his first sight of the shimmering, futuristic New York cityscape from shipboard. But even before the completion of *Die Nibelungen*, Pommer was already telling people about the next Fritz Lang project, " a horror tale of the future," based on a novel written by von Harbou called *Metropolis*. By the time of Lang's return to Germany in December, the hard-working von Harbou had certainly completed her screen adaptation.

Metropolis takes place in the year 2025, in a wealthy city of enormous skyscrapers built over a subterranean "city of workers." The laborers, robotized in their hopeless existence of poverty and slavery, toil in terrible conditions manning huge, dangerous machines that power the city above. In the skyscrapers, the leisure class is presided over by their supreme

The grim underground world of the workers in *Metropolis*

master, Jon Frederson, who is at odds with his spoiled but good-hearted son, Freder. The young man falls in love with Maria, "a daughter of the people," who preaches Christian love and patience to the downtrodden workers in an underground church amid ancient caves and catacombs.

Frederson contacts Rotwang, a mad scientist living in a medieval house in the middle of the city, who lost his only love, a woman named Hel, to Frederson years ago. Hel subsequently died giving birth to Freder.

The master of Metropolis wants his old rival to kidnap Maria and give his robot her face so that Frederson can control what she says to the workers. Rotwang agrees and chases Maria through the underground tombs until he captures her. He then transfers her face, body and voice to his metallic robot using an electrical laboratory with flashing lights and bubbling liquids.

The soulless false Maria soon gets out of Rotwang's control and incites the workers to destroy their machines for the evil glee of it. This causes their underground homes to be flooded. The real Maria escapes from Rotwang, joins with Freder and helps the children of the workers escape the rising water. When the workers realize that the false Maria has caused them to destroy their own homes, they capture her and burn her at the stake. But as she dies, laughing wickedly, she reverts back to the metallic robot.

Meanwhile, Rotwang has gone completely mad and mistakes the real Maria for his lost love, Hel. He chases her to the top of the high cathedral. Freder runs to her rescue. As his terrified father and the workers watch from below, Freder fights Rotwang for Maria. Rotwang falls to his death in the struggle, and Freder saves the girl.

She urges Freder to persuade his father to shake hands with the leader of the workers. "The heart must mediate between the brain and the hands," she tells Freder. On the stairs of the cathedral, as the people of Metropolis watch, Freder pulls his father and the worker together for their historic handshake.

Lang told *The New York Times* that he envisioned *Metropolis* as the "costliest and most ambitious picture ever," with thousands of extras, huge sets and ground-breaking special effects. Even by UFA standards, the projected budget was huge. Never expecting to make a profit, Pommer hoped *Metropolis* would eventually recoup its colossal cost while creating an opening for future German pictures in America.

Pommer persuaded Karl Freund to photograph *Metropolis*, partnered with Gunther Rittau. Freund still blamed Lang for the death of Lisa Rosenthal, even suspecting murder, but Pommer promised that Freund could communicate with the director through an assistant.

Many of the massive sets were actually trick shots supervised by the brilliant photographic specialist, Eugen Schufftan. He had originally invented the "Schufftan process" for an UFA version of *Gulliver's Travels* which was never produced. Instead, he employed it for the first time on *Metropolis*. The Schufftan process composited live action with miniature sets in the same frame. The scaled down scenery was reflected in a mirror placed at a 45-degree angle from the axis of the camera lens. A portion of the mirror was scraped away, and through this clear area, live actors and a matching full-size portion of the set were photographed, blending with the reflected miniature. This in-camera effect saved the expense of huge sets and double exposures.

Lang planned *Metropolis* to be as *avant garde* in design as *Die Nibelungen* had been classical. In the endless, seven-day-a-week preproduction meetings that began in the winter of 1924, his first order of business was the layout of the futuristic cityscape. Lang described his inspiration, the sights of Manhattan, in *Film-Kurier* of December 1924: "...full of turning, twisting, circling lights, like a paean to human happiness," with sky-high towers "picked out of the darkness of night by floodlights."

The director made it his business to become well acquainted with the contemporary schools of art, from Bauhaus to Expressionism and from Cubism to Futurism. All of these elements and more would crop up in the designs for *Metropolis*. While the look of Rotwang's medieval house evokes paintings by Bauhaus director Otto Bartning, the design by Otto Hunte of the Tower of Babel, which is featured in Maria's sermon to the workers, alludes to renderings by the Old Masters.

Expressionist imagery portrays technology as a nightmare. But *Metropolis* incorporates Constructivist influences and its attendant fascination with technology as well. Much of the visual complexity of *Metropolis* derives from this depiction of the simultaneous beauty and horror of its machine world. Nowhere is this combination more apparent than in the design for Rotwang's robot. Blending the shapes of the human female form with a shining metallic surface and a face frightening in its lack of emotion, the robot becomes the embodiment of both German Expressionism and such other *avant garde* movements as Futurism and Constructivism.

Pommer pressured Lang to cease the preproduction meetings and to begin casting and rehearsals. Meanwhile, the miniatures for the establishing shots were constructed in the glassed-in studio and photographed by Freund and Schufftan under Lang's supervision. Toy cars and planes on wires were filmed using stop-motion technique, moving them by hand a short space and then exposing one frame of negative at a time. Although these scenes showing the city would only appear for seconds on the screen, they took months to prepare

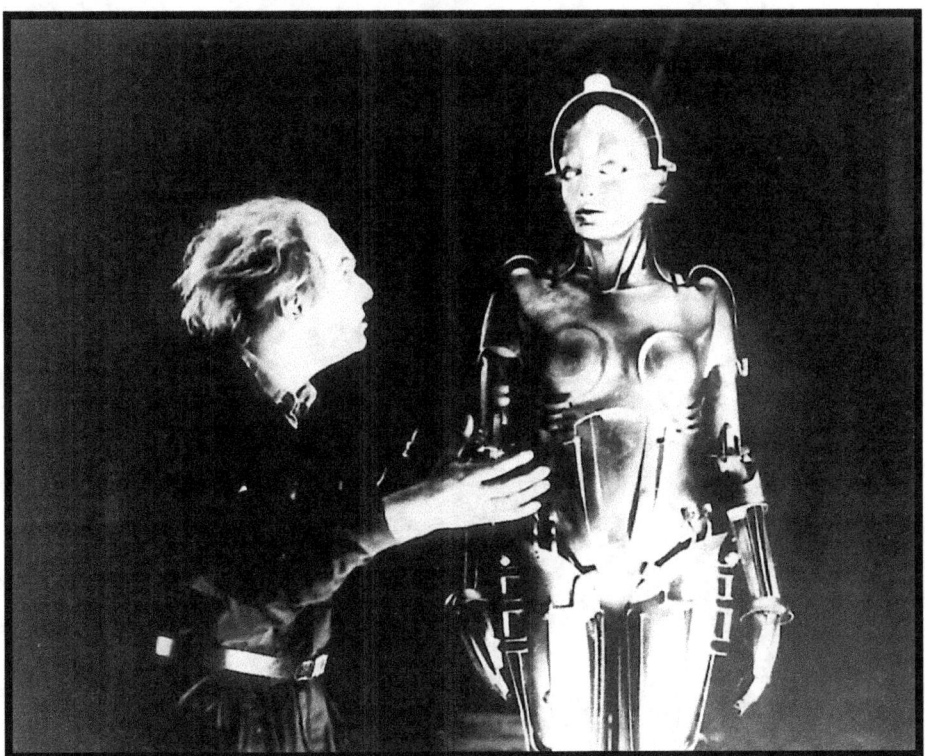

Blending the female form with a shining metallic surface in *Metropolis*, the robot becomes the embodiment of German Expressionism.

and several full days to shoot to Lang's satisfaction. The techniques were so new that the head of the processing lab overexposed the film, and the shots had to be retaken.

Lang cast his own discovery, Brigitte Helm, in the dual role of Maria and the robot-Maria. Born Eva Gisela Schnittenhelm in 1906, she was taken by her rather pushy stage mother to the set of *Die Nibelungen* after Lang had expressed interest in some photographs of her. Lang arranged a screen test and then, a year later, another audition in the presence of Erich Pommer. At this second test, the young girl enacted one of Kriemheld's dramatic scenes from Lang's *Die Nibelungen*. Her portrayal stunned Lang and Pommer, and she was immediately signed to a contract. The producer and director promptly renamed her Brigitte Helm, and Lang took it upon himself to enhance the teenager's sophistication by teaching her dancing and horseback riding.

Principal photography on *Metropolis* began on May 22, 1925. After the first few weeks of shooting, it became evident to Lang that he had made a mistake in casting the young male lead. Thea von Harbou noticed an earnest and handsome young man playing one of the worker slaves. Gustav Frohlich had been a journalist, a vaudevillian and a Volksbuhne actor, and von Harbou convinced her husband to give him the lead in this, his most costly and visionary film. UFA publicity claimed that, apart from the eight principals, which included von Harbou's former husband Rudolf Klein-Rogge as Rotwang, there were 750 actors in small roles, 26,000 male extras, 11,000 female ones, 750 children, "100 Negroes and 25 Chinese." Until his death, Lang could proudly reel off these questionable statistics.

As shooting progressed, Lang was especially demanding with Brigitte Helm. He acted out scenes for her, corrected her every move, tried to calm her nerves, but just as often, lost

In this creation scene in *Metropolis*, rings of light encircle the robot, moving luminously up and down the seated figure.

his temper with her. One of her most difficult trials was wearing the backless robot suit made from "liquid wood." The pieces were form fitted to Helm's body using a plaster cast of her, and she had to wear it for several weeks during the filming of the lab scenes. To make matters worse, the pieces had been sculpted on a standing cast of her, and Lang decided to have her sit during the scene transferring Maria's aspect to the robot. Even though the designers tried to smooth down the most jagged points, Helm had to stay in the same position for hours in the tight, hot, painful armor under blazing studio lights. Already in fragile health, she was constantly monitored by a doctor.

In this creation scene, which prefigures James Whale's similar ones in *Frankenstein* and *The Bride of Frankenstein*, rings of light encircle the robot, moving luminously up and down the seated figure until a glowing circulatory system dissolves over her body. Cameraman Gunther Rittau achieved the ascending and descending circles by moving the camera up and down as it filmed a small, whirling silver ball against a black velvet backdrop. These shining rings were then superimposed over the seated robot with an optical printer.

Lang relentlessly demanded the same perfection from his new leading man as he did from Helm. The director's method was to demonstrate the action he wanted from Frohlich, then insist he repeat it exactly. In the catacomb scene, Frohlich was instructed to fall on his knees in front of Helm and caress her as she stroked his hair. With endless rehearsals and retakes, Frohlich fell to his knees from morning until midnight for two days until his legs were bruised and battered. In another scene, Lang required the young actor to bang on a heavy wooden door with his bare fists. Again because of Lang's exacting standards, the

In *Metropolis*, not only the stars suffered for Lang's art but also the thousands of extras who showed up for work as unemployment soared in Germany.

shot was retaken until Frohlich crumbled, blood running down his arms. When Frohlich's thumb was dislocated in a fight scene with a group of workers, Lang only allowed a half-hour break for the actor to be sedated and the thumb rejoined before calling him back to resume shooting. "Nothing was allowed to seem fake, everything had to look real," wrote Frohlich in his autobiography. "In scenes of physical suffering, he tormented the actors until they really did suffer."

Not only the stars suffered for Lang's art but also the thousands of extras who showed up for work as unemployment soared in Germany. Nearly 500 skinny, malnourished children were rounded up from the Berlin slums to run through geysers of chilly water as the workers' underground city was flooded. In a cavernous, unheated zeppelin hangar turned studio in Staaken, an entire army of nude men shivered in the bitter cold winter of 1925 as Lang shot them marching into the smoking mouth of a giant machine. Scores of extras were suspended on wires and whipped through the air while Lang filmed the explosion of one of the mechanisms.

A thousand men had their heads shaved by hundreds of barbers and dragged huge stones and tree trunks through the desert sand in Rehbergen to enact Maria's parable about the building of the Tower of Babel. Many suffered sunburns to the point where they had blisters on their unprotected heads. Lang optically multiplied the thousand extras to appear to be 4,000 on the final negative. "Malicious tongues whispered that if he could have, Lang would only too gladly, and without any scruples, have someone really shot, stabbed, or strangled—for say, an execution scene, murder or suicide. Then he would have been able

Lang was especially demanding of Brigitte Helm, who played both Maria and the robot in *Metropolis*.

to film — guaranteed for real — the death throes of a human being before his life was blotted out," wrote Frohlich.

After almost a year of filming, the UFA executive board convened in January 1926 to debate shutting down the money-draining project. The board held Erich Pommer responsible and dismissed him as director of productions as of January 22, 1926. Ironically, Pommer had rarely visited the set and then, only to use his diplomatic skills to talk Lang out of further retakes. Pommer left for the United States on April 1 to become a staff producer for Famous Players–Lasky. The new chief of production of UFA, Major Alexander Grau, never imposed himself on Lang, allowing him to finish his film and offering no assistance when Freund and others complained of Lang's methods.

Those methods included continuing to put his star in danger of injury. In the spring of 1926, Lang shot Rotwang's pursuit of Maria up to the cathedral roof. Brigitte Helm had to leap from a staircase to a rope hanging from a giant suspended bell. If she missed the rope, she would fall 12 feet to mattresses, a risky proposition for the leading lady. She managed to grab the rope, which caused the bell to swing back and forth. This whipped Helm wildly from one wall to the other as her hands slid slowly down. When the stunt was finished, she was covered in bruises and abrasions, and her clothes were ripped. She ran from the set in tears, physically and emotionally drained.

But Lang had not finished with her, yet. One night, he rehearsed the angry crowd hauling her to the top of a pyre and binding her to a stake for three hours and 30 minutes. After this was filmed, the pyre was soaked with gasoline and Helm was strapped to the stake to face real flames. During a take, sparks caught her dress, setting it on fire. Lang and the standby firefighters leapt to her rescue, and she collapsed in her director's arms. Fortunately, she was not hurt. Future screenwriter Curt Siodmak, who would pen such scripts as *The Wolf Man* and *Son of Dracula* in America two decades later, was present as a reporter and wrote of the episode: "I don't know how good an actress she was at the time, but here was Svengali and Trilby, and Lang coaxed her into a state of near hysteria." In 1933, Brigitte Helm would tell the Italian magazine, *Cinema Illustrazione*, "*Metropolis* was the worst experience I ever had."

Principal photography officially ended October 30, 1926 after 310 days and 60 nights of filming. The budget had bloated to five million marks or a little over one million U.S. dollars at the time. Of course, UFA had charged some of its overhead to the production, and the total was further inflated by Germany's weak economy.

The premiere took place on January 10, 1927 and was attended by the foremost art and literature figures in Berlin society. A live orchestra accompanied the film with an original score by Gottfried Huppertz. The crowd immediately recognized *Metropolis* as a masterpiece of the cinema. After several of Lang's breathtaking set pieces, the audience broke into spontaneous applause. At the end, they needed no prompting in their thunderous ovation for Lang's greatest achievement in silent film storytelling. The ensemble, including Brigitte Helm and Fritz Lang, took numerous curtain calls as bouquets of flowers were delivered to them on stage.

Unfortunately for UFA, the press was not as appreciative. Responding to the film as an intellectual tract instead of as a piece of cinematic art, the critic for *Die Filmwoche* called Lang's film "lifeless," "dehumanizing" and "unrealistic." Berlin's cultural journal, *Die literarische Welt*, also characterized *Metropolis* as technically and artistically monumental but intellectually empty. The most savage attack came from the visionary science fiction writer H.G. Wells, who was quoted in the *Frankfurter Zeitung* of May 3, 1927 as stating, "I have recently seen the silliest film. I do not believe it would be possible to make one sillier." He found that *Metropolis* consisted of "almost every possible foolishness, cliché, platitude and muddlement about mechanical progress and progress in general, served up with a sauce of sentimentality."

The new board of UFA met in the spring of 1927 to decide what to do with their expensive behemoth. Industrial and communications magnate Alfred Hugenberg assumed obligations as the company's leading investor. An arch conservative who later became a minister in Hitler's Third Reich, Hugenberg's priorities included modernizing the studio and converting from silent productions to sound.

Lang's cut of *Metropolis* ran two-and-a-half hours. This limited the number of showings per day, and the film could not meet the studio's financial expectations. Also, Hugenberg was offended by some of the intertitles that displayed Communist tendencies and heretical religiosity. *Metropolis* was yanked from theaters, condensed to two hours and re-released widely throughout Germany in August, eight months after its initial premiere. No doubt Lang was consulted on the editing, but he had no choice but to comply.

Parufamet, a mutual distribution organization between UFA and America's Paramount Studios, released its own edited version of *Metropolis* in Europe. The box-office proved modest, but the critical reaction was more in keeping with Lang's achievement. *The London Times* celebrated its "remarkable pictorial power," while Iris Barry in *The Spectator* wrote that "there are moments when it touches real greatness." In Paris, the future surrealist filmmaker, Luis Bunuel, reviewed the film for *Gaceta literaria* and raved, "from the photographic angle, (the film's) emotive force, its unheard-of and overwhelming beauty, is unequaled. It

Lang forces the audience to truly care about Freder (Gustav Frohlich) and Maria and their struggle to do the right thing in a world of conflict in *Metropolis*.

is of such a technical perfection that it can stand a prolonged analysis."

All along, UFA had counted on recouping its costs in America. The New York City premiere in March 1927 was preceded by a *New York Times* review from Berlin by Herman G. Sheffauer who hailed *Metropolis* as "a wonderful film, in many ways one of the most remarkable achievements in the history of the 'light play'... (which) will bid fair to become one of the master-films of all times."

But Paramount, which distributed the film in America, also worried about the length. They hired dramatist Channing Pollock, whose play, *The Fool*, had been the hit of the 1922 season, at $1,000 a day to reduce *Metropolis* from two-and-a-half hours to one hour and 47 minutes. Gone were scenes of a subplot involving Freder's assistant, Josephat, played by Fritz Rasp; a spectacular opening sequence showing Freder running a race in a huge coliseum; and all references to Frederson's late wife, Hel, who had been loved by both Frederson and Rotwang. The mad scientist's enormous bust of Hel was one of the film's famous images that Pollock sacrificed. He also changed the characters' names and even altered the story-line by rewriting the intertitles. His take on the plot was summarized in his autobiography: "A greedy employer hoped to grow rich by hiring the inventor to create hundreds of steel workmen. These proved to be perfect, except that they could not be endowed with souls, and the result was catastrophe."

Even in this altered form, the influential Gilbert Seldes in *The New Republic* acclaimed the film as a visionary work of the first order, and Randolph Bartlett wrote in *The New York Times:* "The trimming of this production is said, by those who saw it in its original form, to have improved it. I am willing to wager that *Metropolis*, as it is seen at the Rialto now, is nearer Fritz Lang's idea than the version he himself released in Germany." As for Lang, he felt the editing was handled "dictatorially and carelessly. They had slashed my film so cruelly that I dared not see it."

So, is *Metropolis* silly or a masterpiece? Later in his life, Lang himself had problems with the film, centering mostly around the famous handshake ending. "I have often said that I didn't like *Metropolis*," Lang told the French film magazine *Cahiers du Cinema* in 1965, "and that is because I cannot accept today the leitmotif of the message of the film. It is absurd to say that the heart is the mediator between the hands and the head, that is to say, of course, between employee and employer. The problem is social, not moral." Explaining this change of opinion, Lang declared in 1967, "I was not so politically minded in those days as I am now."

But in the last year of his life, Lang changed his opinion again. In 1976, he said:

> I didn't think in those days a social question could be solved with something as simple as the line: "The mediator between the brain (capital) and hand (working class) must be the heart." Yet today, when you speak to young people about what they miss in the computer-guided establishment, the answer is always, "The heart!" So probably the scenarist, Mrs. Thea von Harbou, had foresight, and therefore was right, and I was wrong.

More important to its value, *Metropolis* is full of Lang set pieces in which he creates atmosphere and propels the story by visual means. For example, Lang designs the amazingly suspenseful sequence in which Rotwang chases Maria through the catacombs by having the panic-stricken girl running in and out of an unrelenting beam of light from the mad scientist's lantern. In another scene, Lang simulates the concussion from an explosion by putting the camera on a swing and pushing it toward Freder and Maria and then allowing it to swing back as they fall. Silently, the plunging and retreating movement compels the audience to experience the force of the blast.

Lang arranges his crowds of workers in architectural patterns or moves them in slow, decorative unison, like dancers in a silent musical. It is no wonder that the film excited Hitler and Goebbels when they saw it together in a provincial theater years before their Third Reich took power. Lang's geometric arrangement of crowds predicts Leni Riefenstahl's choreography of soldiers in her Nazi propaganda film, *Triumph of the Will*, and the manipulative, militaristic world of National Socialism itself.

Metropolis shares with other Lang masterworks many of the themes that obsessed him. Besides his characteristic mood of oppression, he presents contending forces and an enclosing trap as in *Kriemheld's Revenge*, *M*, *Fury*, *Manhunt*, *Hangmen Also Die*, *Woman in the Window* and *While the City Sleeps*. Also in *Metropolis*, Lang portrays individuals struggling with vicious mobs as he would later in *M*, *Fury* and *Hangmen Also Die*. And the controversial handshake is not the only prosaic ending to a tense and bizarre situation as *M*, *Fury*, *Scarlet Street* and, most famously, *Woman in the Window* prove.

Metropolis is not only the most physically impressive, but also the most emotionally powerful of the silent German horror masterpieces. Whereas there is an undeniable chilly remoteness about *The Cabinet of Dr. Caligari*, *The Golem* and *Nosferatu*, Lang's film transcends its formal surface design and its maudlin insistence on profundity to force the audience to truly care about Freder and Maria and their struggle to do the right thing in a world of conflicting political and economic issues. Part of the reason for this success stems from Lang's involving suspense set pieces, but much of it results from the beauty and passion of his find, young Brigitte Helm. Her unwavering physical and emotional commitment to the roles of Maria and the evil robot compel the audience to experience each exciting event with her. After all that has happened to her, Maria's love and virtue at the end is undiminished, and her positive effect on the future of the heartless city becomes the most moving aspect of the famous handshake.

Maria's example may be the only thing standing between us and a *Metropolis*-like future. As Lang ultimately realized, the prophesies of *Metropolis* may not be beyond possibility. There are those who believe that human society is moving toward an ultimate split between impoverished, undereducated workers and a wealthy elite. Lang's "silly" nightmare may yet prove prophetic.

The name of Henrik Galeen was linked with some of the greatest German horror films of the silent era. He wrote and co-directed with Paul Wegener the 1914 version of *The Golem*, co-wrote the 1920 classic with Wegener and wrote both Murnau's *Nosferatu* and Paul Leni's *Waxworks*. Born in 1881 of Dutch origin, he began his career as a journalist and secretary to Hanns Heinz Ewers, the author of the novels *The Student of Prague* and *Alraune*. In 1926 and 1927, Galeen directed and co-wrote with Ewers the finest adaptations of both of these stories.

Cinema technique was in its infancy when Stellan Rye directed the 1913 *The Student of Prague*. The 13 years that intervened between that version and Galeen's saw the invention of the most imaginative methods for film storytelling in the history of the medium. And Galeen's film benefits from almost every one of the new means. His style incorporates a Romantic use of natural locations, cinematic subjective shots and montage, studio-built landscapes of the mind, chiaroscuro lighting and camera-sensitive acting. Whereas Rye in 1913 staged scenes in a single static shot, like illustrations to a storybook, Galeen marshaled all of the arsenal of cinema to involve the audience emotionally in each moment. The result is one of the most moving and filmically complex works of the German screen.

Galeen's expert orchestrations commence from the very beginning of the film. In a series of shots, groups of students are shown marching through the woods toward an outdoor cafe. As their numbers build, so too does the excitement of the montage. The scene introduces gaunt and moody Balduin, played by Conrad Veidt. He sits apart from the carousing students until one of them rudely tears the apron of a pretty dancing peasant, Lydushka. Balduin, the finest swordsman in the land, defends the honor of the girl in an excitingly shot and edited dual. Galeen's coverage concentrates on the happy crowd as Balduin continuously flicks his opponent's sword away from him. The blade keeps flying into the group of watchers, impaling itself dangerously close to them.

Galeen and his cinematographers, Guenther Krampf and Erich Nitzchmann, reveal an eye for natural locations to rival Murnau's. In one impressive shot, Scapinelli, played by Werner Krauss, walks to the top of a hill that features one twisted, windswept tree against an overcast, white sky. Holding his umbrella behind him and looking off toward a fox hunt, the wind whipping his coat, Scapinelli seems to become part of the gothic landscape. The scene continues as Scapinelli uses hand gestures to control the direction of the thundering horses and riders. Galeen intercuts shots of Scapinelli with progressively closer views of the steeds as they move this way and that across the vast fields.

Shots of Balduin and his friends approaching a farm house alternate with tracking close shots of Comptesse Magrit pulling desperately on the reins of her runaway horse. In a series of quick cuts, the horse rears and the Comptesse is thrown from her saddle. In design and execution, the scene presages the even more cinematically elaborate treatment of Tippi Hedren and her horse in Alfred Hitchcock's *Marnie* almost 40 years later.

Balduin (Conrad Veidt) and Magrit are unaware of the shadow stalking them in *The Student of Prague*. [Photofest]

Once Balduin and Magrit meet, Galeen immediately slows the pace. He holds their close shots long enough for the audience to experience the depth of feeling in their faces and glances. Coming on the heels of the quickly edited hunt and accident, the change of rhythm makes a tremendous emotional impact.

Unlike Rye, Galeen uses insert shots to emphasize story points. When Magrit's rich suitor, Waldis, arrives with a huge spray of flowers, Galeen reminds viewers of Balduin's comparatively small bouquet by cutting to close shots of it as Balduin tries to hide it behind his back and in his cap. This allows Veidt to conceal his feelings in this subtle performance, unlike the demonstrative gestures required of Wegener in the earlier, more primitive version. Similarly, Galeen builds the excitement of Balduin and Scapinelli as the old devil pours gold onto the student's table by intercutting close shots of the mounting coins with reactions of the two actors.

Galeen's use of shadows as the embodiment of evil is reminiscent of Murnau's in *Nosferatu*. In a low-angle long shot, Balduin and Magrit appear as two small figures standing together on a high terrace. Scapinelli's enormous shadow rises up the terrace wall and reaches for an incriminating note from Balduin to Magrit on the balustrade. Galeen cuts to an insert of the note which is pulled over the side by Scapinelli's invisible shadow. Scapinelli drops the note on the ground in front of Lyduschka, the peasant girl who loves Balduin, and she takes it to Magrit's fiance, Waldis.

After losing the Comptess, Balduin indulges in a long night of debauchery at a local tavern. Obviously influenced by Murnau's *The Last Laugh*, Galeen depicts Balduin's drunken dizziness in a montage of musical instruments, dancing figures and swirling point-of-view shots. He superimposes the image of a saw blade moving back and forth across the bass viola over a close shot of Balduin's head to simulate his wracking hangover.

The sets were designed by Herman Warm, who had built the Expressionistic world of *The Cabinet of Dr. Caligari*. These constructions are much more realistic in nature, especially the magnificent period rooms of Magrit's castle and the luxurious interiors of Balduin's home after he makes his pact with Scapinelli. Warm does get to design Expressionistically influenced streets for the climactic scene of Balduin being pursued through the windy night by his double. These shots are truly eerie as the camera tracks the fleeing student. The combination of Veidt's panic-stricken performance, the turbulent, studio-created wind, the dark, subtly twisted architecture and the special effects of Balduin's mirror image appearing from nowhere combine to create a frightening nightmare of helplessness.

The following year, Galeen and Ewers collaborated once again for their classic adaptation of Ewers' *Alraune*. The story had been filmed twice previously in 1918, one version of which was directed by Michael Curtiz, who would guide such later genre efforts as *Dr. X*, *Mystery of the Wax Museum* and *The Walking Dead*. Neither 1918 version exists.

Professor Jakob Ten Brinken is inspired by a legend from the early Middle Ages of the mandrake root, a branch that grows under the gallows on the night of the full moon from the spilled seed of a hanged man. If the root is dug up at exactly midnight, it will become a human being and could bring luck to the person who unearths it. "But it could also bring suffering and torment to anyone who tries to own it."

With the reluctant help of his young nephew, Franz Braun, the Professor creates a woman by combining in his lab the sperm of a condemned prisoner with the egg from a prostitute. The result is Alraune, a name which means Mandrake in German, a wildly sexual, manipulative and heartless girl. Ten Brinken raises her to believe that he is her father.

At the Sacred Heart Convent, Alraune persuades a young man from the village to steal bank money from his aging father, the bank guard, and secretly spirit her away.

By the time Ten Brinken locates her months later, she and her boyfriend are part of the circus. The magician and the lion tamer fight for her affection as her young boyfriend watches helplessly. Ten Brinken takes her with him to raise her himself. She shrinks from him, admitting, "I'm afraid of you."

The Professor brings her to a luxury hotel and introduces her to society. Alraune immediately attracts a handsome Viscount. The Professor grows jealous, and when the suitor asks the older man for Alraune's hand in marriage, Ten Brinken refuses. Angrily, Alraune plans to run away with the Viscount that night.

But before she sneaks out, she pulls Ten Brinken's diary from under his pillow as he sleeps. She reads of her origins and breaks down sobbing. She sees herself as "An experiment. A whim of a cynical scientist—child of crime and vice." Like Frankenstein's monster, Alraune swears vengeance on her creator.

But unlike Frankenstein's monster, Alraune's vengeance is sexual. She sets about seducing the man who has acted as her father. First, she makes him jealous by flirting with every man in the hotel. Dressed in a clinging, backless gown, she lures him down onto a couch, then admits that she knows he is not her father. He tries to kiss her, but she teasingly runs from him. Ten Brinken swears that he will kill her if she tries to leave him.

The Professor learns that all of his speculative ventures have failed: he is financially ruined. He takes Alraune to the gambling table, hoping that, as in the legend, she will bring

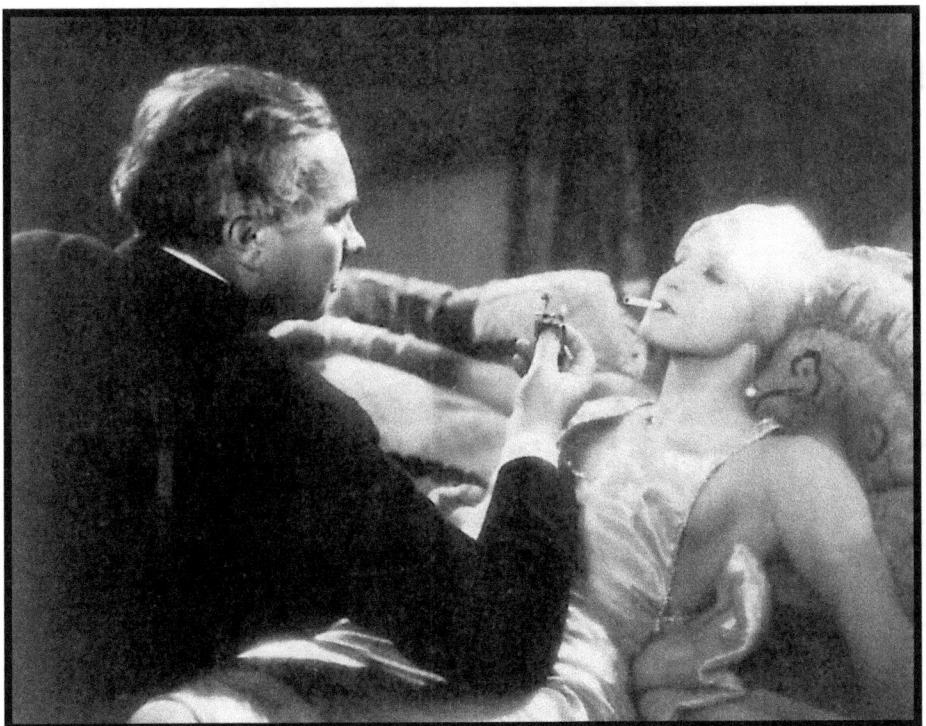

Alraune (Brigitte Helm) uses her sexual wiles to avenge herself on her creator/"father" (Paul Wegener) in *Alraune*.

him luck. While she stands behind him, he wins a huge amount at roulette. But she sneaks away, and on the next spin, he loses it all.

The Professor finds Alraune packing to leave him and chases her with a knife. She is rescued by Franz Braun. "Give me another soul, and a heart so that I might become a human being. And love like one," she sobs to the Professor's nephew. The Professor is left behind "to suffer the Hell of loneliness and insanity."

Finished late in 1927 and released in 1928, this sinisterly romantic *schauerromane* exudes a sense of perverse sexuality that rivals the Pabst films with Louise Brooks. As in *The Student of Prague*, Galeen uses the silent cinema's full range of cinematic technique. *Alraune*'s opening prologue detailing the legend of the mandrake root is shown with Expressionistic long shots of a body hanging on the gallows silhouetted by a full moon. A peasant dressed in fur creeps under the dangling man with a shovel to unearth the magic root.

After the prologue, the style is contemporary and realistic in costume, decor and lighting. But the realism is punctuated with expressive stylistic flourishes. For example, in the circus sequence, Fritz Lang's discovery, Brigitte Helm, who plays Alraune, heartlessly blows cigarette smoke through the bars of the lions' cage. She is shown in a close shot from the lions' point of view exhaling the smoke right at the camera.

Galeen emphasizes the human emotions in his fantasy as when Alraune's young boyfriend is left behind after Ten Brinken, who is played by Paul Wegener, takes the girl away from the circus. Galeen stops the story to allow us to see the boy crying in Alraune's empty

dressing room, holding her costume to his face. He intercuts this with a long shot of a guitar player sitting on the stoop of his circus wagon, strumming a mournful tune.

Galeen uses the moving camera sparingly. When Alraune reads the Professor's diary and learns of her true origin, Galeen tracks back with her as she angrily approaches his sleeping form. For that moment, we are Alraune, experiencing her shame, betrayal and anger. Will she kill this man whom she calls father? Would we?

As in *The Student of Prague*, Galeen again uses shadows to symbolize the evil thoughts of his character. The shadow of Alraune's hands creep up the sheet covering the sleeping Ten Brinken, approaching his throat as if to strangle him. The moment recalls the shadow of Nosferatu moving up the body of Hutter and later, Ellen.

The most cinematic moment in *Alraune* is a close point-of-view shot into a mirrored compact. Alraune's eyes stare back at us from the mirror as she adjusts her makeup. But she tilts the mirror slightly so that she and we see the angry expression of Ten Brinken standing behind her, fuming over her recent flirtations. Another subjective shot is a dream vision from the Professor's point of view. His fascination with his "daughter" has become an obsession. Alone, he envisions the mandrake root that first inspired him. As it revolves, he studies its human-like face and its branches raised over its head as if they were arms. The root dissolves to Alraune revolving, her pose matching the abstract body of the mandrake.

Throughout the film, Galeen gives us sensuous close-ups of Brigitte Helm, blowing smoke from her cigarette, staring invitingly at men, her pale eyes drawing in them and us. When the Professor takes her to a nightclub, she plays with a feathered fan. In close-up, she covers her face with it, then emerges from behind the soft white feathers to stare coquettishly at her prey. Later, as she lays on the couch, posing for her "father," Galeen gives us an extreme close profile. Helm blows her backlit cigarette smoke out slowly, the side shot formalizing her beauty like a perfectly sculpted but marble-cold statue. The incestuous tension in this last third of the film makes *Alraune* one of the silent cinema's most suspensefully sensual works.

The novel on which it was based deals with even more sexual aberration than the movie. The character of Franz Braun, the professor's nephew, plays a much more important part in the book. In fact, many of Ewers' horror novels feature Braun as a sort of wish-fulfillment alter-ego. In the book *Alraune*, it is Braun who suggests the mandrake experiment to his vicious old uncle. While serving his compulsory military term and under arrest for fighting a duel, Braun has run up enormous gambling debts which he cannot pay. His only choices are suicide or help from his uncle. In return for his assistance on the Alraune project, Ten Brinken pays his nephew's debts.

Together, they visit the slums of Berlin looking for the ideal whore. Braun finds the woman and strings her along until his uncle carries her off to his laboratory. Braun leaves the story at this point, as in the film, to return at the end when Alraune is a young woman. In the book, he too falls under her deadly spell and becomes her perverted lover, mixing sex with blood vampirism. In the end, Braun destroys the actual mandrake root that first inspired the experiment. Perhaps because of that, Alraune dies in an accident.

The film was released in Germany by AMA Film. When it arrived in the United States in May 1928, it was surprisingly well received by the critic for *Variety*: "Titillation for the gooseflesh. All the horrors of *Metropolis* and quite a lot more... Hanns Heinz Ewers, scenario writer, makes Edgar Allan Poe look like an amateur... Heinrich Galeen squeezes all the horror juice out of it, and Brigitte Helm, the vamp, is at least 200 percent. When will some American director take a look at this extraordinarily fascinating girl? She has an individuality all her own."

The fact that Ewers was an early member of the National Socialist Party makes his theme of genetic manipulation even more sinister. Ten Brinken is the fictional forerunner of the actual Dr. Mengele, who performed torturous experiments on prisoners in Nazi concentration camps. Ironically, a year after Hitler became Chancellor, Ewers fell out of political favor, and his books were banned and burned. Perhaps the moralizing of *Alraune*, in which the Professor is punished for his attempts to manipulate nature, offended the more "progressive" Fuehrer. Hitler may also have learned that Ewers believed that both Jews and Gentiles were suitable to be members of the Master Race. In his 1922 novel, *Vampir*, Ewers even suggested that the Jews were the best Germans.

The most likely reason for Hitler's ultimate disapproval of Ewers was the author's glorification of the old-guard Nazis in his book and screenplay about Horst Wessel, the storm trooper who was killed in an early street brawl. Many of the heroes of Ewers' biography were Nazis whom Hitler removed from power or ordered murdered. Goebbels accused Ewers of making a "pseudo-artistic or inartistic attempt to exploit the actual political situation."

Or perhaps the Nazi defenders of public morality just felt that Ewers' dark, sadistic, erotic works were "degenerate art," unfit for consumption by wholesome Aryans. After all, the Nazis did label him as "decadent" and a "poisoner of the people," and he was forbidden from publishing his work. For whatever reason, when Ewers died in 1943 in Berlin, it was as an "unperson."

Henrik Galeen made a few more movies in Germany after *Alraune* before emigrating to the United States in 1933 when the Nazis came to power. In America, he made no films and disappeared from public view. He died in 1949.

Galeen, like his mentor, Hanns Heinz Ewers, like Paul Wegener, Robert Wiene, Janowitz and Mayer, F.W. Murnau, Albin Grau, Paul Leni, Fritz Lang and Thea von Harbou, all saw themselves as artists working within the new medium of cinema and shaping it with stories of terror into an aesthetic form to rank beside literature, theater, music, painting and sculpture. These filmmakers truly believed that horror provided the means to delve deeply into the human psyche and to inspire new and effective cinematic techniques. They realized that few other genres depended as much on mood and atmosphere, even more than narrative, and that these were aspects of storytelling that film could render most effectively. Thus, the very root of the horror genre was a self-conscious effort by serious creators to expand the medium to appeal to a sophisticated and discerning audience.

Because horror fiction has been a popular tradition, it is often regarded as low culture. In an attempt to associate them with established and legitimate aesthetic forms, the films of the German artists of the 1920s are sometimes labeled as Romantic or Expressionistic rather than examples of the cinema of terror. But the truth is that each of the German filmmakers sought to disturb and frighten their audience using advanced techniques, and in so doing, they established the tradition of the best horror movies.

CHAPTER 3
EUROPEAN EVIL

The art house horror cinema of Germany influenced filmmakers from other European countries in the 1920s. Benjamin Christensen was born in Viborg, Denmark on September 28, 1879, the youngest of 12 children. Although he studied medicine at the University of Denmark, he was not a diligent student.

A professional opera performer heard Christensen singing in his apartment and insisted that he audition. Christensen got the part and began a career in the opera in 1902. Unfortunately, he only felt comfortable singing when he thought no one was listening, and this nervousness forced him to abandon singing for acting on the stage. The same anxiety caused him to quit this profession, too, and he became the Danish representative for a French champagne company.

But he was drawn to the new art form of the motion picture when he saw the great Swedish film, *The Abyss*, in 1910. Christensen appeared in occasional Danish films as a performer as well as writing scenarios for the pioneer director August Blom. He convinced the studio managers to allow him to direct, and in August 1913, he made an impressive debut helming his own script, *The Mysterious X*, in which he also starred. Christensen worked three months in production when the average Danish feature usually took two weeks, and he spent three to four times the usual cost.

From this first venture, a spy thriller heavily influenced by the flamboyant French detective serials of Louis Feuillade, he revealed an interest in the uncanny and the macabre. Because of the outbreak of World War I, spy films were outlawed in Germany and Austria, so Christensen changed the characters' trade from spying to smuggling. When the film was released in 1914, it garnered rave reviews for its excellent acting and for its directional lighting in which characters sometimes appeared as silhouettes.

Christensen again wrote, acted and directed in 1915 with his second feature, *Night of Vengeance*, a crime drama taking place in the circus. This picture received such impressive notices in America that Vitagraph offered Christensen the post of Supervising Director with authority over the work of every other director in the company. But Christensen turned the job down to pursue his own muse.

In America, while Christensen showed *Night of Vengeance* to a group of prisoners in Sing Sing, one convict knifed another. The incident disturbed Christensen greatly, and he talked it over with the prison warden, the renowned reformist, Thomas Osborn. The Warden shared his theory that even the most hardened criminal possessed depths of feeling that made him reachable on a human level.

Christensen began to think about how a belief in absolute evil caused mankind to dehumanize and persecute those with mental illness, deformity or in poverty. This, coupled with his interest in the supernatural, led Christensen to research a film on the witchcraft hysteria of the Middle Ages. At first, he wanted to collaborate with professional historians so that his film would be as accurate as possible. But the academics refused because of their disrespect for the new art form and because the subject of witchcraft seemed distasteful to them.

Christensen was forced to sell his own studio when World War I made it increasingly difficult to release his products overseas, so he approached Svensk Filmindustri, the foremost studio in Sweden, to finance the project. In 1919, the company not only agreed but gave Christensen full artistic freedom to create what would become his masterpiece: a one-of-a-

***Haxan* turned out to be the most expensive silent movie ever produced in the Scandinavian countries. [Photofest]**

kind dramatized documentary of medieval witchcraft, the Inquisition and modern female neurosis called *Haxan*, which means, "The Witch."

Christensen convinced the Swedish company to allow him to shoot his film at his old studio, north of Copenhagen in Denmark. The financiers not only purchased the facility, but they upgraded it with the latest lighting and camera equipment. Because he felt that he could not bring out the hysteria he needed from his actors in the daylight hours, Christensen insisted on shooting much of the film at night. This caused the budget to bloat with overtime bonuses for the cast and crew. In fact, *Haxan* turned out to be the most expensive silent movie ever produced in the Scandinavian countries.

This remarkable work is a strange combination of naive lecture and spectacularly designed and realized cinema. Christensen presents the material in seven chapters, each lasting a reel of film. The first section consists merely of illustrations by such artists as Bosch, Cranach, Breughel and Durer taken from books. A model and a crudely made chart from cut paper depicts the medieval conception of the universe with the sun and planets orbiting the earth and tiers of angels surrounding the solar system. Pointers and pencils are thrust into shots to emphasize features of the illustrations.

By contrast, the remaining six reels feature dramatized episodes that are examples of the finest filmmaking of their time. The static camera and artistic compositions emphasize the painterly quality of the scenes as if they were illustrations come to life. The lighting by photographer Johan Ankerstjerne creates the moody, firelit atmosphere of Rembrandt.

***Haxan* ended Christensen's film career for two years.**

Exteriors of the witches traveling to their midnight Sabbat utilize silhouetted figures against an overcast sky with superimposed shots of hags on broomsticks flashing by overhead. Seventy-five witches on broomsticks were photographed on separate pieces of film against a black background. They sat suspended between the floor and ceiling of the studio with airplane propellers blowing their heavy period costumes while the camera moved by them from front to back to make it appear as if they were flying. On another piece of film, a huge miniature of a medieval town with houses only two meters high was moved by 20 stagehands on a turntable so that the static camera could photograph it as a background. A pioneering optical printer was built to combine the flying witches with the town in one seemingly moving shot. To get the proper cloud effects for witches flying through the night, Christensen sent a camera unit on a month-long trip to Norway to photograph stormy skies.

The witches' evil revelry is filmed with stark, high-contrast lighting and features shocking makeup and costumes for Satan and his demons. Trees on the studio grounds were uprooted and upended to give the effect of twisted branches surrounding the celebrants. Christensen uses innovative camera techniques such as reverse motion and stop motion animation to create this fantastic world. One beautiful shot shows the nude back of a young woman lying on the ground, her white skin glowing against the surrounding darkness. Carefully placed objects such as a skull and an hour glass complete the composition. A demon hand with long, bony fingers reaches for the girl, gently touching her smooth flesh with its pointed nails.

Christensen himself plays Satan with a bald head, bat-like ears and stubby horns thrusting from his forehead. His fingers have been lengthened into sharp talons, and his blotchy, discolored body is naked. Into long-held shots without movement, he suddenly jumps up from behind window sills and desks, his tongue thrusting in and out of his mouth lasciviously, and his eyes rolled up in his head. The effect is both shocking and comically indecent, like the punch line of a dirty joke. He beckons sleeping women and fat priests to join him in his revels. In one scene, he clubs a nun over the head, causing her to stagger about the convent blindly before possessing her.

Christensen does not shy away from the more disgusting behavior of the damned. Old peasant women kiss Satan's bare, mud-encrusted ass, and two ancient crones urinate in buckets and throw the vile liquid onto the door of their enemy. Fat, naked male demons pump butter churns in obvious pantomimes of masturbation. One shot shows an old woman who has been impregnated by the devil giving birth to a brood of hideous demons who crawl from out of the darkness of her spread skirt. The overall impression is of sex stripped of beauty and romance and made monstrously vile.

Much of the narrative betrays a male paranoia of women gaining independence. A pretty medieval wife sleeps naked in bed next to her husband. Suddenly, Christensen as Satan appears in the open bedroom window. The wife begins to smile and lick her lips, obviously overcome with sexual thoughts. She rises from bed, still asleep, and embraces the devil. Her nude form, in silhouette, sleepwalks through the countryside on her way to the witches' Sabbat, her arms stretched blindly before her.

Unable to control her mind and body in sleep, she becomes vulnerable to frightening impulses. In Freudian terms, her ego can no longer control her id. The women of *Haxan* escape the supervision of their fathers and husbands and secretly follow their deepest desires. Or perhaps, without male figures to watch over them, they are more susceptible to the dark forces. Either way, their independence becomes threatening and immoral, a masculine fear personified.

Having it both ways, the film also portrays the merciless clergy of the Catholic Church persecuting pathetic old crones and wrongly accused young women. An ancient beggar accused of practicing the black arts is bullied by white-robed priests, one fat and cruel and another smiling in sadistic glee. When the innocent and harmless woman refuses to confess, her frail body is subjected to torture. In a series of close shots, Christensen clinically reveals selected instruments for inflicting pain actually used during the Inquisition. Also in close-up, the poor old peasant moans in agony, driving home the point that the Catholic Church demanded obedience and faith through force. When the film was released, the Swedish cen-

Much of *Haxan*'s narrative betrays a male paranoia of women gaining independence.

sors demanded the removal of these tight shots, finding it indecent and unnatural to show the naked human face in pain projected to such a huge size on the screen.

Christensen is not afraid to show the angry determination and smiling glee of the priests as their victims are put to the question. To put an end to her agony, the old woman condemns other innocent females, including the young mother of a newborn. Thus, the injustice of the Church spreads thoughout the village to destroy more blameless lives. Christensen relates the Church to both ignorance and sadism, giving the impression that religion at its core is inseparable from evil.

Also, Christensen visually links the Inquisitors with the wicked demons they fight. If the Black Mass includes wild orgiastic abandon, the repression of the clergy also encourages sexual deviance. After glimpsing a pretty woman who has come to testify to the Inquisitors, a new, fresh-faced priest opens the rectory window on spring blossoms and stares out with carnal longing. Christensen superimposes the white flowers over his unhappy countenance, emphasizing the natural impulse of his feelings. But the celibate's desire is suppressed, expressing itself in aberration. He tells another stern priest of his weakness and begs to be punished. The young man strips himself to the waist and allows the older cleric to beat him with a whip. Christensen superimposes a close-up of the flagellant's face over the scene of his whipping. His expression betrays a combination of pain and orgasm, revealing the young man's masochistic sexual release. When his punisher quits, the flagellant asks longingly, "Oh brother, why have you stopped?"

The director mirrors scenes of demons with later ones featuring members of the Church. At the Witches' Sabbat, a giant, grotesque monster sacrifices an infant as revelers dance wildly to the beating of a fat troll's drum. Christensen later depicts a possessed nun, shut away in a convent, who steals the wooden figure of the baby Jesus from the statue of its mother and carries the lifeless thing in her arms like Satan's human offering. The nun's insanity soon affects the other weak-minded sisters, and they scamper madly around the convent recalling the celebrants at Satan's orgy.

A priest pricks the white back of an innocent young woman looking for the insensitive "devil's mark." The scene dissolves from Satan's taloned hand puncturing the tender flesh on his initiate's back. With purely cinematic means, Christensen clearly communicates his meaning: the Inquisitors have become as monstrous as the demons by assuming authority over God's dominion. Their torment of women and their demand for blind obedience echo Satan's.

With another dissolve, Christensen also associates the priest's methods with those of the modern man of medicine. He depicts a 20th-century doctor pricking the back of a female patient to find the insensitive area caused by her neurosis, mirroring the Inquisition's search for the "devil's mark." In the age of psychoanalysis, the women accused of witchcraft in the Middle Ages would be diagnosed as hysterics. Instead of being handed over to the heartless Church, in modern times, such women would be arrested by civil authority or treated by doctors and clinics.

The film also dramatizes the story of a disturbed modern lady who lights matches while sleepwalking. Again, the male fear of female independence surfaces as she escapes control in sleep and succumbs to the impulses of her unconscious. During the day, she shoplifts uncontrollably. But when she is caught by a store clerk, he shows her mercy, unlike the stern Church of the past. This episode illustrates the theories learned by Christensen from Warden Osborn at Sing Sing: that criminals are not evil, just sick in mind and soul.

Like the women of the Middle Ages, the shoplifter is surrounded by male authority figures who decide her fate. They remind us of the priests of the Church, but also of Satan and his demons. Like the devil, the doctor comes to her at night, but only in her dreams. The woman's doctor is played by Christensen himself, as is Satan, further linking the characters.

Haxan's frequent, though discreetly presented, nudity, lurid detail and criticism of the Catholic Church limited its release to very few countries. Rather than being trimmed, it was more often banned outright. Begun in 1919 but not finished until 1922, the film premiered in Stockholm on September 18, 1922 and in Denmark on November 7. In its countries of origin, *Haxan* was greeted with lavish praise from the critics. Some reviewers disagreed, however. In one popular Copenhagen newspaper, the film's review bore the headline, "Get This Film Off the Screen." The writer objected to the perversion of the subject matter and the nauseating close-ups of suffering women. But unlike in Sweden, Danish censors passed the film without a cut.

Haxan did not open in Germany until 1924 and then only in a heavily edited version with long, pedantic intertitles that slowed the action and blunted the cinematic power. The last title suggested that history would pass the same harsh judgment on victims of World War I as on victims of the witchcraft trials. Even though the writer was probably trying to compare the madness of the witch persecutions with the madness of war, Germans found this allusion distasteful since it seemed to cast aspersions on the dead heroes of the fatherland.

When the film opened in France, Catholic organizations brought a complaint against it with the police that it defamed the Church. *Haxan* did not reach the United States until a severely shortened version called *Witchcraft Through the Ages* was shown in March 1929. In New York City, it premiered with a Laurel and Hardy short called "Liberty."

The review in *Variety* said, "Swedish and Danish pictures easily hold the palm for morbid realism, and in many cases for brilliant acting and production. *Witchcraft Through the Ages*, made by Benjamin Christensen, leaves all the others beaten....Many of its scenes are unadulterated horror." The review concluded that the film was "absolutely unfit for

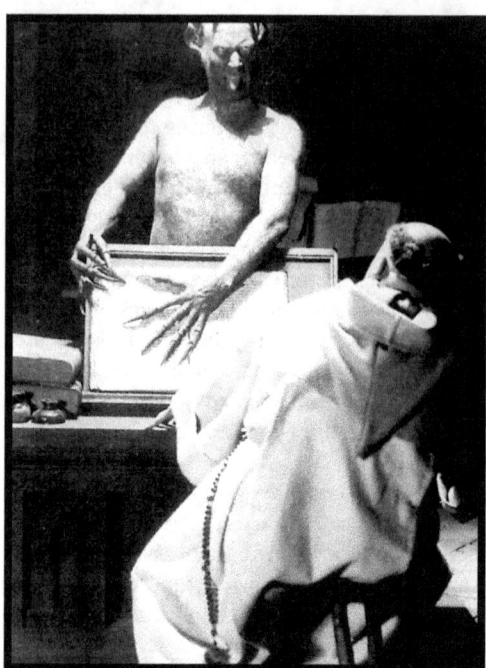

In *Haxan* Christensen himself plays Satan with a bald head, bat-like ears and stubby horns thrusting from his forehead. [Photofest]

public exhibition." *Film Daily* agreed, calling the film's "subject matter too grim for most picture houses." However, *The New York Times* termed the picture "fantastically conceived and directed, holding the onlooker in a sort of medieval spell. Most of the characters seem to have stepped from primitive paintings." Ado Kyrou, the surrealist film historian, described it as an indictment of "the criminal church, its inquisition, and its instruments of torture." He added, "this document should be shown in every school in the world." Despite its critical success, its limited distribution in the United States doomed it at the box-office.

For Christensen, *Haxan* ended his career for two years. Because of the experimental nature of his film, other companies in Denmark and abroad avoided him. He had envisioned *Haxan* as the first part of a supernatural trilogy, the other two movies being *The Saint* and *The Spirits*. The first film would have dealt with religious hysteria, and Christensen actually filmed a few scenes, but the project was never completed. For *The Spirits*, Christensen wanted to set up an experimental laboratory for the finest mediums in the world, especially physical mediums. He felt that film was the best way to break through the barrier that separated the living from the dead. His ultimate goal was to record the materialization of a spirit on film. Unfortunately, Christensen was never again to create a personal film like *Haxan*.

The movie was re-released in Denmark in 1941 during the Nazi occupation. Silent films rarely played during the sound era, but this release succeeded with both critics and audiences. 25,000 people saw it in the first week, a record in the cinema in which it played. The film saw the same triumph across the country. Preceded by a filmed introduction by Christensen himself, this re-release may have inspired Carl Dreyer to make his 1943 masterpiece about witchcraft paranoia, *Day of Wrath*.

Haxan is a one-of-a-kind movie, an experiment in docu-drama unlike any other film in the silent era. Certainly, no feature like it could have been made in the United States or Britain for at least 50 years after its production. Ahead of its time in its criticism of the Church and its depiction of nudity, sexual aberration and the unpleasant realities of the Middle Ages, it is also almost medieval itself in its literal portrayal of Satan and witchcraft. Aside from its warnings about demonic possession, the movie addresses issues that concern society more at the end of the 20th century than at the time of its release. The women's movement of the 1970s would certainly have embraced the message of the film.

The final impression of *Haxan* is that women throughout history have been subjected to the control of men, sometimes mercifully, more often cruelly. Females are tempted and degraded by Satan, unfairly judged and punished by the Church, and diagnosed and shut away in clinics by modern doctors. The implication is that men fear the opposite sex and seek to control them. The final image in the film is a silhouette of the charred bodies of several accused witches bound to stakes after being burned alive: the ultimate method of male restraint and domination.

Over the years, many killers have shocked and fascinated the public, but overshadowing them all in terms of sheer horror was the Victorian fiend known only by his grim nickname: Jack the Ripper. The bloody ferocity of his butchery of prostitutes in the foggy streets of London's East End jolted the staid society of 1888. The mocking letters sent to the Central News Agency and the Whitechapel Vigilance Committee, whether by the Ripper or an impostor, revealed a level of human evil never before encountered by the common populace. But the most haunting aspect of the case was the fact that the Ripper was never caught or identified. He could have been anyone, from any strata of the community, and the possibilities and implications tormented the collective imagination. Naturally, it was not long before writers began to speculate creatively about this human monster's identity. The most famous attempt was Mrs. Marie Belloc Lowndes' short story of 1911 and subsequent novel of 1913, *The Lodger*.

Born in 1868, the daughter of an English mother and a French barrister named Louis Belloc, Marie was a member of a distinguished family. Her great-great-grandfather was Joseph Priesley, the chemist who discovered oxygen; her grandmother was the French translator of Harriet Beecher Stowe's *Uncle Tom's Cabin*; her brother was the famous writer Hilaire Belloc. Marie married Frederic Sawrey Lowndes, a well-known journalist for the *London Times*.

She claimed to have written virtually every day of her life beginning at the age of 16. Rewriting constantly and painstakingly, she still managed to be quite prolific. Even within the genre of suspense and horror, she concentrated on character development and relationships, particularly between men and women.

The Lodger tells the story of Mr. and Mrs. Bunting, former domestic servants, whose livelihood now depends on renting upstairs rooms in their London lodging house. Just when their financial situation appears hopeless, an eccentric gentleman named Mr. Sleuth suddenly takes the rooms, paying a month in advance.

First Mrs. Bunting then her husband begin to suspect that Mr. Sleuth is actually a Jack the Ripper–like killer of women who leaves triangles of gray paper pinned to his victims with one chilling phrase in red ink: The Avenger. The lodger silently slips out at night and sleeps all day. He carries a small black bag just large enough to conceal a knife, brings bundles of old clothes to his room which subsequently disappear, and is caught burning clothes in the kitchen stove one night. The newspaper reports that the Avenger leaves prints from the bottom of rubber-soled shoes, and Mr.

French poster of *The Lodger*

Sleuth promptly disposes of his pair and replaces them with regular boots. One night, Mr. Bunting brushes against the lodger as he returns from one of his nightly forays, and the landlord comes away with a smear of blood on his hand.

Mr. Sleuth also betrays a fear and loathing of women: he turns portraits of early Victorian belles in lace and ball dresses to face the wall, claiming that their eyes follow him about the room. Demanding a Bible be brought to him, he is often overheard quoting passages warning of the evils of the female seducer.

The Buntings cannot afford to turn him out, and their situation is further complicated when Daisy, Mr. Bunting's 18-year-old daughter from a previous marriage, comes to stay with them for her birthday. The couple fear leaving her alone in the house with their sinister lodger. To add to the couple's worries, their friend, Joe Chandler, a detective on the Avenger case, is attracted to Daisy.

Mr. Sleuth invites the family to Madame Tussaud's Wax Museum for Daisy's birthday. There he glimpses the one man who can identify him as the Avenger: a Police Commissioner who knows that he was imprisoned in a mental hospital for similar crimes and recently escaped after stealing some gold sovereigns. Mr. Sleuth, in his paranoid madness, accuses Mrs. Bunting of setting him up and vows revenge. But he escapes from the police and is never seen by the Buntings again.

In late April 1926, Michael Balcon, the head of production for the British company Gainsborough Pictures, assigned the screen adaptation of *The Lodger* to his new, 26-year-old director, Alfred Hitchcock. Destined to become the most famous filmmaker in history, Hitchcock was born on August 13, 1899 in London. His father was a poultry dealer and fruit importer. His Catholic parents enrolled Hitchcock in a strict Jesuit school, Saint Ignatius College. After graduating, he attended a vocational college where he studied mechanics, electricity, acoustics and navigation.

At 19, he took a job as a estimator of electrical cables for a telegraph company. But at night, he attended art courses at the University of London, and this led to his transfer to the telegraph company's advertising department as a sketch artist and assistant layout man.

In 1920, he achieved his dream of entering the film industry when he landed a job as a designer of titles for the new London branch of Hollywood's Famous Player–Lasky. Soon, he headed the title department. Gainborough Pictures, formed by Michael Balcon, took over the Famous Players studio in Islington in 1922. Balcon promoted Hitchcock to assistant director, as well as art director and screenwriter.

Finally, in 1925, Balcon permitted Hitchcock to direct his first feature in Germany, a backstage romance called *The Pleasure Garden*. Hitchcock was finishing post-production on his second feature, *The Mountain Eagle*, when he received the assignment of *The Lodger*.

Unfortunately, *The Pleasure Garden* was judged unreleaseable by the head financier of the distribution company, C.M. Woolf. Hitchcock had been very influenced by German filmmakers such as Murnau and Lang and had even visited the set of *Metropolis* while working in Germany. Woolf felt that the extreme high- and low-angle shots and contrasts in lighting that Hitchcock had borrowed from the Germans would confuse and upset English audiences accustomed to the more simple views of American films. Balcon gave *The Lodger* to Hitchcock for precisely these reasons. He realized that the mystery and suspense of the story would justify Hitchcock's eerie visual touches.

Eager to redeem himself, Hitchcock and his writer, Eliot Stannard, completed the script by the beginning of May. Stannard had already written 50 scripts in his 10 years in the British film industry by the time Balcon assigned him to Hitchcock's first film, *The Pleasure Garden*. Ivor Montagu, who would later re-edit *The Lodger*, described Stannard as a consummate professional whose method "was to sit down and tap it straight out on the typewriter as he thought of it, without change or erase-ment." Hitchcock broke the entire script into separate shots, each of which was sketched by an illustrator. Further, he indicated all the set designs, furnishings and props in the scenario. The art director had only to follow instructions. As Hitchcock would do in his later productions, he almost completely assembled the movie on paper before a roll of film had been exposed.

When Ivor Novello, the Welsh-born, Oxford educated matinee idol, took the part of the nameless lodger, a major script change was demanded because of his enormous popularity. Hitchcock could not conclude the film with the lodger disappearing into the night, his guilt or innocence never clearly resolved, as he had planned. "They wouldn't let Novello even be considered as a villain," Hitchcock said. "The publicity angle carried the day, and we had to change the script to show that without a doubt he was innocent. So I just never even showed the real murderer."

In the end, the lodger's nocturnal prowlings, haunted quality and obsession with the Avenger is explained: his beloved sister was murdered by the Avenger at her coming out party, and the lodger seeks him each night to exact revenge. Hitchcock would be forced to perform a similar rewrite at the end of *Suspicion*, his 1941 adaptation of Francis Iles' *Before the Fact*. Producers felt that the audience would not accept Cary Grant as a murderer, so his elaborate preparations for poisoning Joan Fontaine were explained as arrangements for his own suicide.

The changed scenario of *The Lodger* reflected not only this forced twist ending but the dark and threatening romance that would become part of Hitchcock's personal style. As in the novel, the mysterious stranger comes to lodge with the Buntings at the height of the Avenger murders. Daisy is already living with the old couple, and Joe Chandler is a regular fixture in their home as he courts her. No longer Mrs. Belloc Lowndes' lower- middle-class, uneducated waif, Daisy, as played by the beautiful June Tripp, is a sophisticated high-fashion model. She often laughs at the quaint ways of her parents and even finds funny the handsome lodger's act of turning the pictures of women to the wall. While her mother and father's suspicions grow, she spends time with the lodger, bringing him meals, playing chess and eventually going on a date with him. She is sexually attracted to his dark, mysterious obsessiveness, and not at all intimidated. Hitchcock's theme of the complacency of average people unable to recognize evil has its first expression with Daisy.

Since all clues point to the lodger being the Avenger, his attentions to Daisy seem aberrant and threatening. Hitchcock creates suspense by hinting at the lodger's impending murder of the innocent girl. In an insert shot, he shows the lodger slowly picking up a poker from the fireplace while Daisy concentrates on finding a lost chess figure. Her golden hair, the same color as that of all the Avenger's victims, fills the screen as she bends down for the lost game piece. Also in a close shot, the lodger holds a knife close to her body, then uses it to flick a speck from her clothes. As he watches her modeling the latest fashions, the lodger never takes his eyes from Daisy, not even when he lights the cigarette of a young woman sitting next to him. Twenty-five years later, in *Strangers on a Train*, Hitchcock similarly shows the psychopath, Bruno Anthony, staring at his obsession, Guy Haines, while the heads of all around him look back and forth at the ball in a tennis match.

In *The Lodger*, the mysterious stranger stands at the bathroom door trying to turn the doorknob as Daisy sits naked in the tub running hot water over her body. Does he want to murder her or make love to her? The effect equates sexual desire with the lust to kill, a theme that runs through later Hitchcock films such as *Suspicion*, *Spellbound*, *Psycho* and *Frenzy*.

Another Hitchcock theme that emerges as a result of the change is that of the innocent man wrongly accused of a crime. Joe Chandler grows jealous of Daisy's attentions to the lodger and is only too eager to listen to the old couple's suspicions. He searches the lodger's room and finds a map of the Avenger killings. Even after the lodger emotionally confesses his real quest, Joe insists on cuffing and arresting him. The lodger escapes wearing the cuffs like the heroes of *The 39 Steps* and *Saboteur*, tries to conceal them with the aid of Daisy in a pub, and runs from the police and an angry mob. He hangs, Christ-like, from an iron fence when his cuffs are caught on one of the spikes. At the last minute, Joe hears that the real Avenger has been caught, and he rescues the lodger from the mob surrounding him. "Thank God I was in time," says Joe's intertitle, harking back to the iconography of the Church of Hitchcock's upbringing.

Principal photography began the first week of May at the grimy Islington studios, and Hitchcock followed his designs meticulously. His demand for accuracy meant that a three-sided house had to be constructed in the studio with narrow walls and low ceilings in the exact dimensions of a middle-class home. The difficulties of lighting such a set were considerable. When Mrs. Belloc Lowndes herself visited the studio, she must have been gratified to see that at least the setting of her novel was being accurately followed.

Already interested in revealing narrative through the point of view of a character, Hitchcock created expressive visuals to transfer the Buntings' growing fear of their lodger to the audience. At one point, they hear the lodger pacing back and forth in the room above their heads. Hitchcock cuts to their point of view of the ceiling. It seems to dissolve away, and we are looking up through it at the feet of the lodger as he strides across the floor like a nervous cat.

"I had a floor made out of one-inch-thick plate glass, about six feet square," Hitchcock told Peter Bogdanovich. "This was the visual substitution for sound, you see. Just as much as was the set I had built for when the lodger went out late at night—almost to the ceiling of the studio, showing four flights of stairs and a handrail. And all you see is a hand going down (from a high angle shooting straight down the stairs). That was, of course, from the point of view of the mother listening. Today we would substitute sound for that, although I think the handrail shot would be worthy of today with the addition of sound."

The Lodger was completed by early July at a cost of £12,000. Graham Cutts, a senior director for whom Hitchcock had recently worked as assistant, had often dropped by to watch his former employee's progress. He began to spread rumors at the studio about the incomprehensibility of the film. Hitchcock told Bogdanovich: "When it was finished, Cutts was still in the company and Balcon had gone to America. When he returned, Cutts said to him, 'I've been looking at the rushes and I can't make head nor tail of them—don't know what the hell he's shooting.'"

"He had been perfectly happy with Hitch the young handyman and as his assistant director," Balcon wrote. "Hitch could not understand what he had done to offend Cutts and I had to explain to him that he had done nothing wrong; it was only that Cutts was jealous. Hitch was rising too fast for Cutts' taste and he resented him as a rival director in the same studio... Cutts began to tell

Ivor Novello as the nameless lodger is a little too interested in the innocent Daisy (June Tripp) in Hitchcock's *The Lodger.*

anybody who would listen that we had a disaster on our hands. Unfortunately, one person who listened was C.M. Woolf, who, of course, had the say as to distribution."

On the day that Woolf and the potential exhibitors screened the completed film, Hitchcock nervously took his fiancee, Alma Reville, on an aimless walk around central London: across the Thames, up the Strand, and through the East End. Finally, Hitchcock turned away and said, "They've seen it all by now and had a chance to hash it over. Let's go back."

When they walked into the studio, Woolf announced to Hitchcock, "Your picture is so dreadful that we're just going to put it on the shelf and forget about it." To make matters worse, Woolf also considered Hitchcock's second feature, *The Mountain Eagle*, unmarketable. That meant that Hitchcock's first three films as a director were to be shelved, a crushing personal embarrassment for Hitchcock and a financial setback for the studio. It probably would have signaled the premature end of Hitchcock's career had Michael Balcon not desperately sought a way to salvage *The Lodger*. Not only did Balcon want to recoup his investment in the picture, but he also needed to follow the successful release of Novello's last movie, *The Rat*, with another film featuring the same star.

Balcon canceled the early general trade show to which the press would have been invited and postponed it until late September. Then he contacted 22-year-old Ivor Montagu through London's Film Society. Montagu was the same young Cambridge graduate who had unsuccessfully tried to persuade Florence Stoker to allow a free screening for the Society of *Nosferatu*. The son of the eminent banker Lord Swaythling, Monagu had been raised in wealth in Kensington. He had studied zoology, been a founding member of the London Film Society and had gone to Germany as a correspondent for the *London Times* to cover the growth of their film industry. When Balcon contacted him, Montagu was translating titles and re-editing foreign films in a cramped office behind Shaftesbury Avenue in the heart of Soho.

Balcon screened *The Lodger* for him, and Montagu was very impressed. He suggested reducing the number of title cards from over 300 to about 80 and reshooting a few unclear scenes. He also detected a triangular thematic design, not just in the notes left by the Avenger on his victims, but also as a symbol of the film's three-way love interest. He brought in the

American poster artist E. McKnight Kauffer, who had revolutionized British design, to draw sinister triangular backgrounds to the title cards.

At first resentful, Hitchcock soon saw that Montagu was improving his film artistically, not making it more "commercial." Balcon was so grateful that he brought Montagu in as supervising editor on the next two Hitchcock films at Gainsborough. In September, when the press was finally allowed to see the results, they were thrilled. The *Bioscope* of September 16, 1926 raved: "It is possible that this film is the finest British production ever made."

The Lodger is Hitchcock's greatest silent movie because it is the only one to exploit his talent and passion for the thriller. It is also the only silent British horror film of note, which is ironic for a country whose literature dominated the genre in the 19th and early 20th century. Perhaps the British standard of good taste in the 1920s prevented them from showing what they obviously loved to imagine on the printed page. Hitchcock, a homely, fat young Catholic, seething with unexpressed emotions, was the perfect filmmaker to express England's polite fascination with the macabre. On the strength of this success, Hitchcock became the darling of the British film industry. His first two movies were released in quick succession, and he was offered deals with other studios to direct. Thus, *The Lodger* launched one of the most remarkable film artists of all time and led the way for such future masterpieces as *Shadow of a Doubt, Notorious, Stranger on a Train, Rear Window, Vertigo, North by Northwest, Psycho* and *The Birds*.

Jules Epstein was one of the first film theorists to actually practice what he preached. He was able to turn an occupation writing about cinema into a directing career, a tradition that would later include such moviemakers as Francois Truffaut, Peter Bogdanovich and Paul Shraeder. Born on March 25, 1897 in Warsaw to a French-Jewish father and Polish mother, Epstein took his elementary schooling in Switzerland and lived in France in his teens. He studied biophysics and medicine at the University of Lyons, and worked briefly as a lab assistant and hospital intern before turning his interests to literature and the movies.

Influenced by another film theorist turned director, Louis Delluc, Epstein penned his first work on aesthetics, *Bonjour Cinema*, in 1921. The next year, he directed his initial film, a biography of *Pasteur*. In 1923, he demonstrated many of the stylistic ideas that he expressed in his writings in the visually arresting movie, *Coeur fidele*. After another remarkable work, *La Belle Nivernaise*, he directed several commercial but routine pictures. As a reaction against the course his career was taking, he turned to independent experimental cinema with mystical themes and trick camera work. The high point of this phase of his career was his 1928 adaptation of Poe's "The Fall of the House of Usher." Actually, Epstein's film incorporates Poe's very short story, "The Oval Portrait," into the Usher narrative, retaining almost all of the former while drastically altering the events and themes of the title tale.

In "The Oval Portrait," a traveler notices a striking painting of a beautiful young woman in the bedroom of a deserted house. He reads a history of the painting and discovers that it was done by an intensely dedicated artist who neglected his new bride to obsessively complete her portrait. The bride's vitality seems to seep away as her picture becomes more lifelike. When the work is finally complete, the artist cries, "This is indeed *Life* itself!" He turns to his subject and finds her dead.

Poe's famous tale, "The Fall of the House of Usher," tells of a boyhood friend of Roderick Usher who comes to stay at the decaying mansion of his former companion. He finds that Roderick has changed into a morbid hypochondriac so sensitive he cannot tolerate bright light or colors, sounds of any kind, or even certain fabrics on his skin. His beloved twin sister, Madeline, is quietly wasting away from a mysterious malady and wanders about the house like a ghost. She apparently dies during the friend's visit, and Roderick inters her in the family vault beneath the house. He suffers the tortures of the damned after her burial. During a stormy night, he cringes, terrified, as his friend endeavors to comfort him by reading a story. Finally, Roderick admits that he has buried his cataleptic sister alive, and his acute sensitivity allows him to hear her twisting and clawing in her coffin. At that moment, she appears in the doorway. Roderick screams as she collapses on him, and they both fall to the floor, dead. The mansion itself dies with them, crumbling and sinking into the tarn that surrounds it as the friend flees for his life.

Epstein's script does justice to "The Oval Portrait" while completely altering "The Fall of the House of Usher." Before beginning his Poe pastiche, Epstein's opening even borrows from *Nosferatu*. Roderick's friend, like Hutter in Murnau's film, arouses a fearful response at the village inn when he mentions his destination. This foreshadowing scene, which appears in Stoker's novel but not in Poe's short story, would be used so often in horror films as to become a convention.

When the friend arrives at the house of Usher, he finds Roderick obsessed with painting his wife, Madeline, who appears to suffer with each brush stroke. Opting to go with the relationship in "The Oval Portrait," Epstein does not make Madeline the twin sister of Roderick. This robs the film of the spiritual link of the Usher family to the house itself which is central to Poe's conception.

The aging friend, who is both hard of hearing and slightly dense, finds Roderick so absorbed with his painting that he has little time to socialize. As in "The Oval Portrait," Roderick drains the life from his wife as his picture of her becomes more realistic. When he finally finishes, he exclaims, "Truly it is like life itself!" His friend sees that Madeline has collapsed onto the floor, dead.

Unlike Poe's story in which Madeline is buried in a family vault in the cellars of the symbolic house itself, in Epstein's scenario, her coffin is put in a boat that crosses a lake to her crypt. This allows Epstein some stunningly photographed outdoor scenes that are the cinematic highlights of his movie. The burial party carries the casket past bare trees whose black branches reach into the bald, white sky. Ground mist rises from the horizon. The boat carrying the casket drifts across the rippling lake like a barge on the River Styx.

The most drastic change to Poe's story in terms of theme and tone is the ending. In the author's conception, of course, Roderick and Madeline perish along with the house itself. In Epstein's retelling, Madeline returns from her grave, not for revenge, but to save her husband when lightning strikes the house. As Roderick's friend flees the burning building, Roderick leads Madeline to safety. Her portrait burns in the conflagration, presumably freeing the Ushers from its life-draining power.

This is a far cry from Poe, who suggests that the corrupt and dying spirit of the Usher family is present even in the very walls of its crumbling mansion. Poe also hints that Roderick may have deliberately buried his sister alive when he insists on nailing the lid of her coffin. In Epstein's film, Roderick, in blind hope, fears that Madeline might be prematurely interred. He insists the coffin not be sealed. Without giving a specific answer, Poe's conception forces the perceptive reader to ask why Roderick would want to bury his beloved sister alive. The possible answers add to the tension and the dark relationship of the Ushers. This aspect, of course, is lost in Epstein's version.

What Epstein does offer is a visual *tour de force*. The art direction of the house emphasizes huge open spaces with an impossibly long fireplace burning logs the size of tree trunks. The wide stairway is bordered by high spiked balustrades and a massive chain for a handrail. Curtains hang over all of the walls, constantly billowing in the wind. Wild nature

Madeline Usher (Margaret Gance) is the object of her brother's obsession in Jean Epstein's *The Fall of the House of Usher*.

invades the fragile walls of the house of Usher as leaves constantly swirl through its rooms and across its floors. In one shot, Epstein glides the camera forward at ground level as if it were the wind pushing the rustling leaves before it.

The model of the exterior of the house of Usher is deliberately stylized, with huge patterned stars in the sky like the glowing orbs in a Van Gogh painting. Swirling mist surrounds the model, and a tree bursts into flames in front of the house when lightning strikes it. Madeline's crypt is also Expressionistic with obviously painted foliage surrounding the cave-like entrance.

Using slow motion, expressive dolly moves and symbolic details, Epstein, along with his cinematographers, Georges and Jean Lucas, treat the camera like a living participant in the film. Slow motion shots give the action a dream-like quality: a storm-blown pile of books and a suit of armor float gracefully to the floor. Later, Madeline drifts down with impossible slowness as her life ebbs from her. During Madeline's funeral, Epstein constantly cuts to slow motion shots of the white veil that extends from her coffin drifting like a ghost in the wind or trailing hauntingly in the water. The first appearance of Madeline's resurrection is her white veil fluttering out of the mouth of her crypt.

Epstein utilizes precise editing and shots of Roderick's moving point-of-view to force the audience to experience Usher's obsession. As his elderly friend prattles on, Roderick tries to take his mind off his artwork by playing the guitar. Epstein intercuts inserts of Roderick's hand strumming the strings with quick static shots of the lake, the forest and the sky, simulating the liberating Romanticism of his music. But Roderick's gaze keeps returning to the picture. As he walks away from it, he looks down, and Epstein gives us his moving viewpoint of the palette and brushes, wet with paint. The audience is put into Roderick's mind, reminded constantly of his unfinished artwork, and impatient with his well-meaning friend.

When Roderick returns to his work, Epstein shows him in huge close-up from the viewpoint of the painting. He stares at us with the intense obsession of a monomaniac, and we understand his single-minded dedication.

Epstein also allows us to experience Madeline's dizzy suffering. The director overlaps multiple takes of her swaying weakly back and forth, transparent as a ghost. The last exposure is a negative representing the final stage of her swoon: her own death.

Flickering candles surrounding Madeline represent her existence as they slowly burn themselves out. When Roderick discovers Madeline's body on the floor, he picks it up and carries it blindly, knocking the candles over. Epstein depicts his panicked grief by moving the camera madly around the room with his wide-eyed close-up. As Roderick and the other pall bearers carry Madeline's casket through the countryside, Epstein double exposes long, thin candles against the landscape as if Madeline were still existing on an invisible spiritual plane.

Epstein depicts Roderick's restless sadness after Madeline's burial with a montage of landscapes and objects. He presents the mechanisms of a clock in giant close shots as the seconds and minutes tick away. A pendulum swings slowly back and forth against a black background. As the chimes strike the hour, Epstein cuts to a close shot of Roderick's guitar, and a string snaps, symbolizing Usher's nerves.

Like Murnau with *The Last Laugh* and Ewald André Dupont with *Varieté*, Epstein utilizes the moving camera more frequently than the filmmaking conventions of his time. He constantly tracks back with characters as they move toward us or tracks forward with them as we follow them into a room. There are several moving point-of-view shots, not just for Roderick, but for other characters as well. During the funeral scene, Epstein cuts to low- angle moving shots of tree branches reaching into the sky. These could only represent Madeline's view from the casket, hinting at the false nature of her "death."

Madeline's resurrection to save the man whose obsessive artwork caused her demise is quite Christ-like. Epstein hints at his Christian intentions when he intercuts symbolically regenerative scenes of copulating frogs with double-exposed shots of Madeline's doctor hammering the nail on the lid of her coffin. Also, when the house finally burns to the ground, a cross can clearly be seen amid the stylized stars in the upper right corner of the night sky. Unfortunately, all of this deviates too far from Poe, and the impact of the story suffers.

An acting teacher himself, Epstein gets fine performances from Jean Debucourt as Roderick and Margaret Gance, wife of the brilliant French director Abel Gance, as Madeline. After enrolling in Epstein's acting class, young Luis Bunuel begged the director for a job on his films. By the time of *The Fall of the House of Usher*, Epstein had made Bunuel his second assistant in charge of interiors. One day, Epstein asked Bunuel to assist Abel Gance in auditioning two girls. Bunuel wrote in his autobiography: "With my usual abruptness, I replied that I was *his* assistant and not Gance's, that I didn't much like Gance's movies (except for *Napoleon*) and that I found Gance himself very pretentious.

" 'How can an insignificant asshole like you dare to talk that way about a great director!' Epstein exploded..." Ironically, this "insignificant asshole" went on to become one the great artists of world cinema, winning the best direction prize at the Canne's Film Festival for *Los Olvidados*, the Special Jury Prize at Cannes for *Nazarin*, the Grand Prize at Cannes for *Viridiana* and the Academy Award for Best Foreign Film for *The Discreet Charm of the Bourgeoisie*.

Unfortunately, with all of its cinematic sophistication, Epstein's *The Fall of the House of Usher* ultimately fails as a translation of Poe. The miscalculation of turning Roderick Usher into a tortured romantic hero blunts the disturbing ambiguity of his character as presented in the story. Although the film successfully creates an atmosphere of morbid beauty appropriate to the author, it falters in its ultimate emotional impact of horror by maneuvering the events into a more conventional happy ending. The visitor to the Usher house, the narrator in the story, becomes a passive and almost simple-minded witness, providing no moral or emotional contrast to Roderick, and offering no identification figure for the audience. Only Epstein's inventive visuals involve the spectator in the film, but they are often abstract to the point of confusion. This version of Poe's tale is evidence that cinematic expressiveness cannot overcome a miscalculated story structure.

CHAPTER 4
AMERICA THE HIDEOUS

In the early part of the century, horror was basically un-American. Of the thousands of one- and two-reel films released in the United States in that period, very few were deliberately terrifying. The Gothic tales of the 19th century which provided inspiration for the first horror movies sprang from myth, tradition and legend, fed by centuries of imaginative elaboration. Except for Edgar Allan Poe, most of the authors of the great works of Gothic literature were European, and their stories were set there. The United States was lacking in many of the accouterments: ancestral castles with dank dungeons, superstitious villagers, deranged and sadistic aristocrats.

In addition, the moralistic attitudes of America's Puritan roots were still strong in the culture. When women were given the vote in 1920, even a common vice like drinking liquor could be outlawed. In the United States, horror for the sake of entertainment was frowned upon by this public and often attacked from the pulpit as well. No wonder exhibitors had to be very careful not to offend the vast majority of their customers.

The only regularly filmed horror story in America before 1920 was Stevenson's *Dr. Jekyll and Mr. Hyde*. With its well-defined separation of good and evil and its parable-like consequences of succumbing to sin, the tale contained enough comfortable moralizing to appeal to the most conservative tastes. Like the first version in 1908, all subsequent silent adaptations followed the structure of Sullivan's play rather than Stevenson's novella.

In 1911, Lucius Henderson directed the second American version for the producer Edwin Thanhouser. James Cruze, who would go on to direct such silent features as *The Covered Wagon*, played Dr. Jekyll, and Cruze's wife, Marguerite Snow, enacted the part of his sweetheart, called simply in the intertitles, "the Minister's daughter." In this 15-minute film, white-haired Dr. Jekyll drinks the potion, chokes and sinks into a chair, his head slumped on his chest. A quick frame-cut, and Mr. Hyde rises from the chair with black curled hair, wide eyes and fangs at the corners of his mouth. As called for in the original novella, Mr. Hyde is noticeably shorter than Dr. Jekyll. In fact, he is not even tall enough to see himself in the good Doctor's mirror hanging on the wall at the back of the set. The method for achieving this effect was not disclosed for more than 50 years. In 1963, octogenarian actor Harry Benham revealed that he, and not James Cruze, had played Mr. Hyde.

As in Selig's 1908 version, Jekyll begins to change involuntarily while visiting his fiancee. Hyde attacks the girl but is interrupted by her father. The monster strangles the old man and runs back to his lab. As Jekyll, he feels intense guilt for his crime but quickly turns back to Hyde. His manservant, not recognizing Hyde's voice when he demands an antidote from the chemist, alerts the police. A burly bobby breaks down the laboratory door, but not before Hyde swallows poison and dies in agony.

A review of the times said: "The film is made with a finesse that is typical of the New Rochelle manufacturer."

The next American adaptation of Stevenson's classic would be the first horror film produced by a studio that would eventually monopolize the genre for two decades and create its most lasting icons. Carl Laemmle was born in Laupheim, Germany on January 17, 1867. By the time five-foot-two-inch Laemmle turned 40 years old, he had saved enough cash as a bookkeeper and clothing store manager to buy a nickelodeon in Chicago. Encouraged by the quick returns, he launched another theater two months later. He set up his own distribution company, the Laemmle Film Service, in 1907 and expanded into so many American and Canadian cities that he became one of the leading distributors in the business.

An independent spirit, he defied the pressure tactics of Edison's Motion Picture Patents Company, known in the industry as "The Trust." This conglomerate, whose members included the film companies of Vitagraph, Essanay, Kalem and Lubin, was formed solely to eliminate not only independent film producers but also the several thousand independent theater exchanges and exhibitors. Edison and his group wanted complete control of the growing industry and insisted all licensed producers and exhibitors pay him a fee for his cameras and projectors. The Trust resorted to hiring thugs to break cameras, steal film and harass producers. This was one reason many independents came to Hollywood, far away from the New York offices of the Trust. Laemmle went into production in direct competition with this ruthless company. He called his production entity the Independent Motion Picture Company of America or Imp for short.

Edison's Patents Company producers feared that naming their players in advertising or on the screen would result in them upping their salary demands. Intent on glorifying his company's product, which included 100 shorts in 1910 alone, Laemmle glamorized his players and spent unprecedented amounts on publicity, regularly mentioning his stars by name. In 1912, after winning a court battle that hastened the demise of the Patents Company, Laemmle merged with several smaller firms to form the Universal Film Manufacturing Company, later known simply as Universal.

In 1913, Universal's first foray into terror was, of course, yet another version of *Dr. Jekyll and Mr. Hyde*. Laemmle's virile and handsome leading man, King Baggot, starred and Herbert Brenon wrote and directed. Lured by Laemmle in 1910 after the closing of a seemingly secure stage tour, Baggot's weekly one-reelers won him early international stardom. He was the first star to specialize in character parts, and he became adept at makeup—since actors applied it themselves in the early days.

As usual, the plot follows the basic outlines of Selig's initial presentation. This time, however, Dr. Jekyll is taken further from Stevenson's conception of an aging hypocrite when the film shows the handsome young man operating a free clinic in the London slums. Dr. Jekyll's motive for his experiments is to find a new drug which will rid London's wretched poor of their evil ways. An ironic scene at the end depicts Jekyll's friend, Dr. Lanyon, covering Hyde's corpse with his cloak after the police have broken into the laboratory. When Jekyll's fiancee, Alice, arrives, she pulls back the cape to see the man who killed her father and uncovers the body of Dr. Jekyll.

At 30 minutes, this was the longest and most detailed adaptation yet. In the March 1, 1913 *Moving Picture World*, George Blaisdell commented: "It is seldom that one man dominates a picture. In these two roles Baggot holds the centre of attention all the way... It is a forceful characterization and shows much care and study. It may be said, and said in cold blood, that Mr. Baggot has done nothing for the screen that will rank higher as an artistic piece of work than will his exposition as Mr. Hyde."

For the first time, instead of a matching cut from Jekyll to Hyde, a dissolve was used to show the transition. A dissolve is accomplished by fading out the last image, fading in the new shot and double exposing the fades so that one picture seems to melt into the other. Blaisdell was impressed: "It is through the means of the dissolving process that the transformation is made peculiarly effective. You see the change from the man of good to the man of evil right before your eyes." A British reviewer noted: "We get the real dissolving view as the drug begins to manifest its influence, in the place of the crude facial manipulations employed on stage."

The dissolving transformation was used at Universal the following year when the company made the first human-into-wolf film, *The Werewolf*. Transferring the legend from its origins in Europe to the United States, director Henry McRae's 18-minute film tells of a Navajo witch who thinks she has been deserted by her white husband when actually, he has been killed. She raises her daughter to hate all white men. The daughter dissolves into a real wolf and murders the men that her mother lures to their doom.

The classic and most influential silent film of *Dr. Jekyll and Mr. Hyde* is the 1920 Paramount adaptation by Clara S. Beranger, directed by John Stuart Robertson and starring John Barrymore. At feature length, set in a convincing 1885 London, with atmospheric lighting and composition by Roy Overbaugh, this is the only silent version to do justice to the story if not to Stevenson's intentions.

The most influential silent film version of *Dr. Jekyll and Mr. Hyde* is the 1920 Paramount adaptation starring John Barrymore.

Beranger's scenario strays further from Steven-son's conception of Jekyll than any of her predecessors. In the initial treatment and in the script, Beranger emphasizes that Dr. Jekyll, as played by the beautiful John Barrymore, should be, "almost Godlike." As in the Baggot version, this film shows Jekyll's selfless devotion to his free charity ward. Beranger writes in the treatment: "In this scene in his work among the poor I would play for the effect that an absolute purity of soul has on others." In the screenplay, she even advocates "halo" lighting around Jekyll.

This is a far cry from Stevenson's conception in which Jekyll recounts how his youthful pleasures, which he concealed, hardened into hypocrisy: "And indeed the worst of my faults was a certain impatient gaiety of disposition, such as has made the happiness of many, but such as I found it hard to reconcile with my imperious desire to carry my head high and wear a more than commonly grave countenance before the public. Hence it came about that I concealed my pleasures; and that when I reached years of reflection, and began to look round me and take stock of my progress and position in the world, I stood already committed to a profound duplicity of life." In Stevenson's book, Jekyll's "profound duplicity of life" was present before the creation of Hyde. Mr. Hyde merely gave it a physical reference.

In order to personify the temptation that her Jekyll has completely repressed, Beranger finds it necessary to invent a character to act as a Mephistophelian influence. Actually, she borrows more than invents the personality of Sir George Carew, since his attitude and many of his lines come from Lord Henry, the witty Satanic seducer of Oscar Wilde's *The Picture of Dorian Gray*. In her treatment, Beranger writes, "(Sir George) waxes eloquent in his philosophy of Hedonism."

Sir George is quite eloquent indeed, since his lines are some of Oscar Wilde's most famous epigrams: "The only way to get rid of temptation is to yield to it," he purrs to Jekyll. Sir George tells one of his young female guests, "A beautiful woman like you is Paradise for the eyes—but Hell for the soul." To further corrupt the young man, Sir George leads Jekyll to a low-class Music Hall just as Lord Henry does for Dorian Gray. Actually, Sir George resembles Stevenson's conception of Dr. Jekyll. At the dinner party, he wonders, "What would man be like if he didn't have to answer to society?" and, "Just think of the pleasure of yielding to every temptation—of living life to the fullest." The first time Dr. Jekyll takes the transforming drug, Sir George's smirking face is superimposed over the scene. In Beranger's version, Mr. Hyde fulfills Sir George's dreams more than the desires of Dr. Jekyll.

At the Music Hall, Beranger presents her most influential innovation. She plants Miss Gina, a young and provocative Italian dancer who unsuccessfully tries to tempt the handsome Dr. Jekyll but ends up becoming the sexual slave to Mr. Hyde. The creation of this character places Jekyll's repression and Hyde's liberation firmly in the sexual category, quite against Stevenson's stated intentions.

Writing of Jekyll's earlier scene with Sir George's sweet and innocent daughter, Millicent, Beranger states her concept for their relationship in the treatment: "Here in a scene between them can be shown her entire devotion to him—his interest is friendly rather than amatory." And later, she describes her plan for depicting Jekyll's home, a detail that the director neglects in the film: "Jekyll's living room is an outward sign of his love of the chaste in art. (I would use this room to show the gradual development of his taste along more luxurious, hedonistic lines.)" In other words, Jekyll is a completely asexual character in the beginning. Beranger equates sexuality with evil, and it is primarily this which Hyde embodies.

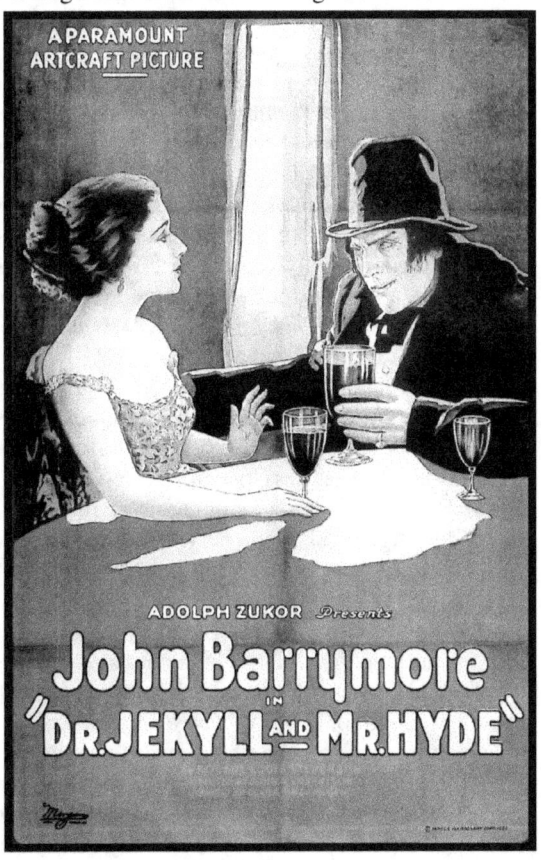

Hyde's sexuality even destroys Miss Gina, Jekyll's temptress. Despite her ripe appearance and forward behavior, Beranger still envisions her as a virgin. She describes Miss Gina this way: "Sophisticated about the world and men, she has managed to keep chaste for the simple reason that she is calculating enough to believe that some day she will find the man who will pay her the price she demands—marriage." Needless to say, Hyde is not that man. Director Robertson shows Gina's degradation as she takes up with Hyde in his dingy Soho apartment by altering her makeup to include dark circles under her eyes and hollows in her youthful cheeks. Eventually, Hyde discards her in favor of a more healthy looking replacement.

Another innovation introduced by Beranger is Hyde's own degradation. Barrymore's makeup is altered as the film progresses and his evils multiply. The shadows on his face become darker, his expressions become more deranged, his overbite becomes more prominent, and he develops a strange point at the balding crown of his head. Beranger indicates her idea in the treatment: "Though at first Hyde is a rough looking individual, misshapen and hideous, he is nothing like the unspeakable vile looking creature that he is at the end of the picture. This should be a gradual development of evil."

Beranger introduces one more idea that would become a convention in retelling the story. After Hyde takes poison and dies, he is shown in close profile turning back into the handsome Dr. Jekyll. Unlike Stevenson's ending, in which Jekyll goes to his grave in the damning form of Hyde, Beranger's Jekyll is symbolically redeemed of his crimes through his self-sacrifice. The audience's last view of Barrymore is this beatific close-up from his most famous angle. Both the Fredric March and Spencer Tracy sound versions would repeat this ending, down to the last glimpse of Jekyll from the side, even without the benefit of Barrymore's famous profile.

Although Beranger follows the structure of Sullivan's play, giving Jekyll an innocent fiancee and a prospective father-in-law whom Hyde murders, she consciously works in scenes from the original novella. For example, she is careful to include the subplot of Jekyll's will naming Hyde as his benefactor. This scene no longer fulfills its purpose as a clue to the link between Jekyll and Hyde as it does in Stevenson because the story is no longer structured as a mystery. Even so, Beranger states in her treatment: "the will to be used here much as in the story of Stevenson." She also dramatizes Stevenson's scene in which Hyde tramples a small child and is forced to pay for damages with a check signed by Jekyll. This complication seems unnecessary, again because it acts as a clue in the novella to a mystery that does not exist in the film. Beranger states her reasons for inclusion in the treatment: "I would use this episode because it is a thing well known to the readers who know the story and because it shows a form of brutality that is different."

The director, John Stuart Robertson, was born in London, Ontario, Canada on June 14, 1878. Highly acclaimed in the silent days for his sincerity and restrained craftsmanship, he was known as Hollywood's most liked filmmaker. Starting as a stage actor, he entered films in 1915 as a performer for Vitagraph but soon became a director. His most famous production was *Dr. Jekyll and Mr. Hyde*, but he also directed major films with stars such as Mary Pickford and Greta Garbo.

His handling of *Dr. Jekyll and Mr. Hyde* is quietly skillful, allowing the atmospheric lighting, the costumes and art direction and the expert playing by his cast to dominate. Following the conventions of the well-made movie of the day, he never moves the camera within a shot, and he uses close-ups expressively and unobtrusively. At one point, when Miss Gina tells Mr. Hyde the story of her ring with the hidden compartment, he cuts to a scene in the Middle Ages. This aside depicts the ring in action as it is used to poison a nobleman's rival suitor. Except for this brief lapse of judgment, Robertson's storytelling is lucid and invisible.

John Barrymore was born John Sydney Blythe in Philadelphia on February 15, 1882. Defying the family tradition of his actor father and mother, Maurice Barrymore and Georgiana Drew, and his actor brother and sister, Lionel and Ethel Barrymore, this youngest sibling started as a cartoonist for a New York daily newspaper. Revealing the true nature of his imagination, his fondest ambition was to create the definitive illustrations to the works of Poe. But in 1903, he finally gave in and made his stage debut in *Magda*. Ironically, he soon surpassed the popularity of his brother and sister, becoming the most respected idol of his day with appearances in such plays as *The Affairs of Anatole*, *Peter Ibbetson* and *Redemption*.

Although most popular in the role of the great lover, Barrymore preferred the bravura of grotesque, tortured parts such as Mr. Hyde in *Dr. Jekyll and Mr. Hyde*. [Photofest]

He entered films in 1913, appearing in mostly undistinguished romantic dramas, comedies and swashbuckling adventures.

Although most popular in the role of the great lover, he preferred the bravura of grotesque, tortured parts. In fact, right after filming *Dr. Jekyll and Mr. Hyde* at the Famous Players studio on West 56th Street in New York, he enjoyed a triumph as *Richard III* at the Plymouth Theater. For four-and-a-half hours each night, Barrymore wore the hunched back and club foot of Shakespeare's evil protagonist and even had to have his black copper armor sprayed down with a hose before he could remove it because of the intense heat of the lights. No wonder he suffered a complete nervous and physical collapse after his back-to-back villainy and needed to recuperate in a White Plains sanitarium.

Barrymore had undoubtedly seen Richard Mansfield's performance as Jekyll and Hyde since John's father, whose real name was Herbert Blythe, had been a close friend. The chal-

Hyde murders Millicent's father Sir George (Brandon Hurst) in *Dr. Jekyll and Mr. Hyde*.

lenge implied by taking the part was whether Barrymore could manage the transformation as Mansfield did, using only facial contortions and lighting. Of course, the medium of motion pictures was much more intimate and demanding than the stage, and Beranger's scenario called for a progressive degeneration of Hyde's appearance.

But Barrymore does accomplish the beginning of the first transformation impressively with nothing but his altered expression. Robertson then cuts to a close shot of Barrymore's hand which dissolves into the deeply shaded, long-fingered talons of Mr. Hyde. When Robertson cuts back to Barrymore's close-up, he wears greasepaint circles around his eyes and shading around his mouth and cheekbones. In a later incarnation as Hyde, he removes his pointed hat to reveal that his head is almost exactly the same shape.

In one surprising scene, Jekyll sleeps in his four-poster bed as a man-sized, transparent spider with Hyde's face crawls in with him and covers him with its disgusting body. The spider is a double exposure of Barrymore wearing his Hyde makeup and an elaborate costume. He expertly mimes the halting movements of the giant arachnid, and it is a highlight of his performance. As the spider fades away, Jekyll involuntarily dissolves into Hyde while he sleeps.

Barrymore does go way over the top on one occasion, actually throwing himself onto the floor in a backflip while painfully transforming into Hyde. In his autobiography, he wrote of the frustrations of acting in silent movies: "In the Silent days, I found myself continually making frantic and futile faces to try to express unexpressable ideas—like a man behind a closed window on a train that is moving out of a station who is trying, in pantomime, to tell his wife, on the platform outside, that he forgot to pack his blue pajamas and that he wants her to send them to him care of Detweiler, 1032 West 189th Street, New York City!"

But the reviews could not praise Barrymore's performance enough. The *Moving Picture World* of April 10, 1920 stated: "Deprived of the blood curdling effect achieved by Richard Mansfield with the fiendish tones of his voice, Mr. Barrymore justifies the terrible repulsiveness of the character by the truth and power of his impersonation. It is worthy to rank along side the Mephistopheles of Harry Irving and the Bertuccio of Edwin Booth. The screen has never before known such great acting." The March 29, 1920 *The New York Times* raved, "It is what Mr. Barrymore himself does that makes the dual character of Jekyll and Hyde tremendous. His performance is one of pure motion picture pantomime on as high a level as has ever been attained by anyone... he creates such a genuinely beautiful Jekyll and compellingly hideous Hyde, and emphasizes the contrast between the two with such a sure eye for essentials, that one must believe in both while he sees them and afterwards admire a work of art... John Barrymore's acting... places the picture high up among screen accomplishments."

Later in his life, Barrymore assessed his own efforts: "The critics said my portrayal of the horrible Hyde was something magnificent. All I did was put on a harrowing makeup, twist my face, claw at my throat and roll on the floor. That, the critics said, was acting. And, may my worthy ancestors forgive me, I began to agree with them."

Actually, Barrymore is quite modest about his accomplishment. His Hyde exudes a repulsive aura of debauchery, especially in his quieter moments, like when he heartlessly trades the corrupted Gina for a healthier prostitute. Smoking a thin cigar and motioning with casual superiority, he seems like an aging pimp who regards women as subhuman commodities for his pleasure. And when he does "twist" his face, he achieves expressions of such surpassing evil, as he does while viciously biting the throat of Sir George Carew, that the visage of his Hyde becomes one of the most memorable nightmares of silent movies.

Despite its liberties taken with Stevenson's intentions, Robertson's film is a brilliant transferal of his work to the silent screen. As written, Stevenson's tale resists a literal adaptation to dramatic mediums because he unfolds his story through anecdotes and suppositions until Jekyll's confession is revealed after his suicide. Beranger elaborates on Sullivan's dramatization, humanizing Hyde as Sullivan did Jekyll and contrasting the difference between the two. Together, the adapters create a vivid world for Dr. Jekyll and Mr. Hyde along with supporting characters to whom they can relate. Jekyll and Hyde become more than intellectual symbols and more than suspects in a mystery. In Robertson's movie, they emerge as human beings, vulnerable and tempted by human passions. The fact that the two most notable sound versions in 1932 and 1941 are virtual remakes of Robertson's film shows the impact of the changes initiated by Sullivan and extended by Beranger.

Surprisingly, another feature-length *Dr. Jekyll and Mr. Hyde* was released simultaneously with the Barrymore version. Louis B. Mayer's Pioneer production was a low-budget attempt to capitalize on the excitement over the Paramount film. Because of a copyright technicality, Mayer set his story in contemporary New York to avoid a possible lawsuit from Paramount's Adolf Zukor. Unlike the Barrymore film, which was told with all the expertise of the silent American cinema, Mayer's movie was so technically poor that the director-screenwriter, Charles J. Hayden, chose not to list his name in the credits. In fact, the style of photography, acting and effects were no better than the one-reeler with James Cruze made in 1912.

Sheldon Lewis played Dr. Jekyll, and his Mr. Hyde was an exact duplicate of his Clutching Hand villain from the 1914 Pearl White serial, *The Exploits of Elaine*. He played the dual role once again in a short sound version released in 1929. Lewis' transformation is accomplished in the easiest and least expensive way: his Jekyll drinks from a test tube, we cut away to the Butler brushing his hat and cut back to Mr. Hyde, crouching and clutching at the air. The intertitle announces him as "An Apostle of Hell!" Hyde, with fangs and scraggly hair, proceeds to "a squalid tenement district" where he indulges in "crimes of his demon nature." Actually, he jumps out at a passing woman and snatches her purse. Nabbed by Chief Barnes of the local precinct, he is given the Third Degree. Finally, Hyde is strapped into the electric chair. At this point, Jekyll awakens in his easy chair and realizes it has all been a dream. "I believe in God!" he cries. "I have a soul—and I shall have you!" he tells his fiancee, and off they go to the opera. With that, the story of *Dr. Jekyll and Mr. Hyde* was put to a well-deserved rest for the remainder of the silent era.

Another American horror film masquerading as a morality tale was the 1926 version of *The Bells*. Emile Erckmann and Alexandre Chatrian wrote the French play, *Le Juif Polonais* on which Leopold Lewis based his adaptation for the famous 19th-century British actor-manager Henry Irving. The grand thespian virtually made his own the part of Mathias, the seemingly kind and generous Alsatian innkeeper who commits the horrible ax murder of a traveling Jewish merchant.

With gold stolen from the victim's money belt, Mathias pays off the mortgage on his inn and influences the townspeople to elect him Burgomaster. The daughter of Mathias becomes engaged to a handsome young officer who is investigating the crime. But Mathias has burned the merchant's body in his lime kiln, leaving no evidence but a hat and some blood in the snow.

Wracked by guilt, Mathias repeatedly imagines that he hears the Jew's sleigh bells as he did at the moment of the killing. The ghost of his victim appears to him, blood drooling from the ax wound on his forehead. Mathias angrily challenges the ghost to play cards with him, and the specter wins.

The dead man's brother comes to town offering a substantial reward for the apprehension of the killer and bringing with him a Mesmerist who can hypnotize a suspect into confessing. Mathias goes mad from fear and guilt before dying of a heart attack.

Henry Irving did not live long enough to record his performance on film, but in 1914, his son, H.B. Irving, played the lead in a primitive British movie version. Like *Dr. Jekyll and Mr. Hyde*, the story's insistence on a moral reckoning for its transgressing protagonist insured its popularity in the Puritanical early American cinema. The United States produced film adaptations in 1913, 1914 and 1918. In 1926, the producer I.E. Chadwick mounted the definitive version written and directed by James Young and starring John Barrymore's older brother, Lionel, as Mathias.

James Young was born in Baltimore in 1878 and followed his early work as a theatrical actor by joining Vitagraph in 1910 as co-director of the series, "Scenes of True Life." These short films re-enacted such famous historical moments as Lincoln's Gettysburg Address. Young performed in the series while co-directing with J. Stuart Blackton, but as his experience and reputation grew, he was allowed to helm many of Vitagraph's more ambitious literary adaptations, including *As You Like It*, *The Little Minister* and *Beau Brummel*, in which he also played the lead. By 1926, the veteran of over 40 films, including the 1923 adaptation of George Du Maurier's *Trilby*, Young was a solid choice to guide Chadwick's production of *The Bells*.

Lionel Barrymore was born Lionel Blythe on April 28, 1878 in Philadelphia. He studied at the Gilmore School in London, St. Vincent's Academy in New York, Seton Hall in New Jersey and the Arts Students League in New York. Although he did not act professionally until his late teens, he did appear with his parents on stage as a child. By 1900, he had achieved

Lionel Barrymore is forced to become a murderer to save his daughter from an unhappy marriage in *The Bells*. [Photofest]

Broadway stardom, often appearing with his mother's brother, John Drew. He took a four-year sojourn to Paris to attempt a career in art but returned to the American stage in 1907.

The new medium of film appealed to Lionel, and he was the first Barrymore to seek a cinema career when he joined Biograph in 1909. Within two years, he began playing leads. He appeared in such early films by D.W. Griffith as *The New York Hat*, *The Musketeers of Pig Alley* and *Judith of Bethulia*. He even wrote scripts for Griffith, including *The Tender-Hearted Boy* in 1913. Despite his legitimate Broadway stardom, Lionel was not above appearing in serials such as Pearl White's 1915 *The Exploits of Elaine* and its sequel, *The Romance of Elaine*. In 1925, he abandoned the theater completely in favor of appearing in films.

In the beginning of *The Bells*, Barrymore portrays Mathias as a smiling and good-natured innkeeper. He is always ready to extend credit to customers in his bar and mill despite the fact that his saturnine landlord, played by Gustav von Seyffertitz, demands either the mortgage on the inn or the hand of Mathias' sweet young daughter in marriage.

Barrymore is so beleaguered, even by his nagging wife, that it is a shock when he sneaks after a kindly Jewish merchant on a snowy night, hops on the back of his sleigh and hits him with an ax. We have not been prepared by anything in the script or performance to think that this generous man would be capable of such a cold-blooded crime for money.

The murder and its aftermath are shown in gory detail unusual for the time. Blood drips from the victim's head wound and spots the white snow as he shakes the sleigh bells at Mathias and dies. When the victim's ghost invades Mathias' room, the blood still shines on his head. Later, Mathias sees blood appear on his own hands as he works on his account books. This effect was achieved by painting blood on Barrymore's hands and shining a red filtered light while photographing them. The red filter caused the blood to disappear. When the red filter was removed and replaced with a green one, the blood seemed to materialize on the hands.

Silent Screams

Barrymore's performance becomes more physical and hysterical as the pressure mounts. Despite his ranting and arm waving, he never seems to go over the top. After all, he is reacting, not only to the investigation, but to his own guilty conscience.

The Bells gave the best part in his silent film career to a man who would become the most famous and respected star of horror movies in the 20th century. Boris Karloff received fifth billing in *The Bells*, but his appearance and performance were eerie highlights of the production and harbingers of things to come from the actor.

He was born William Henry Pratt on November 23, 1887 in Dulwich, a suburb of London, the youngest of a civil servant in the British foreign service. His mother, the sister of Anna Leonowens of *Anna and the King of Siam* fame, died when "Billy" was only five. His father, who was half Indian, wrote a letter to the India Office protesting

Boris Karloff in *The Bells*

the "supercilious commiseration or compassion for the class of Coloured Englishmen to which I belong," and a year later, left England to live in France.

Billy was raised by his half-sister and several brothers, who made sure that the boy was well educated for a diplomatic career. But young Billy was not interested in academics. He preferred theater, music and sports. In 1909, he deliberately failed the civil service exam, spending his time attending theater rather than studying.

With a small inheritance from his late mother, he immigrated to Canada to seek an acting career and escape the influence of his overbearing brothers. On the boat over, he decided to change his name to Boris Karloff simply because he liked the sound of it. In Canada, he found immediate employment doing back-breaking farm work. Karloff answered newspaper advertisements and joined one theatrical touring company after another. For the next decade, he played character parts in repertory all over Canada and the United States.

During a brief stay in Los Angeles in 1918, he worked as a screen extra in a scene being directed by Frank Borzage at Universal. When theatrical opportunities were scarce, he continued to toil as an extra and bit player in several films. His acting career could not support him, however, and he also did hard labor and drove trucks.

Karloff found himself very busy in 1926. At the age of 38, he appeared in 11 movies for 10 different companies, including playing the Mesmerist in *The Bells*. Later in his life, Karloff would recall Lionel Barrymore as "a stimulating man—a marvelous, a great man." It was Barrymore who sketched the look of the Mesmerist while discussing the part with Karloff and director Young. Obviously influenced by the makeup and costume worn by Werner Krauss as Dr. Caligari, Barrymore drew Karloff with top hat, black-framed round glasses and long black cloak.

Karloff plays the part with the quiet, smiling menace for which he would later become famous. Early in the story, before Mathias commits the crime, the Mesmerist invites him on stage at the town fair. The Mesmerist wishes to use Mathias to demonstrate that under hypnosis he can "make criminals confess and the good tell of good deeds." Mathias angrily refuses, denouncing the Mesmerist for practicing witchcraft. After the murder, the Mesmerist returns to town with the brother of the victim, seeking to use his powers to help find the killer. From his chair of authority as Burgomaster, Mathias again threatens the Mesmerist with accusations of sorcery. Karloff merely smiles inscrutably at Barrymore's histrionic tirade.

At the end of the film, Mathias dreams of his trial in a huge, black, Expressionistic courtroom. His unsympathetic former landlord is the judge, and the accuser is the victim's brother. The Mesmerist hypnotizes Mathias into revealing how he burnt the body on the night of the killing in his lime kiln. In a shocking flashback, we see Mathias dragging the corpse to the flaming oven and forcing it inside.

In his dream, the merchant's brother thrusts the victim's sleigh bells into Mathias' face. When Mathias awakens in his room to the sound of the bells, he falls on his knees in front of a statue of the Virgin and begs for forgiveness. Convinced that he has been absolved, he clutches his chest and dies of a heart attack.

The movie holds the interest and is efficiently, if not always stylishly, made. Unfortunately, the climax seems abrupt and disappointing, denying the audience the spectacle of Mathias' public unmasking and the reactions of those closest to him. But like Dr. Jekyll, Mathias satisfies the pervading morality by paying the ultimate price of guilt and death for his sin.

Aleister Crowley, who called himself the Great Beast after the horrendous, horned creature predicted to rise from the sea in the Bible's book of Revelation, was to the 20th century what the Marquis de Sade was to the 18th century. Satanist, magician, pornographer, drug addict and sexual degenerate, Crowley represented everything that the Judeo-Christian culture openly despised, yet secretly found fascinating. It was with a combination of revulsion and affection that the newspapers dubbed him "the worst man in England."

He was born Edward Alexander Crowley on October 12, 1875 to Edward Crowley Sr., who made his fortune from Crowley's Ales but retired to preach the doctrines of the Plymouth Brethren. Aleister's mother was so Puritanical that it was she who first called her child "The Great Beast." Perhaps it was not surprising that Aleister, who had been subjected to daily Bible readings at home, turned against organized religion, particularly Christianity, from an early age. His father died in 1886 when Aleister was 11, and the boy shifted his attention to the dark lore of Biblical teaching: to the "Scarlet Woman," to Satan and the Great Beast whose number was 666.

From the age of 14, he was sexually voracious. As an act of rebellion, his first experience was with a servant girl on his own mother's bed. He later wrote, "Love was a challenge to Christianity. It was a degradation and a damnation."

After a traditional education at Trinity College, Cambridge, he turned to the Order of the Golden Dawn for the information he most valued. The Order was a magical society founded in 1887 by Scotsman MacGregor Mathers and chronicled by the convert and brilliant poet William Butler Yeats. By personally translating and interpreting the occult rituals in such ancient texts as the *Key of Solomon*, the Caballa, the elaborate Enochian system devised by the Elizabethan astrologer Dr. John Dee and other lesser-known manuscripts, Mathers, a Mason, attracted to his Order over a hundred intelligent and influential people including the writers Arthur Machen, A.E. Waite and Algernon Blackwood.

From one of the texts translated by Mathers, *The Book of the Sacred Magic of Abra-Melin the Mage*, "as delivered by Abraham the Jew unto his son Lamech, A.D. 1458," Crowley learned how to summon the Holy Guardian Angel in a secluded place after a long period of personal purification. He moved to Boleskin House on the cold, lonely shores of

Loch Ness in Scotland and set about performing the elaborate rituals required. According to his own account, he was only able to invoke a horde of demons. Strange shapes began to haunt the house, and his workroom grew dark even on the sunniest days as he spent hours writing down magical formulas. The Boleskin House groundskeeper went mad and tried to murder his own family.

Crowley fled to the hot, dry climate of Mexico where he perfected such feats of magic as making his own reflection disappear from a mirror. He charged Mathers with lying to the members of the Order and sent demons to plague him in revenge. After taking his pretty but unbalanced wife, Rose, the daughter of the vicar of Camberwell, on a world tour of mountain climbing and spiritual seeking, Crowley finally met his Holy Guardian Angel, which introduced itself as Aiwass, in 1904 in his Cairo apartment.

Explaining that it came as a "messenger from the forces ruling the world at present," the Angel dictated in a musical voice what became the central text of Crowley's philosophy: *The Book of the Law*. Its single most important tenet was, "Do what thou wilt shall be the whole of the Law." Crowley declared that his would be the age of the will; the age in which man could express his innermost self, unrestrained by church or state. "Be strong, O man!" he rejoiced, "lust, enjoy all things of sense and rapture; fear not that any god shall deny thee for this." With these words, Crowley embarked on a notorious career of black magic, drugs and sexual sadism, converting others to his Inner Order of the Great White Brotherhood and bestowing the "serpent's kiss" on the wrists or necks of his female disciples with his sharpened canine teeth.

In 1902, the celebrated British writer William Somerset Maugham met Crowley at a restaurant in Paris called *Le Chat Blanc* and a sort of friendship began. Maugham wrote that he "took an immediate dislike to him, but he interested me and amused me. He was a great talker and he talked uncommonly well." The Great Beast made such an impression on Maugham that the author used him as the subject of a melodramatic novel called *The Magician*, published in 1908.

Maugham was born in Paris on January 25, 1874, making him more than a year Crowley's senior. His father was solicitor to the British embassy in Paris. Orphaned at 10 and raised by his uncle, a vicar, he entered King's School, Canterbury in 1887 and attended lectures at Heidelberg University in 1891 when he decided to become a writer. However, he returned to London to study medicine at St. Thomas' Hospital and practiced as an intern in the Lambeth slums, which became the background for his first novel, *Liza of Lambeth* in 1897.

Threatened with tuberculosis, he moved first to the south of France, then to Paris, where he took up writing in earnest. It was there that his path crossed with Crowley's. Maugham achieved his first theatrical success with *Lady Frederick* in 1907, which ran simultaneously with his *Jack Straw*, *Mrs. Dot* and *The Explorer*, all in 1908. Of course, his great works, such as the play, *The Moon and Sixpence*, the semi-autobiographical novel, *Of Human Bondage* and the short story, "Rain," were all ahead of him when he met and wrote about Crowley. In fact, *The Magician* was one of Maugham's least successful early novels.

In Maugham's book, Aleister Crowley becomes Oliver Haddo, a mad sorcerer in modern Paris obsessed with following a ritual in an ancient manuscript to create artificial life using the heart blood of a maiden. He finds a young woman, Margaret Dauncey, who is engaged to Dr. Burdon, a surgeon who repaired her spine and saved her from paralysis after an accidental injury. Knowing Margaret is a virgin with fair hair and skin and blue eyes as the ritual demands, Haddo contrives meetings with the young woman and eventually puts her under his hypnotic power. On the eve of Margaret's wedding to Dr. Burdon, Haddo wills her to marry him instead. Of course, the marriage is not consummated because Haddo needs a maiden. He takes her to his mountain retreat to perform the ritual while her fiance and her uncle, Dr. Porhoet, race to find them before it is too late.

Crowley read the book the year of its publication. He wrote:

> The title attracted me strongly, *The Magician*. The author, bless my soul! No other than my old and valued friend, William Somerset Maugham... So he had really written a book—who would have believed it!... the Magician, Oliver Haddo, was Aleister Crowley... The hero's witty remarks were, many of them, my own... I was not in the least offended by the attempts of the book to represent me as, in many ways, the most atrocious scoundrel, for he had done more than justice to the qualities of which I was proud... *The Magician* was, in fact, an appreciation of my genius such as I had never dreamed of inspiring.

In the mid-1920s, the novel came to the attention of the American director Rex Ingram, who had set up his own studio in Nice on the French Riviera to turn out features for Metro Goldwyn. In setting and subject matter, the story appealed to this artist whose Irish heritage ensured his fascination with the bizarre and the grotesque.

He was born Reginald Ingram Montgomery Hitchcock in Dublin on January 15, 1892, the son of a clergyman and grandson of Dublin's fire chief. Before immigrating to the United States in 1911, he studied law at Dublin's Trinity College. At Yale's School of Fine Arts, he sculpted while supporting himself as a freight clerk in New Haven's railroad yards.

Ingram became an actor, a writer and a set designer for Edison's motion picture company in 1913 after a chance meeting with the famous inventor's son, Charles. He worked in the same capacities for Vitagraph in Brooklyn and for the Fox studios. In 1916, he moved to Universal-Bluebird as a writer-producer-director. Ingram left show business to serve as a second lieutenant with Canada's Royal Flying Corps in World War I and was badly injured in an air crash.

After joining Metro in 1920, Ingram was assigned to direct Valentino in *The Four Horsemen of the Apocalypse* on the insistence of its influential screenwriter, June Mathis. The enormous critical and commercial success of the film established Ingram as a leading Hollywood director. Metro allowed him to set up his own production unit on the lot, free from studio interference. Ingram chose director of photography John F. Seitz and screenwriter Willis Goldbeck as his collaborators and his own wife, Alice Terry, as his frequent leading lady.

While creating more successes for Metro such as *The Prisoner of Zenda* and *Scaramouche* with Ramon Novarro, Ingram indulged in bizarre personal projects and behavior. For a time, he employed a dwarf as his valet. He also remade one of his earliest and weirdest films as a writer-director, *Black Orchids* from 1917, into *Trifling Women* in 1922, with Barbara LaMarr as a necromancer-vamp. The production featured poisoning, Satanism and necrophilia and was one of Ingram's few commercial disasters. Even his more mainstream projects contained moments of dark fantasy such as the ride of the Four Horsemen in the Valentino picture and the transparent and taloned specter of greed that brings about the death of Ralph Lewis as the miser in *The Conquering Power* in 1922.

Ingram's greatest professional disappointment came when Louis B. Mayer passed him over in favor of Fred Niblo to direct the gigantic production, *Ben-Hur*, despite promising Ingram the assignment. No less a filmmaker than Erich von Stroheim talked him out of retiring because he regarded Ingram as "the world's greatest director." Later, Ingram cut von Stroheim's masterpiece, *Greed*, from 24 to 18 reels when Mayer refused to release it.

Ingram no longer trusted Mayer, and in 1924, he and Alice Terry took their production unit to Nice to avoid studio politics. His films continued to be financed and distributed by Metro Goldwyn, but Ingram was given complete autonomy as an artist.

Since *The Magician* involved the mystical and the macabre, was written by one of the world's great authors, and took place in Paris and the south of France, it was the perfect project for Ingram. He adapted the novel himself, cast his wife as Margaret Dauncey and gave the great German actor, Paul Wegener, the part of Oliver Haddo. Reliable collaborator John Seitz was director of photography. The look and scope of the film were aided enormously by using actual Paris and Monte Carlo locations for the exteriors.

The first scene sets the tone of menace, occasionally seasoned with dashes of visual humor. In her Paris studio, beautiful Margaret sculpts an enormous clay satyr as her plain girlfriend, Susie Boyd, works on a painting of the Seine at sunrise. After looking long and hard at her stylized work, Susie changes the name to "Seine at sun*set*." In a long-held and suspenseful close shot, Ingram shows the huge head of the sculpted satyr start to move as if the clay were slowly coming to life. A crack appears, and the heavy piece breaks off, falling on Margaret.

She is unconscious, and her spine is injured. Dr. Burdon performs surgery on Margaret in an enormous operating theater with a glass-walled observatory. In one of his few moving shots, Ingram tracks across the viewers as they watch the procedure, spellbound.

One of the spectators is Oliver Haddo, "magician, hypnotist and student of medicine." Wegener cuts an enormous figure, his body towering over the other doctors and his sharp cheekbones, slanted eyes and down-turned mouth seeming to be carved in stone like the face of a gargoyle. His hands press against the glass eagerly as he watches the operation.

In a deep-focus composition that will be echoed later when Haddo wills Margaret to come to his apartment on the eve of her wedding, Ingram shoots past the magician looming in the foreground to see the small figure of the patient being wheeled out. In this introduc-

The Magician (**Paul Wegener**) **intends to create life in his lab.**

tory scene, Ingram and Wegener tells us much about Haddo. We see his obsessive nature, his arrogance and a hint of his power.

At an elaborate fair, Haddo attempts to impress Margaret by allowing a Mideastern fakir's poisonous snake to bite him on the hand. Haddo wills the wound to disappear and suffers no effects of the poison. The scene is noteworthy for the way that Ingram again adds dashes of humor to the melodramatic situation. Susie's date accidentally puts his hat on a balloon which floats to the top of the tent. The date cannot find his hat so a sailor flicks his cigarette at the balloon, it pops and the hat falls neatly on the date's head.

This comic relief contrasts sharply with the fatal biting of the fakir's young and pretty female assistant by the snake. Wisely, Ingram does not allow his lurid story to become too heavy-handed in the first act, even portraying Haddo as a slightly ridiculous figure who indignantly throws his cape around himself when Margaret says that he looks like he stepped right out of a melodrama.

But Haddo becomes a much more threatening presence when he visits Margaret to apologize for the episode with the fakir's assistant. Alone with her for the first time, he hypnotizes the frightened young woman and shows her visions of Hell with himself as Satan and Margaret as a sexual sacrifice to the evil god Pan. In conception, art direction and execution, the scene is extraordinarily perverse for its time.

Margaret's hallucination begins with a close shot of Pan staring directly into the camera, smiling wickedly as he blows on his pipes. The camera pulls back to reveal the Hellish landscape of a Black Sabbath. Sulfurous clouds billow around half-naked men and women who run, cavort and make love around the stationary figures of Haddo and Margaret, who

Haddo (Paul Wegener) and his dwarf assistant perform the ritual for the creation of artificial life as lightning flashes outside. Margaret (Ruth Terry) is unconscious on a slab in the sorcerer's laboratory in *The Magician*. [Photofest]

watch from beneath a twisted tree. Haddo's hair forms two horns on the top of his head, and his face is lit from below, making it appear even less human than usual, while Margaret's blonde tresses are down, and she wears a long gown of virginal white.

Haddo motions for Pan, played practically nude by a sinewy American dancer from the *Folies Bergere* named Stowitts, as the creature forces himself on one of the females. Margaret stares with horror as the satyr runs to her, grabs her and bends her back to kiss her passionately. She awakens in her apartment, watched closely by Haddo. When she collects herself from the erotic Satanic experience, she angrily orders him out of her house, but she cannot order him out of her mind.

The last act takes place in and around the "magician's stronghold," a tower that rises over a small French village. Haddo and his dwarf assistant perform the ritual for the creation of artificial life as lightening flashes outside. Margaret is unconscious on a slab in the sorcerer's laboratory. The creation requires great heat, and Haddo works the bellows for a huge, blazing furnace.

A tremendous fight follows with Dr. Burdon finally pushing Haddo back into the flames. The doctor pulls Margaret out of the tower before it explodes in a rain of stone and mortar. After such an exciting and spectacular ending, Ingram again allows the audience the relief of laughter when he shows the dwarf assistant, still alive after the explosion, hanging from a branch on the mountainside, his clothes shredded to tatters.

The Magician is no masterpiece, but Ingram presents settings, characters and situations that would recur endlessly in the horror genre as it develops in the early American talkies. James Whale, who would direct the first sound *Frankenstein* and its sequel, *The Bride of Frankenstein*, would be especially influenced by *The Magician*'s third act setting of the tower laboratory, as well as the figure on the slab, the slightly comic dwarf assistant, the creation of life on a stormy night and the final explosion of the lab. The humorous asides, lightning the melodrama and ironically commenting on it at the same time, also influenced Whale, who shared with Ingram a sophisticated approach to the outré.

On the other hand, the narrative of *The Magician* remains vague as to Haddo's ultimate goal. We never see the homunculus that he attempts to bring to life, and this decreases the urgency of his mission for the audience. Despite Wegener's dark force and subtly self-deprecating humor, Haddo never becomes more than a melodramatic villain. His megalomaniacal charms come more from the larger-than-life actor portraying him than from any moments in the scenario. Margaret is never seriously attracted to him. His manipulation of her results solely from his powers as a hypnotist. Before that, she and Dr. Burdon react with disgust toward his overbearing egotism. How much more complex and interesting the film would have been if his mysterious darkness had drawn Margaret to him.

Unfortunately for Ingram, his vision came too soon for popular acceptance. Reviewers rained a barrage of criticism on *The Magician*, mostly because of its perceived tastelessness, which sank it at the box-office. As Ingram's films indulged his personal interests, the popularity of his work declined. Instead of going to the expense of equipping his tiny studio in Nice for sound, he chose to write and sculpt. He did direct one sound film on location in 1933 called *Love in Morocco*, but then he retired from films for good. Ingram made exotic North Africa his home and, according to some, even converted to Islam. Eventually, he returned to the United States where he died in 1950.

CHAPTER 5
GENIUS OF THE GROTESQUE

America did not escape the Great War unscathed. Because of advances in medical science, soldiers, who in previous conflicts would have died from their disfiguring wounds, were kept alive and assimilated back into society in unprecedented numbers. They could be seen with their missing limbs, smashed features and broken teeth riding in Armistice parades, living symbols of the sacrifices made on behalf of their country's international politics. Along with the physically impaired, even more of this "lost generation" bore invisible mental scars from their helpless subjugation to modern mechanized warfare.

Perhaps this large, maturing audience partly accounted for the incredible popularity of an actor who was not handsome and seldom heroic, who often played men crippled and hideous and seething with vengeful rage. Although he never appeared in a movie in which his disfigurement was blamed on battle, his physical and mental victimization in story after story clearly struck a chord in this post-war audience. In both 1928 and 1929, theater owners voted Lon Chaney the most popular box-office attraction.

He was born Alonso Chaney on April Fools Day, 1883 to deaf-mute parents in Colorado Springs, Colorado. To communicate with his mother and father, he became adept at pantomime and facial expressions. He worked at the Colorado Springs Opera House as a stagehand, scene painter and property boy, occasionally playing small parts. When he was 17, Chaney wrote a play with his brother and took it on the road.

After spending several unsuccessful touring seasons in musical comedy, he married cabaret singer Cleva Creighton on May 31, 1906. They had a son that year, Creighton Chaney, and the family struggled together until Cleva attempted suicide. On the night of April 30, 1913, Cleva stood in the wings of the Majestic Theater on Broadway in Los Angeles while Chaney was working and swallowed a vial of bichloride of mercury. She recovered, but the attempt destroyed her vocal chords. Chaney divorced her, got custody of their son, and never spoke to her again, even encouraging their son to believe she was dead.

Because of the bad press connected to Cleva's attempted suicide, Chaney lost his job in the theater. Out of necessity, he entered motion pictures in 1913 as an extra at Universal, which was then located at the corner of Sunset Blvd. and Gower Street. Chaney worked his way up to playing character parts, many showcasing his incredible talent with makeup. He even directed films for the Victor Company at Universal in 1915, writing the scenarios and acting in some. On November 26, 1915, he married Hazel Hastings, a chorus dancer, whose previous husband had been a legless man who ran a cigar counter in San Francisco. Creighton came home from boarding school to live with them, and the Chaneys became a family again.

Chaney took his first role as a cripple in 1919 when he played Frog, a conman who is able to twist his legs and body to appear disabled, in George Loane Tucker's film of Frank Packard's novel, *The Miracle Man*. In one scene, Chaney "unwinds" as he pretends to be cured by a blind faith healer. As the old man prays over him, Chaney first snaps his wrist from a coiled position and moves it around. He slowly and painfully untangles his twisted legs and stands. As he rises, Chaney thrusts his spine and right leg into place. The performance was so convincing that many reviewers believed that Chaney was either double-jointed or a contortionist, neither of which were true.

The following year, Chaney gave a terrifying performance as a vengeful legless criminal in *The Penalty*. The ferocity of this Satanic character coupled with his physical and mental

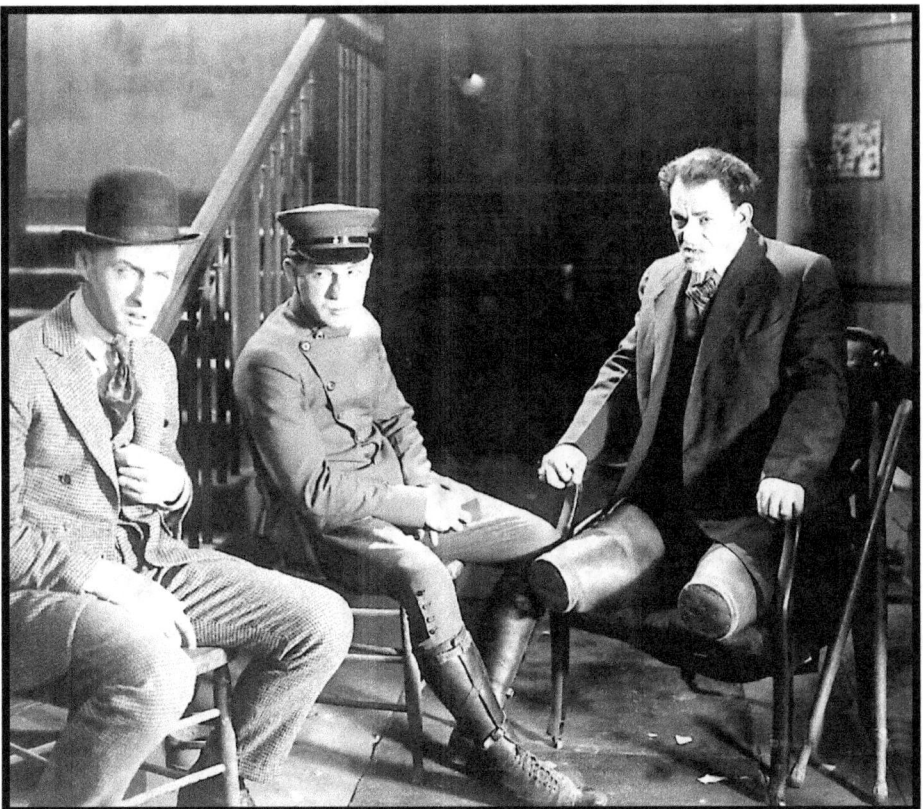

The ferocity of Chaney's Satanic character in *The Penalty*, coupled with his physical and mental aberration, certainly qualifies it as Chaney's first "horror" role.

aberration certainly qualifies it as Chaney's first "horror" role. Samuel Goldwyn bought the rights to the 1913 novel by Governeur Morris and Goldwyn's studio manager, Abe Lehr, signed Chaney to star on the strength of his portrayal in *The Miracle Man*. Chaney accepted a salary of $500 a week. Afterward, he overheard Lehr talking with the studio casting director, Clifford Robertson, father of actor Cliff Robertson, congratulating himself on Chaney's price when they were prepared to pay him $1,500 a week.

Chaney set to work designing the harness and costume necessary to give the illusion of being a man with both legs missing below the knees. As he would do in his later, more famous, portrayals, he closely followed the author's description of the character and the original illustrations in the book, in this case rendered by artist Howard Chandler Christy for the Charles Scribner's Sons edition of 1913.

Chaney devised leather belts to strap his legs up behind him. The pants of his costume were sized so that they could fit the doubled-up legs. He then placed his bent knees into leather stumps which had straps running up the pant legs to a belt worn around his waist. A padded chest piece under his shirt gave Chaney's upper torso a fuller look, and the overlong jacket helped to hide his strapped legs. Chaney walked on his knees with the aid of weighted crutches, practicing at home for several weeks prior to filming. He found that the device caused lower back pain, and he could wear it for only 20 minutes before having to unstrap himself and have his legs massaged.

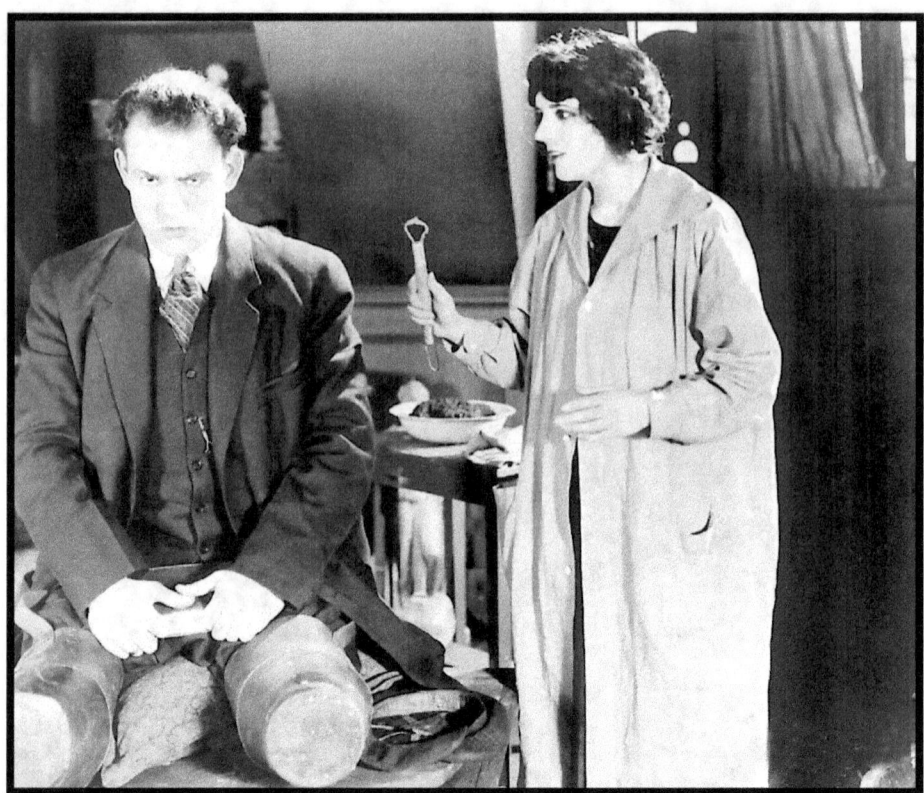

Blizzard (Lon Chaney) plans to use the doctor's pretty young daughter, Barbara (Claire Adams), and ingratiates himself to her by posing for her bust of "Satan, After the Fall" in *The Penalty*.

Charles Kenyon and Philip Lonergan's screenplay begins with a chilling scene of modern horror and tragedy:

A boy has been hit by a car, and young Dr. Ferris has amputated the boy's damaged legs just above the knees. But when an older doctor examines the limbs, he realizes that the amputation was unnecessary. Unfortunately, the boy awakens just in time to hear the two doctors arguing about the bungled operation. When the hysterical child tries to tell his parents, the older doctor denies the conversation, saying that the boy is obviously still dreaming from the anesthetic.

Years later, the boy has grown up to become the feared ruler of the San Francisco underworld. He calls himself Blizzard, and his criminal activities are driven by a demented plot to revenge himself on Dr. Ferris. Blizzard plans to use the doctor's pretty young daughter, Barbara, and ingratiates himself to her by posing for her bust of "Satan, After the Fall." She finds his embittered face Satanic enough, and Blizzard sets about charming her as she sculpts him. Her fiance, Dr. Wilmont, warns her to stay away from Blizzard, but Barbara is fascinated by the criminal.

Meanwhile, Rose, a female agent for the government, manages to get a job in Blizzard's warehouse making hats along with a room full of other women. Blizzard reveals intense cruelty in his treatment of these women, threatening them, bullying them and even hitting them when their work fails to please him.

Rose finds Blizzard's secret basement beneath a fireplace that slides up into the chimney. There, she discovers more workers and rooms full of weapons. Blizzard suspects Rose's treachery but refrains from killing her because she is able to artistically manipulate the foot pedals of his piano while he plays, an activity that soothes his demented mind. Rose learns that Blizzard plans to loot the city with the help of an army of disgruntled foreigners, but she has fallen in love with him and refuses to turn him into the police.

Blizzard kidnaps Dr. Wilmont and holds him hostage. He summons Dr. Ferris and demands that he graft Wilmont's legs onto his own stumps. Dr. Ferris agrees, but instead of carrying out that insane operation, he performs brain surgery, relieving pressure caused by the car accident long ago. Blizzard awakens from the procedure a new man: he is no longer compelled to do evil. When Rose and the other government agents arrive, Dr. Ferris urges them to give Blizzard the chance to lead a normal life so that he can be of use to society.

Rose and Blizzard marry and, with Dr. Ferris, plan to do great things for the world. However, Blizzard's former gang members fear being betrayed by the reformed criminal. While he plays the piano and Rose manipulates the pedals, Blizzard is shot by a drug addict who used to be his hit man. Despite his newfound virtue, Blizzard's former crimes demand that he pay the ultimate penalty.

The first draft screenplay ends differently, with Blizzard recovering from his surgery and returning to Barbara's studio to finish posing for her bust of Satan. In the presence of Rose and Dr. Wilmont, Barbara struggles with the sculpture until she finally throws it to the floor in frustration. The evil expression has left Blizzard's face, and she cannot recapture it in clay. Barbara and Dr. Wilmont embrace as Blizzard and Rose smile. After forcing the audience to wallow in Blizzard's evil, the writers ultimately realized that this conclusion could not work.

In fact, the graphic depiction of Blizzard's criminal world tested the boundaries of censorship at the time. The film begins with Pete, Blizzard's heroin-addicted hit man played by James Mason, knifing a prostitute who has tried to leave Blizzard's gang. Later, Blizzard sadistically tantalizes Pete with a portable dope kit before rewarding him for his services by handing it over. Even an establishing shot of Barbara's studio featuring a nude model would not have been allowed a few years later when the Hays Office prevented such sights on the screens of America.

Goldwyn chose a veteran actor, producer and director of the New York stage, Wallace Worsley, to direct. Worsley was born on December 10, 1878 at his Aunt Mattie Goring's estate at Wappingers Falls, New York. His father was the engineer who installed the original electrical system in the United States Senate. Wallace grew up in Washington society and, in 1896, entered Brown University in Providence, Rhode Island. In his sophomore year, he volunteered for the Army, and on July 20, 1898, he was wounded in battle in Puerto Rico during the Spanish-American War.

Returning home, he entered the American Academy of Dramatic Arts in New York City, studying to become an actor. In 1901, he met his future wife, Julia Marie Taylor, and upon graduation, they both became professionals: Wallace as the juvenile with Willie Collier and Julia as the leading lady with Richard Mansfield's traveling Shakespearean company. They were married in 1904. From 1912 to 1914, they had a summer stock company in Pittsfield, Massachusetts at the Colonial Theater. Wallace then became a producer and director of vaudeville and theatrical productions for the Shuberts and Charles Frohman.

In 1916, while producing shows for the Kirke-Lashell Stock Company, he was asked by Robert Brunton of the Brunton Studios, later to become Paramount, to come to Hollywood as a contract actor. Within a year, Brunton made him a director. From 1917, Worsley

Chaney makes a powerful impression as the criminal Blizzard in *The Penalty*.
continually worked and was soon one of the most successful directors in the industry.

He shot *The Penalty* in 49 days from February 7, 1920 to April 2 at a cost of $88,868. Some exteriors were actually filmed on location in San Francisco, giving the movie an atmosphere of seedy reality. The temperamental Chaney got along so well with Worsley that they made four more films together, including *Ace of Heart* in 1921 and *Voices of the City* in 1922. Worsley was a competent craftsman and most importantly, his invisible style allowed Chaney to be the major attraction in each of their films.

And in *The Penalty*, Chaney makes a powerful impression. His Blizzard rules the world of prostitution, murder, drugs and larceny with ruthless strength. When he enters the room where his women labor over straw hats, he climbs onto the table with his stumps and angrily examines their work. Finding a defect in one of the hats, he grabs it away from the girl and viciously slaps her across the face with it. The other workers shrink back in terror while Blizzard snarls at them. Blizzard starts to leave the room and, as an afterthought, tells them about one of the females who tried to quit his employ. Now, he says with a sneer, she sleeps on a marble slab at the morgue, then he exits laughing.

In another scene, Blizzard meets Dr. Wilmont for the first time at Barbara's art studio. He tells the young doctor that he has "an admirable pair of legs." Glancing down at his own stumps, he adds, "I gave mine to science," and laughs sardonically.

As Blizzard enjoys his growing influence over Barbara, he dares to profess his feelings for her. He sits on a platform as she sculpts him and begins to confess his love with intense passion. But his pleading frightens and repulses the young artist. She laughs nervously, which enrages the cripple. With explosive fury, Blizzard reaches for her and actually falls from the platform.

Standing on his stumps without the aid of his crutches, he tries to grab her, but she easily backs away from him. His twisted expression betrays the depth of his anger as only Chaney can. When Blizzard realizes that his feelings are jeopardizing his revenge, he suddenly stops. Chaney communicates through his expression that he is now in control and insincerely professes deep remorse for his actions. He holds his head down as he apologizes, then slyly glances up to see if his performance is working on the young woman.

In such scenes, Worsley cuts from long-shot masters, allowing us to see Chaney's amazingly agile use of his restricted body, to medium close-ups to show the privileged moments of his facial expressions. The coverage and cutting are standard for this

Chaney and Claire Adams take a break from the intensity of *The Penalty.*

period of filmmaking, but Worsley wisely knows that Chaney's performance guides the camera at all times. By using the wide shots, Worsley enables Chaney to impress us with his strength, as when he walks up a flight of stairs on his stumps, pulls his body to a window by grabbing pegs in the wall and descends a pole using only his arms.

Chaney's intensity and the startling reality of the criminal setting are offset by some unforgivable contrivances and implausibilities in the story, even for melodrama. The complete impossibility of Blizzard's schemes of robbing the entire city of San Francisco and forcing Dr. Ferris to graft Dr. Wilmont's legs onto his stumps can be excused by the cripple's insanity. The very grandiosity of his revenge makes him a fascinating madman in the tradition of the genre.

But Rose's sudden change from a tough undercover government agent aware of the evils of Blizzard's criminal reign to a lovesick woman willing to risk her life and the future of the city because of her sympathy for this monster makes her seem as crazy as Blizzard. And even his insanity would not allow him to spare this woman so she can destroy everything he has planned merely because she pushes the pedals of his piano well. How could he have built such a powerful secret empire if he lets himself be swayed by this kind of sentiment? We have already seen and heard of him killing for much less than Rose's complete betrayal.

Dr. Ferris' plea on behalf of the reformed Blizzard ignores the extent of the cripple's former evil. He has been responsible for crimes that cannot be forgiven, and the government agent's immediate willingness to pardon Blizzard after fighting him for years strains credulity

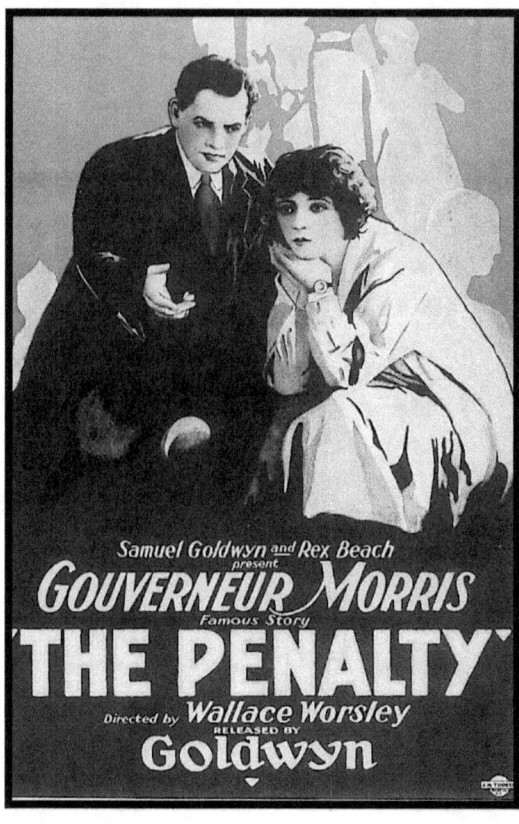

to the breaking point. In a less realistic and contemporary setting, this might have been acceptable as the logic of melodrama, but within the atmosphere so carefully and luridly established in *The Penalty*, it cannot work.

The film was released on November 21, 1920 and garnered Chaney some impressive reviews. *Motion Picture World* said, "Lon Chaney, whose work in *The Miracle Man* won so much praise, portrays a role that might have been written for him... He is wicked and cunning, but in the end he wins sympathy and applause. Chaney makes splendid use of every opportunity." *Wid's Film Daily* raved, "Hats off to Lon Chaney! As 'Blizzard,' the deformed ruler of the Barbary Coast's underworld, he gives one of the screen greatest performances... up to almost the very conclusion the gripping melodramatic incidents hold securely and Chaney's work is so unusually fine that it will probably hold the production for all that is necessary." *Variety* wrote, "It is needless to say that the picture is Chaney more than anyone else," while *The New York Times* observed, "In the midst of a purely mechanistic arrangement of incidents and surrounded by puppets, Chaney creates a character... [Chaney] has another vivid impersonation." Finally, *Photoplay* took a tack that would be adopted by *Variety* for some of Chaney's later high-profile exercises in terror: "Here is a picture that is about as cheerful as a hanging—and as interesting... It is a remarkably good performance this actor [Chaney] gives... Wallace Worsley's direction helps the picture a lot."

By 1921, Samuel Goldwyn had been replaced as head of his own company by F.J. Godsol. Even though neither Chaney nor Worsley were under contract to Goldwyn Studios, readers were instructed to find projects for the team. Early in 1921, they collaborated on another movie based on a story by Gouveneur Morris called *Ace of Heart*. That same year, Chaney and Worsley worked together again on *Voices of the City*. Of course, Chaney acted for other directors as well, since he was now considered a box-office attraction. And at a salary of $1,000 a week, Chaney took as many pictures as his schedule would permit. By the time he made *A Blind Bargain* with Worsley in October, he had already appeared in eight movies that year.

A Blind Bargain was based on a novel called *The Octave of Claudius* written by Barry Pain and published in America by Harper and Row and in England by Holden and Hardingham Ltd., in 1897. Pain, who was born in Cambridge, England on September 28, 1864, was a journalist, humorist and widely read short story writer. As a satirist, his work included *Old Robinson Crusoe*, written in 1907 and *The New Gulliver*, written in 1913, both of which concerned the adventures of their title characters returning to Edwardian England hundreds of years after their famous exploits. His novels of the supernatural included *The Shadow of the Unseen*, written in 1907 with James Blyth, which dealt with witchcraft and *An Exchange of Souls*, written in 1911, about a man with wings. Many of his short stories also involved the supernatural, and he was hailed for a time as the greatest short story writer of his day.

The Octave of Claudius concerns a young man named Claudius Sandell who is rescued from starvation in Wimbledon Common by Dr. Gabriel Lamb. Dr. Lamb takes the unconscious man home to his religiously obsessed wife, Hilda. The physician no longer loves his wife, who is slowly going mad because of the death of their child at birth. Dr. Lamb devotes himself to experiments with animals to help speed and improve evolution and make mankind the master of his own destiny. As Claudius recuperates at their home, Hilda starts to secretly fall in love with him.

The young unfortunate tells them his story: he was educated at Eton and Cambridge University. But because Claudius opposed his father's support of a spiritual medium named Miss Comby, he was cut off without finances, and his father made Miss Comby sole heir to the Sandell fortune. Unknown to Claudius, Miss Comby happens to be Hilda Lamb's sister! Claudius attempted to write a novel, but it was refused for publication.

Dr. Lamb makes Claudius a proposition. Knowing the debt of gratitude that Claudius feels and the young man's sense of honor, the doctor offers Claudius an eight-day holiday with £8,000 to spend if Claudius will return to him on the last night to be used by Dr. Lamb for his experiments. The eight-day holiday resembles the "octave" that the church gives to its saints. Claudius agrees and promises to return.

Before Claudius leaves, Hilda begs him to back out of the bargain. Alone with her husband, Hilda has a hysterical breakdown which Dr. Lamb stops by beating her with a buggy whip.

In London, Claudius meets Angela Wycherly, the daughter of a prominent family, and the two fall in love. Claudius' father reconciles with his son when he receives an anonymous letter sent by Mrs. Lamb exposing Miss Comby. Claudius tells Angela of his agreement and writes to Dr. Lamb trying to cancel it. The scientist refuses.

When he returns on the eighth night, Claudius finds Hilda completely insane. She warns Claudius again before being taken to her room kicking and screaming by a nurse. Dr. Lamb explains to Claudius that Hilda thinks she hears her dead baby crawling around the house.

The doctor reveals his plan to Claudius: after taking his young subject to a house in the country, he will operate. Although Claudius will be under anesthetic, he will awaken for about 50 seconds in tremendous pain, and then he will die. Dr. Lamb cheerfully tells Claudius to settle his affairs in the next few days before they move.

But that night, as Claudius and Dr. Lamb sleep, Hilda escapes from her room. She steals a surgical knife from the lab, and, as the awakening "Dr. Lamb began to move his head, she flung herself upon him and thrust and hacked and pulled."

Claudius wakes up to find the house on fire. Hilda is dragged from repeated attempts to run back into the blazing inferno. Finally, she is imprisoned in Broadmoor asylum, and Claudius returns to Angela.

Goldwyn Studios paid $2,000 for the story rights, and the adaptation was assigned to J.G. Hawks. The screenwriter was fascinated by the scandalous papers being published by the brilliant French surgeon, Dr. Serge Voronoff, who claimed that he could correct birth defects and prolong life by grafting the glands of animals onto other animals and even humans. Since the experiments of the story's Dr. Lamb were rather unspecified, Hawks combined

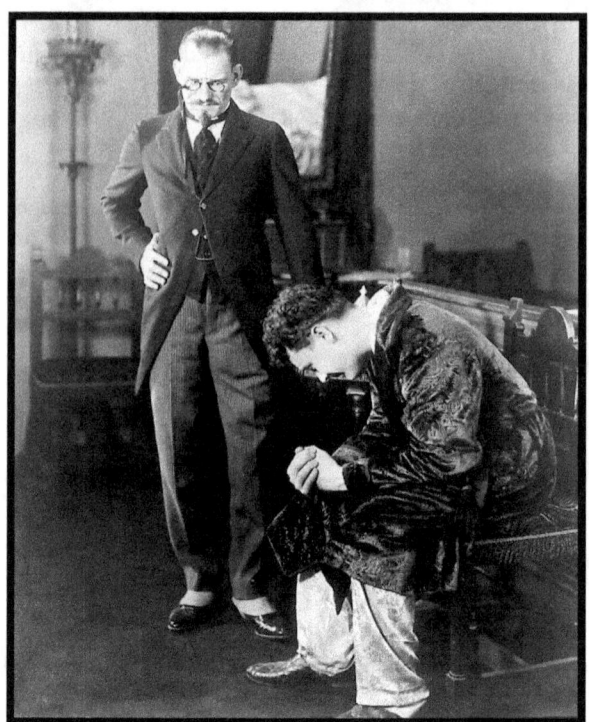

Chaney as Dr. Lamb and Raymond McKee as Robert in *A Blind Bargain*

him with the real Dr. Voronoff, whose visionary theories most people at the time found insane and vaguely immoral.

To give the film a contemporary edge, Hawks changed the young hero into a veteran of World War I and played up his struggle to become a published novelist. The biggest implausibility in Pain's story was the hero's willingness to make a blind bargain and stick to it just as a matter of personal, upper-class honor. To strengthen his motivation, Hawks gave him a dying mother whom the brilliant surgeon cures in exchange for the son's cooperation. Also, in the screen adaptation, Dr. Lamb has the utmost faith in his operation on the young man, confident that his patient will not only survive but be stronger and live longer as a result. The fact that the scientist keeps two half-human mutants as living evidence of past failures increases the hero's uncertainty about his agreement.

As writer-director Tod Browning had done in the 1920 crime melodrama, *Outside the Law*, Hawks lured Lon Chaney with two different roles. Not only would the actor play the mad but well-intentioned Dr. Lamb, but he would also be one of the failed experiments in gland transplantation: a mute, simian humanoid created by combining ape glands and monkey blood with a man. This would allow Chaney to create one of his famous makeups and extravagant characterizations.

The revised story moved swiftly and eliminated many of the coincidences and implausibilities in the source material. The setting was switched to the suburbs of New York in the early 1920s. The hero's name was still Claudius in the script, but by the time the title cards were filmed, it had been changed to the more modern sounding Robert.

Despondent over his unpublished novel and his mother's declining health, Robert tries to rob a theatergoer. His intended victim overpowers him and turns out to be the fanatical surgeon, Dr. Lamb. When Robert tells him why he needs the money, the doctor performs a life-saving operation on Robert's mother on the condition that, after eight days, Robert deliver himself to Dr. Lamb to do with as he pleases.

Both Robert and his bedridden mother move to the Lamb estate and are watched over by the doctor's kindly wife as well as a grotesque ape-man who is the result of one of the scientist's experiments. The surgeon also arranges for Robert's book to be published through the Wytcherly Publishing Company. During his eight days, Robert meets and falls in love with Wytcherly's daughter, Angela.

The biggest implausibility in Pain's story was the hero's willingness to make a blind bargain and stick to it just as a matter of personal, upper-class honor in *A Blind Bargain*.

On the night of Robert's operation, the ape-man shows him a hidden prison in which are kept half-human, half-animal creatures: the results of Dr. Lamb's former procedures. The doctor discovers the two and fights with Robert, attempting to get him onto the operating table. The ape-man releases a powerful humanoid creature from one of the cages, and it snaps the doctor's back. Robert is set free from his bargain and, with the success of his book, is able to take care of his mother and romance Angela.

The film employed split-screen double exposure so that both characters played by Chaney could be in the scene at the same time. As the ape-man, prophetically called the Hunchback in the script, Chaney wore a closely cropped black wig with a low hairline and extended his eyebrows across the bridge of his nose. He puffed the bags under his eyes by molding them in layers of cotton-wool which he stiffened by painting them over with collodion. In addition, Chaney broadened his nose by cutting about three-eighths of an inch off the ends of rubber cigar holders and placing them in his nostrils. This also allowed him to breath freely. A set of false teeth gave a simian protrusion to his upper lip. He padded a slight hump to his back and walked with a stooped, ape-like gait. By contrast, as Dr. Lamb, Chaney slicked back his hair and added a mustache, trimmed goatee and pince-nez. He wore a high celluloid collar, tie, frock coat, vest and spats. A separate title card in the opening credits read: "Presenting Lon Chaney in the dual role of Dr. Anthony Lamb and the Hunchback."

Wallace Worsley's method of directing was to do extensive research and intense preplanning and then to allow the actors and technicians freedom to create within those guide-

Chaney works on his makeup for *A Blind Bargain*.

lines. He had the reputation of bringing pictures in on time and under budget. Worsley shot *A Blind Bargain* from early October through early November 1921 at a cost of $84,719.26.

Unfortunately, when the picture was sneak previewed twice, it met with little positive response from the audience. In fact, the film's theme caused a major uproar. Fundamentalist church groups had begun to grow in power in the United States around the turn of the century. By the 1920s, they had published a 17-volume book of dogma banning all but the strictest interpretation of the Bible. A portion of the public felt that *A Blind Bargain* promoted the theories of evolution and Darwinism as well as using the forbidden subject of vivisection of human beings as a story element. Just the year before, New York banned Chaney and Worsley's film, *Voices of the City*, because of its portrayal of drugs, prostitution and underworld connections to city politics. Goldwyn Studios could not afford another boycott.

A Blind Bargain was immediately withdrawn and recut. The vivisection theme was reduced along with almost all of the footage of Robert living it up during his eight-day "octave." Robert did not meet Angela during his eight days but was engaged to her before the story began. His novel's title changed from *Silver Seas* to *A Sacrifice for Science*. Publication of the book was moved to take place after Dr. Lamb's death so that Robert's motives for breaking his promise were strictly for survival and not because of his newfound success. The character of Angela's mother was completely removed as was some comic relief with Dr. Lamb's maid. The total running time dropped to 52 minutes so additional footage of a fashionable Charity Ball attended by Robert, Angela and Dr. Lamb was added and hand-colored. The final release print was still reduced from six reels in the original cut to five reels. Four different versions of the title cards were drafted before the film received its final approval on February 15, 1922. *A Blind Bargain* finally opened at Goldwyn's Capital Theater in New York City on December 3, 1922, over a year after principal photography had wrapped. It was released nationally on December 10 and worldwide one year later.

As with *The Penalty*, Chaney received better reviews than the picture. *Photoplay* said, "Lon Chaney's fine acting in two widely divergent roles is the outstanding feature of this picture... There are many thrills—illogical, perhaps, but now and then breath taking." *Variety* agreed, noting the emergence of the genre: "Another addition to the 'horror' situation so prevalent in fiction, theatre and on the screen for the past year... beyond the work of the star himself, there is nothing to raise this film above the average feature... Chaney, doubling as the doctor and the hunchback, gives a credible performance and allows for some double photography that is by no means unworthy of mention. Always at his best in a grotesque makeup, Chaney predominates in the character of the man-ape, using the ungainly lope of the supposed animal as a means of locomotion throughout the interpretation of the character." *Exhibitors Trade Review* summed it up: "One merely has to say 'Lon Chaney' and mention next director Wallace Worsley. The former has given the picture its greatest power to interest the spectator and the director has contrived many scenes of photographic distinction and dramatic effect... Mr. Chaney essays the dual role assigned to him with that fine assurance which marks all his work. His makeup is of course wonderful and one marvels at the contrast between the Doctor with his erect and distinguished carriage and the deformed little man victimized by the surgical experiments."

For the first but not the last time, the studio proposed that theater owners hold an amateur makeup contest to promote the picture. One prize would be given for the most original character and another for the best disguise which could be applied in the shortest time. Over the years, similar contests would be repeated by numerous theaters to capitalize on Chaney's growing reputation as "the man of a thousand faces."

In 1931, after silent films were no longer commercially viable, MGM, which took over Goldwyn Studios, destroyed the negative of *A Blind Bargain* along with other silents to conserve storage space. Unlike *Nosferatu*, no complete prints were known to survive.

As early as 1920, Lon Chaney stated publicly that he desired to play Quasimodo in an adaptation of Victor Hugo's sprawling novel from 1831, *Notre Dame de Paris*. The actor optioned the film rights for 60 days in June 1921 for $500. Over the next 14 months, Chaney and

Chaney's performance received better reviews from critics than *A Blind Bargain*.

his business manager, Alfred Grasso, held meetings with potential financiers in the hopes of funding the project independently.

Unfortunately, the trial of popular Hollywood comedian Fatty Arbuckle for manslaughter occurred at the same time. The scandal destroyed Arbuckle's career as a performer and nearly took Hollywood with him. Civic groups and leagues of decency across the country condemned Arbuckle and the "immoral" Hollywood lifestyle he symbolized. Eventually, Paramount Pictures, the studio that produced and distributed the comedian's films, banned him from motion pictures.

The Motion Picture Producers and Distributors of America was created, and Will Hays, the former Postmaster, oversaw a strict censorship code which the producers agreed to follow. Studios included a "morals clause" in each star's contract binding them to conduct themselves correctly even in their private lives. In this shaky climate, potential investors started having second thoughts about committing the large sums of money needed to produce a motion picture. Consequently, Chaney's three separate deals with financiers evaporated.

In late April 1922, the independent Chelsea Pictures Corporation announced that Chaney would star in *The Hunchback of Notre Dame* to be directed in Europe by Alan Crosland as part of a 20-picture schedule. This heralded the first trade announcement linking Chaney with the project, but it also fell through due to funding difficulties.

As early as May 1921, Chaney and Grasso held discussions with Universal's young production executive Irving Thalberg regarding the film. At one point, they considered making the movie on a three-month schedule in Germany, but this idea was rejected by Chaney.

In the early 1920s, Universal typically filmed low-budget programmers, Westerns and serials, designed for neighborhood theaters and small towns. Universal owned no theaters of its own and went mostly unrepresented in the larger urban markets. Instead, they sold their pictures in packages to exhibitors.

The films were graded as to budget, the top line being designated as Universal Jewels, then Junior Jewels, Specials, etc. In an attempt to gain industry credibility in comparison to the larger films regularly released by Paramount, Metro and United Artists, Carl Laemmle created a line of high-budget productions called "Super Jewels." These included only a few movies such as Erich von Stroheim's *Foolish Wives* and *The Merry Go-Round* and Tod Browning's *Outside the Law* with Lon Chaney. Thalberg envisioned *The Hunchback of Notre Dame* as a "Super Jewel."

Irving Thalberg was born May 30, 1899 in Brooklyn, New York of German-Jewish parentage. Frail with a rheumatic heart condition, he spent months in bed with a succession of ailments during his childhood. He claimed that one of the books he read while bedridden was *The Hunchback of Notre Dame*. Since doctors told him he might not live to be 30 years old, Thalberg skipped college, learned shorthand and speed typing and went to work after high school with a small trading company.

In 1918, he began working for Carl Laemmle, a friend of the family, at the Universal Film Manufacturing Company, initially as secretary to Laemmle's assistant, then as private secretary to Laemmle himself. At the company's headquarters, then situated on Broadway in New York, Thalberg became indispensable to Laemmle due to his quick grasp of the film business.

In 1915, Laemmle opened Universal City on Lanchershim in Hollywood, a 230-acre production center. By 1919, the management of Universal City had fallen into disarray, and Laemmle appointed his 20-year-old secretary as head of production. Thalberg soon established a reputation as a capable administrator, a tough taskmaster and an intuitive judge of commercially viable story material. Thalberg's handling of the brilliant but indulgent director Erich von Stroheim on the "Super Jewel" productions of *Foolish Wives* and *The Merry Go-*

Round enhanced the young executive's reputation in Hollywood. A former Universal writer penned a story for *The Saturday Evening Post* called "The Boy Wonder" about a producer patterned after Thalberg, and the name stuck to Thalberg himself.

For *The Hunchback of Notre Dame*, Thalberg offered Chaney $2,000 a week, but no percentage of the film's earnings. Chaney had hoped to participate in the profits if he secured his own financing, but in order to see his dream become a reality, he sacrificed his cut. The actor signed his contract on August 15, 1922. On August 26, Universal announced the production in the trades, stating, "the continuity is being whipped up into shape, and the location and production departments are taking the preliminary steps necessary for the construction of the various sets." Ultimately, the film's budget would reach a whopping $1.25 million.

Chaney knew the novel well and insisted on working closely with screenwriters Edward T. Lowe, Jr. and Perley Poore Sheehan to make sure nothing would be deleted that might hurt the story. However, changes were inevitable. The screenwriters had to pare down the mammoth number of events and characters to achieve a practical length for the screen. Also, Thalberg felt that audiences of the time would not accept some of the unrelieved gloom of the piece, especially the downbeat ending in which Esmeralda was rejected by the heartless captain whom she loved and died despite the best efforts of Quasimodo to save her. Hugo's criticism of the Catholic Church had to be softened so as not to offend the devout. The villain of Hugo's novel was Dom Claude Frollo, the archdeacon of Notre Dame, and Hugo exposed his ruthless hypocrisy as he lusted after Esmeralda. The screenplay did not risk offending the Church and made the villain the archdeacon's non-ordained brother, Jehan. The archdeacon himself was portrayed as gentle, wise and pious.

Thalberg concentrated on finding a director for the project who would be acceptable to Chaney and who could shoot the movie quickly and economically. Chaney preferred a well-known filmmaker such as Maurice Tourneur, Frank Lloyd, John S. Robertson, Chet Withey, Emile Chautard, Raoul Walsh and especially Frank Borzage. Thalberg considered Erich von Stroheim but quickly rejected him as too costly and demanding. Chaney angrily told his business manager that he would refuse to work with any of the directors Universal had in mind. He even asked Grasso to find a way to break his contract so that he could take the project to Louis B. Mayer's

Irving Thalberg and Norma Shearer

Chaney faithfully recreated Hugo's description when designing his makeup for Quasimodo in *The Hunchback of Notre Dame*.

company for Fred Niblo to direct. "I want you to be sure and tell Thalberg that and let me know what he has to say. I am not going to stand for any of their foolishness or stalling," Chaney wrote to Grasso.

Ultimately, Thalberg chose Wallace Worsley, who was not on Chaney's preferred directors list. In an early letter to Grasso, Chaney conceded that Worsley was "as good as any of the second raters or better but for God's sake don't tell them so." Thalberg knew of Worsley's reputation as a reliable craftsman who did not expand a film's budget or schedule. Of course, Worsley had also directed Chaney in four successful films so Thalberg was sure he could handle the demanding star.

Chaney faithfully recreated Hugo's description when designing his makeup for Quasimodo. As reference, Chaney also consulted the 36 unsigned illustrations for the George Routledge and Sons edition of the novel. The actor wore a 20-pound plaster hump on his back which was held in place with a leather harness. This harness fit around his waist like a belt. Straps over his shoulders attached to the front of the belt and kept him bent forward. Between takes, he sat on a special stool with armrests.

Chaney built up his cheekbones with layers of cotton stiffened with collodion just like the bags under his eyes in *A Blind Bargain*. The resulting pieces were more resilient than if they had been shaped from nose putty or mortician's wax, and they could be reused for several days in a row. Chaney closed his right eye with adhesive tape and covered it with nose putty. The resultant strain on the sight of his left eye forced him to wear glasses for the rest of his life. Again as in *A Blind Bargain*, he distended his nostrils by placing pieces of cigar holders inside them. He elongated the tip of his nose with putty. Crepe-wool was used for bushy eyebrows, and a matted wig covered his hair.

James L. Howard, D.D.S. helped Chaney create teeth for the character. In a 1930 article in the trade journal *Oral Hygiene*, Howard explained:

> ...He seemed depressed for fear he could not live up to his own hopes for the part... I thought it over and advanced, as a result of long observation, that from what I had seen, hunchbacks had a large lower jaw... I made an upper plate to fit over his own teeth, but left the molars [back teeth] off. In the lower jaw I made a plate to go over his own teeth and extend well down on the buccal sides [the sides of the mouth facing the cheek], forcing his cheeks down half an inch, or perhaps three quarters of an inch. I put no teeth in the lower plate, but cut the front out, letting the natural anterior [lower front teeth] show. The effect was exactly what he wanted, but the problem was how to hold the lower contraption in his mouth.
>
> ...Then I took two pieces of alarm clock spring, each about two inches long, vulcanizing [hardening] one end of each spring to the upper plate in the molar regions and letting the lower ends slant down and rest on the occlusal [top] ridges of the lower appliance. This caused strong pressure on the lower and permitted the mouth to open and close, at the same time forcing the muscles of the cheeks down, thereby accomplishing the purpose of characterization.

Nineteen-year-old Patsy Ruth Miller was cast as the Gypsy girl Esmeralda after a lengthy talent search. According to her autobiography, *My Hollywood*, the young actress did not remember meeting Wallace Worsley when she tested for the role. Chaney himself came down to the set and quietly explained the part to her.

Elmer E. Sheeley designed the sets with Sidney Ullman as his first assistant. Their designs were translated into plans, blueprinted and delivered to technical director Archie Hall, who supervised set construction. Carpenters and masons then transformed 19 acres of land on Universal's backlot into 15th-century Paris. To lay out the cathedral, one flank of a mountain had to be cut away and a large swale filled in.

The recreation of Notre Dame itself ended just above the massive Gothic doors, but was still 60 feet high. Finn Frowlich, a well-known sculptor, supervised the making of the bas-relief, embellishments, saints, martyrs and gargoyles that covered the structure. For long shots of the cathedral, the remaining 165 feet above the doors was actually a hanging miniature which was placed in front of the camera and aligned precisely to blend with the full-scale set. Sections of the upper part of the cathedral were built on a hill to enable low-angle shots and, as Patsy Ruth Miller said, "so that you wouldn't hurt yourself if you fell."

More than two acres of cement and one acre of cobblestones paved the huge square of the Palace du Parvis in front of the church as well as the other medieval streets. Sixty workmen hauled in the cobblestones from a river 20 miles away. The settings and properties cost about $500,000, with $342,869 of that going for the 11-acre Palace du Parvis set.

Production began on December 16, 1922. The casting call went out for background performers, employing over 2,000 extras. Such a huge number of atmosphere players necessitated construction of a building to house their period costumes. Because the schedule called for over two months of night filming, over 700 lights were needed. Every light Universal owned, along with many borrowed from other studios, was used, requiring 230 electricians, seven motor generators and five miles of cable.

More than two acres of cement and one acre of cobblestones paved the huge square of the Palace du Parvis in front of the church in *The Hunchback of Notre Dame*. **Chaney with Patsy Ruth Miller**

In her autobiography, Patsy Ruth Miller recalled, "It seems to me, in retrospect, that Lon did as much directing as Mr. Worsley did... for our personal scenes I seem to remember Lon giving advice or suggestions more than Mr. Worsley... During the courtroom scene where I, Esmeralda, was being questioned by the judge, it was Lon who made the suggestion that I should underplay the scene, being more exhausted than frightened and it was Lon who came to me, between set-ups and told me that I had caught the mood and to keep it... Lon was at the studio every day, even when he wasn't working; he stood behind the camera and okayed the set-ups and occasionally even made suggestions about the lighting. In the torture scene... it was Lon who commended me for turning my head from side to side, because, he said, people did that to escape from pain. ... During one of the more emotional scenes... Lon came to me and very quietly said, 'You don't have to cry real tears. I hate these people who brag that they can cry at the drop of a hat. The point is not for you to cry but to make your audience cry. So you must be in control...'

"Never, to my knowledge, was there any friction between Lon and Mr. Worsley; they often sat together riffling through the pages of the script, or, when Lon was not in makeup, having lunch together in the commissary."

Robert E. Newhard was named first cameraman. However, the production was so large and took such a long time that almost every other cameraman at Universal had a hand in it at various times. Chaney demanded that Virgil Miller shoot all of his close-ups. Miller had photographed Chaney in *The Trap* the previous year, one of the earliest pictures to use panchromatic film. Miller also shot some special effects and large action scenes for *The Hunchback of Notre Dame*.

To communicate with the cast and crew on the large set, the studio employed the Western Electric Public Address System for the first time. Previously, a director would shout his orders through a large megaphone, hoping he could be heard by the most distant member of the company. Lighting director Harry D. Brown recalled that during lunch, the radio would be turned on over the speaker, which not only provided entertainment, but also kept the extras from wandering away.

Tay Garnett, just out of the Naval Air Service and later to be the director of such films as *The Postman Always Rings Twice*, recalled visiting Patsy Ruth Miller on the set one chilly

Esmeralda and Quasimodo

night. He observed that even the most jaded extras would avoid looking at Chaney in his makeup. That night, there were numerous delays in shooting the scene. First, the camera had problems. Then, a light went out. Each time something went wrong, the extras would douse their torches and sit down, complaining about the long hours. When preparation finally came together, the assistant director yelled at the extras, "Light up your torches and pull up your tights!" The line made such an impression on Garnett that he used it as the title of his 1973 autobiography.

When the studio doctor first saw Chaney's makeup and body appliances in pre-production, he insisted on a clause in Chaney's contract: "Should the artist suffer any physical incapacity or disfigurement materially detracting from his appearance as a motion picture actor, or interfering with his duties hereunder, the producer need pay him no compensation during the period of such incapacity or disfigurement and in the event that such incapacity or disfigurement continues for a period of more than one week, the producer at its option may terminate the employment herein provided for." Chaney side-stepped this clause by hiring Joe Bonomo, who had previously worked with him on *The Light in the Dark*, to double him as Quasimodo for the more hazardous stunts.

Another stuntman attempted the long slide down a hanging rope when the Hunchback rescued Esmeralda. He ended up in the hospital with severe rope burns on his hands and legs. Bonomo had aluminum foil sewn into the tights of his costume and into thick leather gloves. He accomplished the slide without injury. Stuntman Harvey Perry doubled Chaney in other scenes, and Chaney personally applied Quasimodo's makeup to Perry's face in case the camera caught a glimpse of him.

Principal photography finally ended on June 3, 1923. Four months previously, in February, Thalberg severed his ties with Universal when Laemmle insisted the "boy wonder" marry his daughter, Rosabelle, before getting a raise. Previous to his departure, Thalberg persuaded Laemmle against releasing *The Hunchback of Notre Dame* as part of their regular schedule, preferring to sell it at road-show prices. Laemmle immediately offered Thalberg's post to Wallace Worsley, but the director was too busy completing the film. Laemmle then tried to reverse Thalberg's plans for *The Hunchback of Notre Dame*, and Worsley was caught in the middle.

At this point, Laemmle was made aware of the clause in Chaney's contract giving him full control of final cut and titles. No amount of talk, money, or threats could sway Lon Chaney from finishing the picture the way he and Thalberg originally planned it. Laemmle forced Worsley to try to persuade Chaney to compromise. Chaney took this as a betrayal to Thalberg and never spoke to Wallace Worsley again. The director was hurt by Chaney's reaction, both personally and professionally. After *The Hunchback of Notre Dame*, he never directed another film of its magnitude.

Editors assembled the final print in 12 reels, running just over two hours. Program pictures usually numbered between six and eight reels with an average screening time of about 70 minutes. Universal planned an enormous premiere on September 2, 1923 at Carnegie Hall in New York to benefit the American Legion and even persuaded the publicity-shy Chaney to attend. A brass band greeted the actor and Alfred Grasso as they disembarked from the train at Grand Central Station on September 1. Both the picture and Chaney's performance were hailed as triumphs. The film played for 21 weeks to receptive crowds at New York's Astor Theatre.

Upon general release, it was cut down to 10 reels so that exhibitors could book more showings in a day, and in this form, it played throughout the world during the 1920s. Most of the cut footage dealt with actor Ernest Torrance's scenes as Clopin, the King of Beggars, whose performance was hailed almost as much as Chaney's at the preview. Several cut scenes dealt with Clopin teaming with evil Jehan to steal the King's treasure from Notre Dame. The beggar also belittled Esmeralda in front of the other Gypsies after dragging her away from Phoebus' party, treating her more like a frustrated lover than a protective father as the cut print suggested. Clopin even considered trading her to Jehan for the King's treasure.

Jehan's use of the black arts to turn lead into gold was also cut. His primitive laboratory, in which Jehan concealed Satanic symbols behind a black curtain, was no longer glimpsed in the shortened version.

Editors deleted the scenes revealing Jehan's jealousy of his saintly brother, Dom Claude. Jehan even attempted to murder the archdeacon when the priest refused him the key to the King's treasure room during the climactic battle.

Phoebus' dream scene was excised in which he serenaded Esmeralda with a lute, unaware that Quasimodo had rescued her.

Even a few brief scenes with Quasimodo fell away from the release prints. While the Hunchback hid Esmeralda in the tower, he visited a merchant to trade his collection of candle-ends for some clothes for her. The merchant tried to cheat him, and the Hunchback nearly strangled the man. In another deleted scene, Quasimodo crept into Esmeralda's old room in the Court of Miracles and returned with the young Gypsy's little caged bird.

The reviews of the time were mostly positive. *Motion Picture World* said, "Here, then, is a picture that will live forever. Lon Chaney's portrayal of Quasimodo, the hunchback, is superb, not only a marvel of makeup such as is seldom seen upon the screen and stage, but a marvel of sympathetic acting."

Exhibitor Trade Review agreed: "A stupendous production!... The Quasimodo of Lon Chaney is a creature of horror, a weird monstrosity of ape-like ugliness, such a fantastically effective makeup as the screen has never known and in all human probability will never know again. Add to this the wonderful agility and terribly intense pantomimic ability of his impersonator, and you face a Quasimodo such as can only be imagined under the stress of a peculiarly vindictive nightmare."

Photoplay, *Time* and *Harrison's Report* all printed remarkably similar reviews, praising the impressive spectacle and sets, marveling that Hugo's melodrama, despite liberties taken by the screenwriters, provided such a sound story backbone and mostly, praising the incredible appearance and performance of Chaney's Quasimodo.

The most prominent naysayer was the show business newspaper, *Variety*. Sounding like the French nobility, preferring not to dwell on the unpleas-

This scene from *The Hunchback of Notre Dame* fell to the cutting room floor.

Chaney's version of Hugo's *The Hunchback of Notre Dame* is a notable achievement of the silent film in America.

antness of the lives surrounding them in the streets, *Variety* said, "...the total achieved seems to have been a huge—mistake. *The Hunchback of Notre Dame*... is a two-hour nightmare. It's murderous, hideous and repulsive. No children can stand its morbid scenes, and there are likely but few parents seeing it first who will permit their young to see it afterward. Mr. Chaney's... makeup as the Hunchback is propaganda for the wets. His misshapened figure from the hump on his back to the deadeyed eye on his face cannot stand off his acting nor his acrobatics, nor his general work of excellence thoughout this film. And when the hunchback dies, you see Jehan stab him not once, but twice and in the back or in the hump. Knives were plentiful in the reign of Louis XI, 1482, in France. So were the tramps, with Clopin as King of the Bums making the misery stand out. *The Hunchback of Notre Dame* is misery all the time, nothing but misery, tiresome, loathsome misery that doesn't make you feel any the better for it."

Actually, Chaney's version of Hugo's novel is a notable achievement of the silent film in America. Cinematically not as stylish or exciting as the epics of Griffith or De Mille, it still impresses with the accuracy and size of its sets and the direction of its crowds. Although the screenwriters blunt the tragedy of Esmeralda's story, the poignancy of the melodrama continues to move audiences, especially concerning the fierce but pathetic Quasimodo. Because of the repellent makeup and the intense anger of his performance, Chaney loses some of the sadness that would enhance Charles Laughton's later portrayal, but he certainly fascinates. Even the 1923 review in *Photoplay* notices this, stating, "He falls short, perhaps, in creating the sympathy which is due of the *Hunchback*, but he more than atones for this by the wonderful acting." When Chaney is on screen, the film is mesmerizing and surprising.

When he is not, at least the parade of characters and events hold interest until he appears again. The film suffers in comparison with the stylish 1939 remake by William Dieterle starring Laughton, but that version has the benefit of all the resources of a Hollywood sound studio at its artistic peak. Taken on its own, Chaney's version justifies the obvious care and labor in its creation.

The writer of *The Phantom of the Opera*, Gaston Leroux, was born on May 6, 1868 in Paris. His father, who did not marry his mother until June 13 of the same year, spent much of Gaston's childhood rebuilding an ancient castle near a small town called Valery-en-Caux where the future novelist's boyhood imagination ran free. Gaston graduated with high honors from his secondary school in Caen. His first article was published in the college paper, and his first short story saw print in the newspaper, *La Republique Francaise*.

He moved back to Paris to complete his studies, and on October 30, 1889 he received his law degree. When his father died the same year, Gaston's share of the estate came to over a million francs. He set the practice of law aside forever and pursued his love of writing. Unfortunately, he also loved the nightlife, and his penchant for gambling and bad investments eventually dissipated his inheritance. To make a living, he began what became a distinguished career as a crime reporter and war correspondent.

Leroux married a strict Catholic who became frustrated with his preoccupation with death, reincarnation and parallel universes. Shortly after he was named a "Chevalier of the Legion of Honor" for outstanding journalism, he and his wife separated. During his travels, Leroux met an adventurous woman named Jeanne Cayatte. Both Catholics, they kept their love affair discreet. However, their union did produce a son and a daughter.

After his first serialized novel was published in *Le Matin*, the paper for which he worked as a journalist, Leroux quit his job and concentrated on becoming a writer of fiction. Inspired by Poe's "The Murders in the Rue Morgue," Leroux wrote a locked-door mystery called *The Mystery of the Yellow Room* to "out-Poe Poe," as he told Jeanne. It concerned a young police reporter and amateur detective named Joseph Rouletabille, patterned after Poe's first literary crime-solver, C. Auguste Dupin. The serial became an overnight sensation, and Leroux wrote 26 more novels by 1924. In 1913, French producer Victorin Jasset made Leroux's *Balaoo* into a film, the first of 27 to be based on his work.

In 1909, Leroux, Jeanne and their children moved to the French Riviera and set up a home on Mont-Boron overlooking Nice. There, he wrote his most famous novel, *The Phantom of the Opera*.

Through one of his many contacts from his press days, Leroux gained permission to explore the depths of the Paris Opera House. With a few guides, he toured the scene docks, then wished to go into the lower cellars extending as deep as 70 feet below ground. The dark maze of labyrinths enthralled him.

During the Franco-Prussian war in 1870, the working class of Paris, calling themselves the Communards, revolted against the government of Napoleon III. They set up their headquarters in the unfinished Opera House and used the cellars to imprison and torture enemies of the people before being routed by the National Guard.

Leroux imagined a child being forgotten below after the prisoners were freed. The boy eventually went insane and lived in this underworld. Maybe as an adult, he became an architect and designed secret rooms and traps. He could use the old torture chambers on any unwanted intruders who might stumble into his dark domain.

Five stories below the stage, Leroux and his guides found a black lake which could only be viewed from above through barred grills. In the summer of 1861, only a few months after construction of the Opera House began, workers unearthed an underground stream which flooded the site. Charles Garnier, the designer of the theater, built a concrete foundation, sealed it with coal pitch and shifted the stage directly above the lake he had created. This allowed him to use hydraulics to operate the stage lifts. The guides showed Leroux the mechanisms by which the lake could be drained and the walls inspected. Workers used a small boat to travel along the lake. It was rumored that there was a secret room under the water that could only be entered when the lake was drained.

Leroux began to imagine what type of person could survive in such a gloomy and haunted atmosphere. A physician friend visiting Leroux gave him the physical and mental details. In an early German medical journal supplement called *Strahlentherapie*, he found photographs of victims of a disease known today as congenital porphyria. The symptoms included loss of muscle bulk which resulted in a skeletal appearance; severe sensitivity to sunlight which worsened the disease; a tendency for skin lesions and ulcers to mutilate the nose, ears, eyelids and lips; mental disorders ranging from mild hysteria to manic-depressive psychoses and delirium; and a jaundice producing pale yellowish skin.

Borrowing from the French classic, *Beauty and the Beast*, Leroux imagined a hideous genius whose obsessive love for an innocent young soprano caused him to unleash a reign of terror on the Paris Opera. He based this fiend partly on the legend of Faust. Faust was a brilliant and admirable man, but because of his old age, he could never attract the love of a beautiful girl. He made a pact with Satan, regained his youth and beauty, but his evil, selfish side controlled his behavior.

Erik, the Phantom of the Opera, has also turned away from God, in his case because of the repulsive features that have kept him from being loved. He is a brilliant man, a master of music and architecture and he indulges in evil to win the heart of a beautiful girl. His talent and intelligence allow him to become a law unto himself, living outside of society's rules. In the end, despite Erik's crimes, the innocent girl's single act of kindness to him causes him to question his hatred of man, his belief that love cannot exist for him, that there is no God and therefore, no good in the world. The revelation shatters his reality, and he dies, like Faust, repentant.

The book received a small printing in France in 1910 and did not sell well. In 1911, the Bobbs-Merrill Company published a translation in America that was positively reviewed, but again, the print run was very small. The book was soon out of print and forgotten—except by one of its 11-year-old readers, Irving Thalberg.

Over a decade later, even before the first day of production on *The Hunchback of Notre Dame*, Thalberg ordered a treatment and continuity script for *The Phantom of the Opera* by writer George Bronson-Howard. On December 1, 1922, as production geared up for *The Hunchback of Notre Dame*, Howard suddenly died. Thalberg set aside his screenplay for *The Phantom of the Opera* and concentrated on the picture at hand.

After the success of *The Hunchback of Notre Dame* and Thalberg's departure from Universal, Carl Laemmle needed to secure Lon Chaney for another movie. He had lost not only Thalberg, but directors Eric von Stroheim, Clarence Brown and Tod Browning to the new MGM. Chaney still freelanced, but Thalberg would definitely try to persuade him to sign a contract with his studio.

After learning that Thalberg had already started on the screenplay to *The Phantom of the Opera*, Laemmle ordered the new production chief, Julius Bernheim, to continue developing the project to lure Chaney to Universal. The first 11-page treatment by writers Bernard McConville and James Spearing was submitted on October 12, 1923, a month after the release of *The Hunchback of Notre Dame*. This version took numerous liberties with Leroux's story, making his young and innocent ingenue into a desirable diva who is interested in the occult and excited to be loved by Erik until she unmasks his monstrous face.

Aware of Thalberg's efforts on the property, Chaney was also interested in securing *The Phantom of the Opera* for himself. On November 22, 1923, he wired the Bobbs-Merrill Company inquiring as to the availability of the novel and price for the worldwide rights to the novel.

Chaney signed a one-picture deal with MGM to star in their first production, *He Who Gets Slapped*. Before the actor became an exclusive MGM player, Universal acted quickly. Negotiations between Chaney and Universal's New York office began in January 1924. Chaney wired his business manager, Alfred Grasso: "I was up to Universal and they wanted me to do *The Phantom of the Opera* for $100,000. Can we do it?" Grasso replied that the film could not be made for under $200,000. In fact, even that number was grossly inadequate if the production were to include even a fraction of the lavish sets and period costumes of *The Hunchback of Notre Dame*, which ended up costing $1.25 million.

Universal executives then rejected the treatment of *The Phantom of the Opera* as being too morbid and unbelievable for modern audiences. Instead, Bernheim offered Chaney $2,000 a week to star as Gwynplaine in an adaptation of Victor Hugo's novel, *The Man Who Laughs*. The story concerns a young prince whose mouth is cut into a permanent grin by Gypsies. The boy, Gwynplaine, is befriended by an old man. Together with a beautiful blind girl, they tour the provinces for years in a tent show. The blind girl and the grown-up Gwynplaine fall in love.

Laemmle, who had been disturbed by the darkness, violence and horror of *The Hunchback of Notre Dame*, loved what he considered a sweet story of a "laughing boy" and a kindly old man. Unfortunately, no one at Universal had bothered to secure the rights to the novel from the Duc d'Ayens, president of France's largest film studio. Universal managed to extend the deadline with Chaney to secure another title. This amendment to Chaney's contract cost them an additional $500 a week for his salary, and Chaney could pick his own project. He chose the novel Thalberg had bought for him in 1922, *The Phantom of the Opera*. Chaney rejected the treatment by McConville and Spearing, insisting that the script remain true to Leroux's original.

By July, Chaney was booked by MGM for *He Who Gets Slapped* to be followed by a vacation. On December 22, he was scheduled to begin *The Unholy Three* at MGM for director Tod Browning and then *The Monster* for Roland West in January 1925. This only gave Universal from October to December to finish their scenes with Chaney for *The Phantom of the Opera*. Laemmle ordered completion of the script, as well as all sets and scenes that did not include Chaney to be ready by August 1, 1924.

For the director, Laemmle chose Rupert Julian. He was born Percival T. Hayes on January 25, 1889 in Aukland, New Zealand. His father was a sheep and cattle ranchman who sent him to the Catholic Seminary to train for the priesthood. Not suited for his father's ambitions, he joined the Australian army to fight in the Boer War instead. He was captured by the Boers, escaped and worked his way back to South Africa as a seaman. Having reached the rank of Lieutenant, he left the army to try several careers, including barber, sailor, gold prospector and tea salesman. Finally, he joined a traveling show as an actor and stagehand. He was engaged by the J.C. Williamson Company and eventually appeared with Tyrone Power, Sr. on Broadway in *Julius Caesar*.

When the company arrived in California, Julian met Philip Smalley and performed in some of his pictures for Universal. Eventually, Julian not only acted, but directed and produced as well. His film, *We Are French*, became a big hit for Laemmle who offered him a steady job. Julian went with the Smalley Company to Famous Players–Lasky, instead and did not return to Universal until two years later as a contract player. Specializing in heavies, he came into contact with Chaney, with whom he often competed for the same parts.

By 1918, Julian reached the top of Universal's directors list after starring in and directing *The Kaiser, the Beast of Berlin* in which he cast Chaney in a bit part. In 1922, when Irving Thalberg fired Erich von Stroheim as director of *The Merry Go-Round* for insisting on shooting in sequence, the project was given to Julian to complete. The picture did well at the box-office, and Julian was given full credit even though much of von Stroheim's footage remained. Julian was given a raise and permission to film a story that he co-wrote called *Love and Glory* in 1923, followed by *Hell's Highroad* in 1924.

Carl Laemmle, Jr. recalled how Julian got the job of director of *The Phantom of the Opera*:

> There were some problems with the rights to *The Man Who Laughs* and everyone was in a panic. My father had bought thousands of uniforms, guns, swords and boots from the deposed Austrian Emperor Karl—he even bought his Imperial coach—all for use in *Merry Go-Round* for von Stroheim. They were actual things used in the war. Now they were just sitting in the prop and costume department gathering dust. My father was not well at this time and didn't have his usual patience during the bickering and sniveling at the executive meetings—all he knew was that Thalberg had bought *Phantom*, they had no rights for *The Man Who Laughs* and he had committed to theater owners that Lon Chaney would make another picture. Julian had simply suggested that since all the props and costumes that HE used on *Merry Go-Round* were just a wasted expense sitting in that warehouse, that they could be modified to look French if they make *Phantom*. That was all my father needed to hear—a way out! and a way to save money! and that's how Julian got the job—just luck, being able to grovel at the right time with the magic words.—SAVE MONEY—I personally would have chosen (Tod) Browning or (Clarence) Brown, but that's hindsight and I was more concerned with my father's health and not involved in making pictures at that point. Chaney directed all the good scenes that remained in the picture anyway.

To get ready for the August 1 start date, the script department took the project from McConville and Spearing and gave it to Raymond L. Schrock. This writer called his version *The Phantom Swordsman*, and he attempted to make it a historical picture in the vein of *The Hunchback of Notre Dame* by setting it during the war between France and Prussia in 1870. Leroux's ineffectual hero, Raoul, became a vigorous man of action in the Douglas Fairbanks mold; Erik, disfigured by a bayonet when he was three, disarmed Raoul in a sword duel; and there were numerous battle scenes and real historical characters such as Victor Hugo and Napoleon. The scope of the picture and the deviations from Leroux's original made this version unacceptable to Laemmle and the heads of the scenario department.

The next writer assigned was Grant Carpenter, an acquaintance of Chaney's since they made *Bobbie of the Ballet* 10 years earlier. After discussing the script with Chaney, Carpenter reinstated elements of the book including the ending where Christine's kiss destroys Erik. The Franco-Prussian War subplot was removed and the story trimmed to enhance the love interest and prevent the project from reaching the budgetary highs of *The Hunchback of Notre Dame*.

Carpenter's 10-page treatment was given to Rupert Julian's choice for writer, Elliot Clawson. Clawson had been writing scripts at Universal since the opening of the studio in 1915. He was one of the first to adopt Thalberg's method of writing by having as much

Filming of *The Phantom of the Opera* was worked around Lon Chaney's busy schedule.

information on paper as possible. In that way, the script could be a blueprint for all departments involved in production. Working directly from the book, Clawson turned in a first draft shooting script on August 22, 1924.

The August 1 deadline was pushed back because of an inability to find a suitable ending. In one version, the Phantom steals Christine and drives wildly through the streets of Paris in a stolen coach as the angry mob pursues him. When the coach crashes, the Phantom attempts to climb a building but is shot by the leader of the mob. In a rewrite, the Phantom finds refuge in Christine's home after the coach crashes but dies as Raoul, the Persian and the mob break in. The third ending had the Phantom freeing Christine and Raoul from his underground lair after she gently kisses him, and the mob arrives to find him dead at his organ from a broken heart. Since this conclusion was closest to Leroux's novel, it was the first one approved for filming.

Extensive production meetings had been underway even before Clawson's first script. Three art directors shared credit on the film. E.E. Sheeley, who designed most of *The Hunchback of Notre Dame* and his assistant, Sidney Ullman, secured a copy of the blueprints for the Paris Opera, which were published by the architect. With these, which were mounted in a huge book about four feet by five feet, they were able to reconstruct the Grand Staircase of the entrance, the Auditorium of the Opera, the exterior and the surrounding city. The first steel and concrete stage was built on the Universal lot expressly to house the interior of the Opera House and the Grand Staircase sets. Eleven sculptors and scenic artists designed the ornate interior of the Opera House, the Grand Staircase and a full-scale reproduction of the Apollo statue for a scene atop the roof of the Opera House.

But much of the action took place backstage and in the Phantom's underground world. Ben Carre, who was listed initially as Art Director and ultimately given credit as "Consulting Artist," designed the underground and backstage sets. Carre was born in Paris in 1883. He began working in 1900 as an assistant for Antelier Amable's Artists Studio in Paris. Inspired by the early films of Lumiere and Méliès, he took a position in 1906 at Gaumount Studios painting backdrops and designing sets. When the studio opened a branch of their Eclair Productions in Fort Lee, New Jersey, Carre went to America with them. His work with director Maurice Tourneur eventually brought him to Hollywood. His designs could be seen in Tourneur's *Treasure Island* with Lon Chaney in 1920 and in *The Light in the Dark* in 1922, also with Chaney.

Carre recalled his assignment on *The Phantom of the Opera*:

> Gaston Leroux's *Le Fantone de l' Opera* had been one of my favorite books.... I had hoped that Tourneur would be the director, for I knew it was a natural for films. Once we arrived in Hollywood in 1918, I suggested it to him many times....
>
> In 1924, I was about to sail for Nice when I received a telegram from Universal asking for my help. One of the art directors knew that I had worked on the actual sets at the real Paris Opera House... Knowing the original props and backdrops for the operas that were performed at the Paris Opera, the costume, dummy, prop rooms, as well as having seen the original underground lake which protected the Phantom in the book gave me a marvelous opportunity and I agreed to the project.
>
> I did a total of 24 sketches, but even though I knew the real building, many of my designs were right out of imagination. I knew the book well also, and tried to envision Gaston Leroux's original novel for the Phantom's chambers, five floors beneath the Opera stage. Well, I was and am very pleased with the results, for they did not use my sketches as a basis to design the sets—they copied them exactly; to the point where people are still searching the real Opera House for the rooms that came out of my imagination!

Along with Chaney's incredible makeup and performance, the sets and shots designed by Ben Carre helped Rupert Julian create one of the most visually memorable movies of the silent era. Not only were the sets constructed exactly as Carre designed them, but they were also filmed from exactly the angle of his sketches, creating such unforgettable images as the Phantom's shadow glimpsed backstage by the ballerinas in the mouth of a giant prop dragon from Wagner's *Der Ring des Nibelungen*; the Phantom's dark figure running across a suspended catwalk after the fall of the chandelier; the mechanism and long stone stairway behind the mirror in Christine's dressing room; the Phantom leading Christine on a black stallion down the ramps used to move animals up to the stage; the Phantom and Christine gliding in a gondola along the still, inky underground lake that reflects the stone arches around it; and a stagehand cranking a huge wheel to raise the curtain which slowly reveals the shadow of a hanging man on the backstage wall behind him.

For the Phantom's appearance, Chaney created what is, along with Jack Pierce's concept for the Frankenstein Monster, the most brilliant makeup design in film history. In the novel, Leroux described the Phantom as looking "extraordinarily thin and his dress coat hangs on a skeleton frame. His eyes are so deep that you can hardly see the fixed pupils. You just see two big black holes, as in a dead man's skull. His skin, which is stretched across the bones like a drumhead, is not white but a nasty yellow. His nose is so little worth talking about that you can't see it side-face; the absence of that nose is a horrible thing to look at."

The sets and shots designed by Ben Carre for *The Phantom of the Opera* create one of the most visually memorable movies of the silent era.

As in all of his work, Chaney tried to duplicate the author's description as closely as possible. To create the prominent cheekbones of a skull, he used the same cotton and collodion method as in *The Hunchback of Notre Dame*. Shading around his eyes with a dark color liner gave a recessed look which was further emphasized with a thin line of highlight under his lower eyelashes. The jagged teeth were made of gutta-percha and were accentuated by using a dark lining color on his lower lip. A skull cap higher than Chaney's head had a wig sewn into it and a fine piece of muslin on the edge so that it could be blended onto Chaney's forehead. His ears were glued back to make his face appear even longer and thinner.

In an article written in 1974, Charles Van Enger, the director of photography, explained some of Chaney's methods: "He suffered like hell too. He had two wires under his nose that pulled up—that went up the bridge of the nose, were taped down with makeup to hide them and then up under his bald wig where they were tied, like an Indian headband with a thin leather strap. Some days that thing would bleed like hell. This thing with the nose up like that all the time and these rubber stoppers shoved in his nostrils; his ears taped back and those wires in his mouth to hold the (lips) back—I don't know how he stood the pain. But he did and we never had to stop shooting any of his scenes. We all had such respect for him that no one would dare make a mistake in lighting or with the camera. Everything was checked and double checked before he even got on the set."

The actor had a clause in his contract forbidding publication of photographs of his makeup before the film had played for a specific time. This included advertising posters as

Leroux described the Phantom as looking "extraordinarily thin and his dress coat hangs on a skeleton frame. His eyes are so deep that you can hardly see the fixed pupils."

well. Reporters were so curious during filming on the closed set that Chaney was forced to make a public statement: "It is not fair to have me experiment, work up a makeup that is really something of an achievement, then spoil the public's appreciation of it by broadcasting pictures of it, so that by the time the picture is released there is no surprise to it. In fact, it is old news. I suffer a lot in this makeup and it's hard work to apply and to wear. Why should I lose its value to me as an actor?"

Principal photography finally began on October 29, 1924 and lasted for 10 weeks. As Charles Van Enger remembered: "Chaney and Julian hated each other from the start. First Julian would go to the front office and complain about Chaney. Then when they went to

Chaney—and they had to go to him if they wanted to talk to him—he would blow a gasket. When Chaney had some personal family trouble, Julian gave him a bunch of crap about leaving the set. Chaney was too much of a professional to walk off the picture, but the argument that followed sent even the strongest grip running off the set... So they asked me to be the messenger boy. Julian would tell me to go in and tell Chaney to do this, and Chaney would say, 'Tell him to go and screw himself. I'll do it the way I want to do it.' Now that went on the whole picture... After the major blowups between the cast and Julian, we set up our own formula to keep things going on schedule. Julian would take care of most of the scenes for Mary Philbin, Chaney would direct his own big scenes and the assistant directors would handle the crowds."

Like Patsy Ruth Miller on *The Hunchback of Notre Dame*, Mary Philbin, the 21-year-old actress from Stroheim's *The Merry Go-Round* who was cast as Christine in *The Phantom of the Opera*, remembered Chaney's direction more than Julian's. She wrote in 1989:

> I do not remember much about Rupert Julian. Mr. Chaney used to insist that we speak all of the lines that were written in the script. Sometimes he would have pages of *The Phantom of the Opera* book copied by the typist and distribute them to give us ideas on what was happening—to give us some background on what our reactions would be. It was almost like a play where we had rehearsals, learning lines. Often we were on the sets for 18 hours! I do not have too many vivid memories of Mr. Chaney away from the studio. But I do remember the scenes he directed...

According to Philbin, Chaney talked her through their scenes together when his face was concealed by the mask. She wrote, "Since he had the mask on, no one could tell that he was talking to me and after all we didn't have to worry about the microphones, for there were none—we could say whatever we wanted. When it came to the famous unmasking scene I did not have to act. What I mean by that is, Mr. Chaney never prepared me for his makeup for the Phantom. I knew it was horrible and I could see the yellowish color of his skin behind his neck... Well, all you have to do is look at the picture and you can see my reaction when I first saw what he had done to his face! But it wasn't just his face. I will never forget the horrible rage that came from his eyes and the cry that he let out just before he turned around seemed to come from all around the set. Not from him. It was almost inhuman."

Charles Van Enger also remembered that scene: "I could see Lon getting into the part before she even got close to the mask. His feet were tensing and jerking under the organ bench. His breath was contained and it looked like his back would explode any second. I don't know what or who he was thinking about, but I wouldn't want that fury directed at me. So by the time Mary rips the mask off, I thought she was going to faint dead away. She almost did."

Chaney also directed Philbin's reaction shot to her first sight of the Phantom. Charles Van Enger recalled, "...Julian couldn't get through to her. So Chaney waits until Julian is gone and asked us not to strike the set. It was the end of the day and I was told not to shoot anymore. But this was Lon asking so we waited. The next day Mary shows up and takes her place on the floor, only with Lon directing. He tells me to keep the cameras rolling and before Mary knows what is happening, he walks up to her so fast, hot as hell and stops right out of camera range. He lets out a tirade of profanity that you wouldn't believe. He told her that she was the worst actress he'd ever seen. She was wasting everybody's time. She should get on the train and go back to wherever she came from and on and on. Finally little Mary,

Mary Philbin as Christine

almost bursting into tears, starts to get up and said something like she was going to tell Mr. Laemmle and Lon spins around, raising his hand like he is going to hit her. 'You ain't gonna do nothing when I'm through with you!' Mary must have thought he would really have hit her, for she fell back holding her hand in front of her face in mortal terror... and that is the scene that is in the picture. When it was caught on film, Lon instinctively knew it and in an instant the rage stopped and he comforted Mary, explaining what was really going on and from that point on she opened up to him and listened. Out of respect, not fear... He never really let her get too comfortable so that her fear would always project to the theater audience."

The first take of the unmasking shot was lit for and photographed in two-strip Technicolor. Dr. Herbert Kalmus, Daniel Comstock and W.A. Wescott formed the Technicolor company in 1915. Their camera utilized a beam splitter behind the lens which exposed two separate positive films simultaneously but separately, one sensitive to reds and the other to greens. By 1924, Dr. Kalmus, the inventor of the process, had begun using a special stock made for him by Eastman Kodak which was thinner than standard 35mm film. The two thin films were cemented together, combining the reds and greens into a single strip. The one problem was the thickness of the cemented film.

Dr. Kalmus had guaranteed Laemmle that his own men would be waiting to rush replacement prints anywhere in the country if the thicker Technicolor scenes spliced into prints of *The Phantom of the Opera* caused damage when they hit the projector sprockets. Despite the fact that the process was three times as expensive as black and white and required three times as much light, Laemmle ordered the ballet, opera and Masked Ball sequences shot in Technicolor.

After the first Technicolor take of the unmasking, Chaney decided not to use the process for that shot. Charles Van Enger explained: "He used a combination of silver and yellow, which came out looking like a corpse in black and white, but he did not like the results in the early Technicolor. You could see the lines where his skull cap fit his head and when he put the bobby pins or wires in his nose and taped them down, the Technicolor lights were so hot that the putty kept melting and it would come off. One person that you did not want to see mad was Chaney, and anything that held up production made him mad so no color unmasking!"

Ironically, even though the original 1925 release contained a black-and-white take of the unmasking shot, the 1929 re-release used a black-and-white print of the color take so

"Mary must have thought [Chaney] would really have hit her, for she fell back holding her hand in front of her face in mortal terror... and that is the scene that is in the picture."

as not to cut up the original negative. Comparing the two versions, which were from very similar camera angles, Chaney's expression in the color take was much more ferocious and frightening.

Principal photography was completed shortly before the new year. Editors began assembling domestic and foreign negatives from the 350,000 feet of exposed film. Posters of the Phantom in the costume of the Red Death began appearing thoughout New York City, and two of Broadway's largest electric light signs proclaimed that the picture would premiere in February at the Globe Theater.

The premiere cut ran 12 reels, slightly over two hours. In order to gauge an audience's reaction, Universal arranged a sneak preview at a Los Angeles theater on January 7. Even before the unmasking, Universal executives felt the movie was too intense for its audience.

In an early scene, Christine visits her father's grave at Perros after dark. She believes that his spirit has sent her the Angel of Music who coaches her from behind the walls of her dressing room. Actually, of course, her Angel of Music is the homicidal Phantom. As Christine prays by her father's tombstone, Raoul secretly watches her from the dark. We see the shadow of the Phantom against the church wall playing a violin for his protege whose father is buried with his own violin. When Raoul attempts to catch the Phantom, the madman disappears. Skulls roll from a heap of bones to Raoul's feet. As Raoul spots the Phantom at the church door, the fiend suddenly turns, holding a skull in front of him so that it looks like he has the skull for a face. Then, the Phantom throws the death's head at Raoul.

The Phantom of the Opera's **Masked Ball was filmed in Technicolor**

Several people in the Los Angeles audience were so disturbed by this scene that they left the theater or fainted. Universal settled some lawsuits out of court as a result. Even Chaney agreed on the scene's removal so as not to take away from the impact of the later unmasking.

The Perros graveyard scene was followed by the Phantom dropping the giant chandelier on the audience, the Masked Ball with the entrance of the Phantom disguised as the Red Death and then the Phantom's kidnapping of Christine and the unmasking shown in flashback when Christine tells Raoul about it on the roof of the Paris Opera. Executives felt that this was too much unrelieved tension.

Another frightening scene occurring early in the preview showed the strangulation of Joseph Buquet as he descends through a trap door while investigating the sound of the Phantom playing the violin. This scene also was eventually cut.

Toward the end, when Raoul and the Persian are venturing into the dark catacombs, the Opera rat catcher appears from the shadows. His lantern illuminates only his face as he drives something forward with a stick. Raoul and the Persian look down to see a horde of rats scurrying before him. After a reaction of disgust from the preview audience, all shots of the rats were removed, but the scene was retained. The title card was rewritten, identifying the mysterious figure as a "messenger from the shadows" who warns them to turn back. Strangely, the reaction shot of Raoul and the Persian looking down at the rat catcher's feet in horror was kept in the final version.

The biggest disappointment for the preview audience was Chaney's preferred ending. The viewers' cards from the preview were summed up in a memo from Universal's New

The Phantom takes Christine to his underground lair in *The Phantom of the Opera*.

York office: "The ending is not logical or convincing. A monster such as the Phantom, the official torturer, etc. and who delighted in crime, could not have been redeemed through a woman's kiss, nor could a girl who had witnessed his diabolical acts have been moved to kiss him merely because he dropped his head sadly. His death rang false moreover. Better to have kept him a devil to the end."

Some re-editing was ordered and another preview was held in Los Angeles on January 26. This time, in the end, the Persian shot the Phantom while he sat at the organ. Again, the audience felt let down. Preview cards were sent to a furious Carl Laemmle in New York. His personal secretary, Miss Hughes, recalled, "He had always felt that Lon Chaney would make up something too horrible for the post-war public, and now he felt he was right."

The February New York premiere was canceled, and production chief Julius Bernheim was replaced by John Wray. Lon Chaney himself went on radio on February 14 to promote the film. Chaney's radio address caused excitement from the public, but Wray had no idea what to do with the movie.

Laemmle quickly replaced John Wray with Raymond Schrock, one of the first writers on the project. Schrock convinced Laemmle that what the picture needed was more action, comedy and romance. He hired Ernest Sedgwick, who had written and directed 20 low-budget, highly profitable Hoot Gibson westerns, to guide the new material.

Comic actor Chester Conklin played Raoul's valet for laughs, as did Vola Vale as his maid. Schrock hired Ward Crane to play a Russian Count who competes with Raoul for Christine's affections. In a series of silly complications unrelated to the main story, a double playing the Phantom hires an Apache to stab Raoul in a bar which causes a brawl. Despite agreeing to fight him in a dual, the Count helps Raoul duke it out in the barroom since they are both of the nobility. The next morning, the Count shoots Raoul during the dual, deliberately hitting his rival in the belt buckle to spare his life.

Even with the introduction of sound and color, the various remakes have never equaled this perfect match of form and content achieved by the 1925 *Phantom*.

Sedgwick also filmed a clearer explanation as to why Christine initially replaces Carlotta. As Carlotta walks back from the manager's office, the Phantom grabs her arm and warns her not to sing. She runs away screaming and informs the managers that she is too ill to go on. Later, she suspects that it was Raoul who threatened her in order to advance Christine's career.

The Phantom's first kidnapping of Christine and the unmasking were put in chronological order instead of being told as a flashback at the Masked Ball. The Perros graveyard and Joseph Buquet's strangulation were removed, never to be seen again.

Julian had originally shot an alternate ending in which the Phantom flees from the mob in Raoul's commandeered coach. The carriage turns over, and the Phantom runs from his pursuers until he is chased down a landing to the Seine river. In one last desperate gesture of defiance, the Phantom takes something from inside his coat that the crowd assumes is a grenade. When he laughingly opens his hand to reveal it empty, the Phantom is attacked by the mob, beaten to death and thrown into the river. This exciting and satisfying climax replaced the ending in the Phantom's lair.

Universal planned another premiere, but by now, all of the major theaters in New York and Los Angeles were booked months in advance. Desperate to find a city, Universal finally settled for the Curran Theatre in San Francisco. The gala opening took place on April 26, 1925. Unfortunately, the Universal publicity department's advance advertisements claiming that the picture was "proving a sensational success... playing twice daily to exceptionally large audiences at prices ranging up to $1.50 per seat" proved to be premature. In fact, in one week, the film took in a paltry $5,000 while other films earned three and four times that amount in San Francisco theaters. The Curran Theatre was locked into a four-week exclusive contract, and the film limped along until finally finishing its engagement on May 23.

Of course, audiences and critics were completely confused and impatient with almost everything added by Schrock and Sedgwick. In an effort to appeal to every taste, they had diluted the strong flavors of mystery, suspense and horror that were the film's strengths. By now, the project had cost so much money that the future of the company depended on its success. It was booked into the Astor Theater in New York for yet another "premiere" in September, and Laemmle ordered Schrock to pull it into a showable form.

Schrock handed the problem over to editor Lois Webber. She immediately removed all of Sedgwick's new footage with the exception of some additions to Julian's mob chase ending. Shifting scenes around to efficiently and suspensefully tell the story, she ordered new title cards. She even briefly considered reinstating the Garden of Perros scene, but Chaney still felt it muted the unmasking.

The Phantom of the Opera **emerges from its troubled production history as the greatest horror film of the silent era.**

When Laemmle viewed Webber's final cut, he was overjoyed. The movie worked! It was mysterious, romantic, frightening and spectacular. In New York, he launched the biggest merchandising campaign in the history of motion pictures, slapping the title on everything from shoes to candy to radios to lip rouge.

The reviews were positive with very few exceptions. *Film Daily* said, "A marvelous money getting picture. Chaney's makeup and character, while repulsive to perhaps some, is a great piece of work." *Exhibitors Trade Review* agreed: "A super ghost story has been made into a really great picture. It will thrill and chill audiences with its fascinating horror. And they'll like it...Chaney is wonderfully effective in the title role. His much heralded makeup for the part is sufficiently repellent to satisfy the greatest cravings... He is indeed a forceful villain and at all times dominates the action."

The film's effectiveness as a horror movie was emphasized in many of the reviews. *New York World* said, "If this boy (Chaney) doesn't thrill you with his underground-kidnapping of the beautiful Parisian opera singer he will positively, and I guarantee it, send you home determined to leave the lights burning all night long." And *Harrison's Reports* wrote, "If you have been looking for a thriller, the kind that will make your patron's hair stand on end, *The Phantom of the Opera* is the one...Mr. Lon Chaney's role is terrible; the makeup of his face is hideous; but he is fascinating."

As with *The Hunchback of Notre Dame*, *Variety* was offended by the picture: "Universal has turned out another horror...Lon Chaney is again the 'goat' in the matter, no matter if it

The Phantom of the Opera **finds its perfect expression in the silent cinema.**

is another tribute to his character acting...It is impossible to believe there are a majority of picturegoers who prefer this revolting sort of a tale on the screen. It is better for any exhibitor to pass up this film or 100 like it than to have one patron pass up his theatre through it."

Variety was definitely in the minority, however. *The Phantom of the Opera* was chosen as one of the top 10 movies of the year by *Film Daily*, *Photoplay*, *Movie Monthly*, *Screenland*, *Motion Picture News*, *Moving Picture World*, *Exhibitors Trade Review*, *Reel Journal*, *Motion Picture Bulletin*, *Film Mercury* and *National Board of Review*.

And Laemmle's investment finally paid off. After eventually costing $632,357 with retakes, the film grossed over two million, more even than *The Hunchback of Notre Dame*, giving the Laemmles a year that was never topped in profits and box-office receipts. To ride on the success, Universal quickly reissued their other Chaney films, *The Hunchback of Notre Dame*, *The Shock* and *Outside the Law*.

Even though the picture was a whopping success in America, a botched publicity stunt killed its chances in England. When the film was sent to Britain with studio executive James Bryson, Laemmle feared that the print might be stolen. Scotland Yard refused to help, and England's War Office also denied cooperation.

An unnamed employee of Universal's London office told the local territorial regiment in Southampton that they would be filmed by a Universal newsreel if they would accompany the print to London. As the cameras turned, Bryson and the film were greeted by the sort of fanfare reserved for royalty. The regiment escorted Bryson and the cans of celluloid by train. When the armored car detachment was canceled, the regiment proceeded by foot with the print to London, all captured by the Universal newsreel. Unfortunately, the English press and government were less than amused by this misuse of official troops. Calls for an inquiry and boycott resulted in Universal being forced to pull the picture from the English

market, costing the company huge revenues. In 1930, Britain finally allowed the re-edited, part-talkie version to be shown, but that was little consolation to Laemmle.

The Phantom of the Opera emerges from its troubled production history as the greatest horror film of the silent era. As in a dark legend or fairy tale, the power of its mysterious, shadowy setting and grandly demented villain overcome any lapses in logical story development or character motivation. The rendering of these elements by Chaney and Carre are appropriately larger than life. Ironically for a story involving singing, *The Phantom of the Opera* finds its perfect expression in the silent cinema. The grand, unrealistic gestures and visuals match the romantic passions of Erik, Christine and Raoul. Chaney understands the type of gothic atmosphere appropriate for these wild events and directs his movements like a ballet, posing Mary Philbin as his dancing partner in melodrama. Even with the introduction of sound and color, the various remakes have never equaled this perfect match of form and content achieved by the 1925 version. Bravely trying to rewrite the story to make sense logically and psychologically, they only succeed in blunting the power found in the original.

CHAPTER 6
THE WEIRDEST SHOW ON EARTH

Charles Albert Browning was born in Louisville, Kentucky, on July 12, 1880. Infatuated with a dancer in a sideshow, he left home at the age of 16 to literally join the circus, or more precisely, a traveling carnival, as a roustabout and occasional barker. He changed his name to "Tod" Browning, started performing as a clown, then as a contortionist, and even allowed himself to be buried alive for one or two days as the "Hypnotic Living Corpse." He eventually entered vaudeville where he performed the same acts on stage as well as doing comedy and song and dance.

He met D.W. Griffith in 1913 and joined his fledgling team of filmmakers as an actor, stuntman and assistant director. After journeying with Griffith to Hollywood, he began directing his own two-reelers such as *The Lucky Transfer*, *The Living Death* and *The Burned Hand* in 1915.

Browning's new income allowed him to indulge his love of gambling, liquor and fast cars. On the foggy night of June 16, 1915, Browning drunkenly plowed his roadster into a flatbed car loaded with street rails, killing his passenger, Griffith actor Elmer Booth, and severely injuring himself and second passenger, George A. Seigmann, another member of the Griffith unit.

Film historians have theorized that the accident may have resulted in the loss of Browning's genitals, a trauma that turned him to alcoholism and an obsession with stories of sexual frustration and symbolic forms of castration. He never had children, but he remained married to the same woman until the end of his life, certainly a disconcerting situation for her if the castration tale is correct.

Browning wore full dentures from an early age, possibly as a result of the collision. According to Freudian psychology, dental injuries usually have disturbing implications in the unconscious mind. For men, teeth can symbolize hardness and aggression. The loss of a man's teeth might be experienced as a kind of castration. Whether the emasculation was real or psychological, it continually showed up as a theme in Browning's work as writer and director.

After a long convalescence, Browning returned to movies, writing films such as *The Mystery of the Leaping Fish* for other directors. The plot of that particular work involves Douglas Fairbanks as private detective Coke Ennyday who shoots cocaine into the palm of his hand periodically to assist him in solving a case involving opium smugglers. Ironically or deliberately, Griffith cast Browning less than a year after the accident as the driver who recklessly races Mae Marsh to save her husband from the gallows at the conclusion of his masterpiece, *Intolerance*.

The following year, in 1917, Browning co-directed his first feature, *Jim Bludso*, a Civil War drama. He then moved to Metro Pictures where he directed *The Jury of Fate* in 1917, *The Legion of Death*, *Revenge* and *The Eyes of Mystery*, all in 1918. The last was a haunted house melodrama that would foreshadow his more macabre work to come.

In 1919, Universal hired Browning to finish *Which Woman* for ailing director Harry A. Pollard. Browning stayed at Universal to direct *The Wicked Darling*, a gangster story that initiated his long collaboration with Lon Chaney. In their first effort together, Chaney was the villain opposite Universal star Priscilla Dean, who played a female jewel thief with a heart of gold.

Browning's alcoholism led to his work becoming sporadic, though his first epic, *The Virgin of Stamboul*, was released to great success in 1920. His next picture reunited him

Chaney portrayed a Chinaman and a gangster in the Tod Browning–directed *Outside the Law*.

with Chaney, who played both a kindly Chinaman and a vicious gangster in the Priscilla Dean vehicle, *Outside the Law*. After a tremendously violent gunfight at the end, Browning used editing to show the Chinaman kill the gangster, both played by Chaney. The Chinaman's character, Ah Wing, was billed as "Guess Who?" The film received generally positive reviews and did extraordinarily well at the box-office.

Nevertheless, Universal no longer considered Browning dependable due to his drinking. His last film for the company, *The White Tiger*, sat on the shelf for over a year, unreleaseable in the form in which Browning delivered it. The director's alcoholism cost him the assignment of Universal's biggest picture, *The Hunchback of Notre Dame*, even after the studio trade publication had announced him as its director.

"I made an ass of myself," Browning later admitted. At a New Year's Eve party at the St. Francis Hotel in San Francisco, Browning became so drunkenly obnoxious that an assistant manager of the hotel asked him to keep it down. In a tellingly symbolic gesture worthy of one of his later films, Browning yanked out his false teeth, both uppers and lowers, threw them at the man and told him, "Go bite yourself!"

Alice Browning, who had given up her own prospects as an actress to help support her husband's career, learned that Browning had indulged in an affair with beautiful 15-year-old Asian starlet Anna May Wong. What type of affair was this if the castration theory was true? Be that as it may, Mrs. Browning still had her family to support her and in late 1923, she left him. Browning managed to secure a one-picture contract with Goldwyn for *The Day of Faith*, which received scathing reviews and flopped.

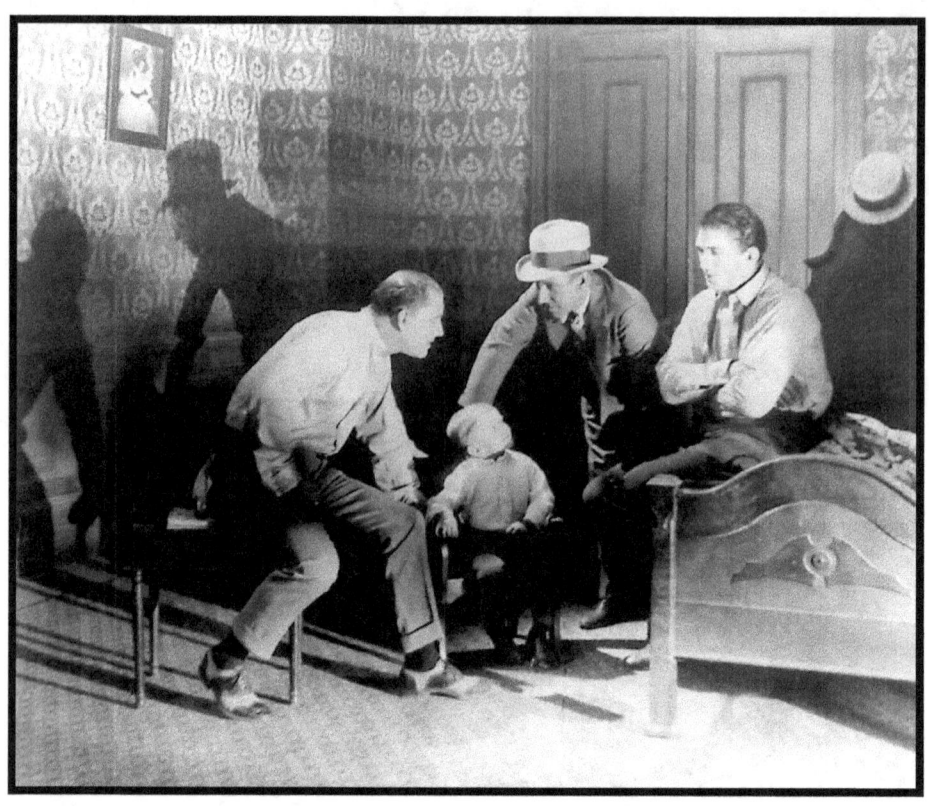

Lon Chaney and Harry Earles (center) in *The Unholy Three*

Finally taking stock of his failing fortunes, Browning stopped drinking for good. He successfully completed *The Dangerous Flirt* for Gothic Pictures, a film that was surprisingly adult regarding the sexual problems of a newly married couple. Seeing that her husband had given up the bottle and gone back to work, Mrs. Browning returned to him and received a part in his next movie, *Silk Stocking Sal*, another story about jewel thieves.

In 1925, Browning approached Irving Thalberg at the newly formed Metro-Goldwyn-Mayer studios to sell him on a film of Aaron "Tod" Robbins' strange best-selling novel of 1917, *The Unholy Three*. Thalberg saw the potential of the story as a Lon Chaney vehicle, and he bought the rights for $10,000. The young production head warily offered Browning a one-picture contract at a salary of $6,500, less than half his price at Goldwyn, plus a $3,500 incentive bonus if Browning completed the picture on time and on budget.

Browning could not quite manage to do that, but he did create a stunningly original crime story that proved a critical and box-office sensation. Chaney plays a ventriloquist dressed as a kindly old lady who sells supposedly talking parrots to rich customers. When the parrots cannot talk once taken home, Chaney and his partners, a vicious midget dressed as a baby and a simple-minded strongman who protects the little man, visit the wealthy families and secretly clean out their safes of jewelry.

The film generated a spectacular profit for MGM of $328,000 even after the deduction of studio overhead. In addition, it instantly re-established Browning as a commercially viable director. The studio exercised its first three-picture option on Browning's services, raising his salary to $10,000 per film. This was the beginning of a Browning-Chaney association at MGM that would produce some of the best films in both men's careers: *The Blackbird*, *The*

Road to Manderlay, *The Unknown*, *London After Midnight*, *The Big City*, *West of Zanzibar* and *Where East is East*.

Like *The Unholy Three*, most of these movies involve bizarre characters or subject matter, but only three of them cross over into the morbid to qualify as horror. The first and perhaps most powerful of these is *The Unknown* in 1927. Still an extraordinarily disturbing and fascinating work, it literalizes Freud's psychological theories from his 1919 essay, "The Uncanny," while rendering the classic Browning atmosphere of backstage life at the circus.

In his essay, Freud wrote that "dismembered limbs, a severed head, a hand cut off at the wrist... all these have something peculiarly uncanny about them... As we already know, this kind of uncanniness springs from its proximity to the castration complex." The original story by Browning on which he based *The Unknown* was called "Alonso the Armless," and that title gave a more accurate description of the Freudian nightmare cooked up by this carnival barker turned filmmaker.

The story begins in a Spanish circus which features an armless entertainer named Alonzo, played by Chaney. Alonzo performs a precision knife-throwing and sharpshooting act, handling the blades and rifles adroitly with his bare feet. In the opening scene, Alonzo fires knives and bullets with unerring precision at his beautiful assistant, Nanon, played by young Joan Crawford, while the two revolve on a rotating platform. The phallic barrage severs articles of her clothing and at the end of Alonzo's symbolic undressing of her, she is attired only in revealing undergarments.

In fact, Alonzo does have arms. Only his sinister dwarf assistant, Cojo, knows this fact. Every day, Cojo must bind Alonzo's arms into a tight leather corset to maintain the deception. Alonzo has two reasons for this illusion. First, on one of his hands, he possesses a double thumb. The prints from this distinctive anomaly could identify him as the perpetrator of previous, unidentified crimes. The second reason for Alonzo's disguise is that it keeps him close to Nanon, whom he secretly desires, for this lovely young performer suffers from a morbid repulsion to men's hands. "Men! The beasts!" she tells an approving Alonzo after being groped by the handsome strongman, Malabar. "God would show wisdom if He took the hands from all of them!"

In the original story, Browning and his scenerist, Waldemar Young, intended that Alonzo have a claw. The final choice of a double thumb seems yet more evidence of the possible influence of Freud's essay on Browning. In it, Freud writes that doubling is an imaginative defense against the feared loss of the self, or a part of the self.

Chaney as the "armless" Alonzo in *The Unknown*

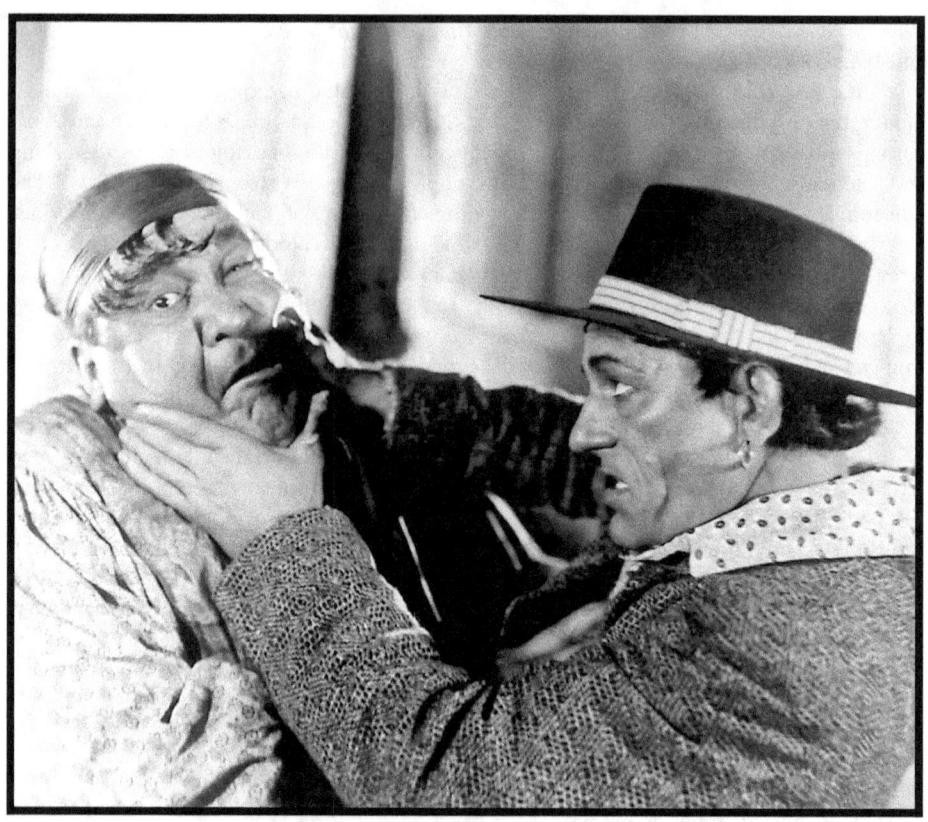

Alonzo strangles Nanon's father in *The Unknown*

The reason for Nanon's phobia is never overtly stated, but the behavior of her violently possessive father gives the perceptive viewer a clue. Even though Alonzo can only sympathetically listen to Nanon's complaints, her fat father, the owner of the circus, jealously orders her out of Alonzo's wagon and beats the armless man with a whip until he is restrained by the strongman. The implication is that Nanon's extreme neurosis results from the conscious or unconscious memory of her own father's hands on her.

One night, the owner catches Alonzo with his arms unlaced. Alonzo strangles the man outside of Nanon's wagon. She glimpses his distinctive double thumb but not his face as he squeezes the life from her father. Alonzo offers to take care of Nanon after her father's death and he, Cojo and the girl stay behind as the circus leaves town. Unfortunately, Malabar also remains to court the young woman. Crazed with jealousy, Alonzo does the unthinkable: he blackmails a surgeon into actually amputating his arms so that he can win Nanon without revealing his terrible secret.

But with the death of her father and the love of Malabar, Nanon overcomes her fear of the strongman's hands. Meanwhile, Alonzo recuperates in the hospital after his amputation. When he returns, Alonzo finds that Nanon is engaged to Malabar. The truth slowly dawns on Alonzo in a long-held close-up as he initially mistakes the couple's talk of marriage as his own union with Nanon.

Alonzo attempts to wreak revenge on Malabar by arranging the destruction of the strongman's arms. During the show, a pair of white stallions on treadmills are strapped to

Crazed with jealousy, Alonzo does the unthinkable: he has his arms amputated so that he can win Nanon (Joan Crawford) without revealing his terrible secret in *The Unknown*.

Malabar's wrists, and he restrains them as a scantily clad Nanon whips them into a frenzy. Backstage, Alonzo pulls the lever on the treadmills, stopping them so that the horses will rip Malabar's arms from his sockets. But in preventing Nanon from helping Malabar, Alonzo falls in front of one of the rearing steeds, and it comes down on his chest, crushing him to death.

The Unknown began filming on February 7, 1927 and wrapped six weeks later on March 18 at a cost of $217,000. Like his other leading ladies, Joan Crawford, who was only 18 when she played Nanon, had few memories of her director but clearly recalled working with Chaney. She said, "I was so eager to learn my craft in those early days...that I did more observing of acting than I did of directors and directing techniques." However, unlike Miller and Philbin, Joan Crawford did not give the impression that her co-star was the guiding force on the set. She remembered "how very soft-spoken, quiet and sensitive Tod Browning was and how very knowledgeable." According to her, Browning was "concerned that all of us were comfortable in our scenes...he was very patient with me, a newcomer."

A. Arnold Gillespie, the unit art director under Gibbons, also remembered Browning. "Tod was one of only a few 'complete directors.' By complete I mean from original story selection—sometimes his own—to script construction and cast selection, from star or stars to bit players, wardrobe, sets, dressing of sets and of course, direction and finally, film editing. He was thorough in all of these facets. In my opinion an 'auteur,' as they say today."

Of Browning's relation with Chaney, Gillespie wrote, "Tod's direction of Chaney, as I remember, was generally accepted by him. But not always! Lon *lived* the character he was depicting, and any out-of-character suggestions Browning might make were vetoed, though amicably, by the master of character. He was very much his own man."

Following Chaney's death, Browning himself told journalist Adela Rogers St. John that Chaney "never said anything to me on the set except, 'Yes, boss.' We used to argue a bit before and after hours. But on the set he was a good soldier." But St. John added, "Argue! They fought like a couple of sea lions. They yelled and cussed each other out plenty. But just let anyone else interfere. Let any executive or writer attempt to take advantage of the apparent friction. They soon found out it was a very private fight. Tod and Lon instantly ganged up on the intruder, who decided that he would be better occupied elsewhere."

Joan Crawford recalled Chaney's masochistic need to wear the leather harness tightly binding his arms to his body as "agonizing... When he was not before the camera, Mr. Browning would say to him, 'Lon, don't you want me to untie your arms?' And Lon would answer, 'No, the pain I am enduring now will help the scene. Let's go!'" The young starlet remembered him keeping his arms bound one day for five hours, "enduring such numbness, such torture, that when we got to this scene, he was able to convey not just realism but such emotional agony that it was shocking... and fascinating." She thought her co-star to be "the most tense, exciting individual I'd ever met, a man mesmerized into his part." When he acted, "it was as if God were working, he had such profound concentration. It was then I became aware for the first time of the difference between standing in front of the camera and acting."

Chaney wore no unusual makeup for the part, aside from the wax double thumb affixed with spirit gum over his own thumb. The studio eagerly publicized that Chaney learned to throw knives, light cigarettes, mop his brow and even sign autographs with his feet for the role. In some long shots, Chaney did use his own feet, but Browning needed a double for the close shots of Alonzo dexterously manipulating objects with his toes. The upper part of his body hidden below Chaney and the camera, a real armless man named Paul Dismute enacted Chaney's fancy footwork. Chaney's face was matted over Dismute's head in the shots where he threw knives with his feet on the revolving platform. Dismute worked at a salary of $150 a week for seven weeks. He later used the credit to get a job with Al G. Barnes Circus and Sideshow, billed as "The Man Who Doubled Lon Chaney's Legs in *The Unknown*."

The power of the film derives from its surreal obsession with arms, an obsession it shares with its two principal characters, Alonzo and Nanon. This single-mindedness springs from the very inception of the piece. Browning stated that when he was working on a story for a Chaney film, the character would come first, and the plot would grow from that character. "When we're getting ready to discuss a new story," Browning told the press, Chaney would "amble into my office and say, 'Well, what's it going to be, boss?' I'll say, 'This time a leg comes off, or an arm, or a nose'—whatever it may be." In the case of *The Unknown*, Browning said that he merely came up with the idea of an armless man and then created startling dilemmas for a person with such a problem. The character of the beautiful girl repulsed by men's' hands was a brilliant inspiration as a romantic goal for Browning's armless man. As an added turn of the screw, Browning then decided that the man secretly would have arms. Why would he want to hide his arms? Because he is a criminal and could be identified by his peculiar hands. And what would this character do when faced with such a condition for the love of the woman he desires? He would have his arms amputated, of course. This type of insane logic seems to follow naturally in the story, so relentless is its construction around one single idea. Every subsequent plot twist puts another pressure on the man with no arms. What is the worst thing that could happen to him upon having his arms removed for the girl he loves? She overcomes her fear of arms and falls for the strongman, of course.

Chaney, shown with John George, wore no unusual makeup for the part, aside from the wax double thumb affixed with spirit gum over his own thumb in *The Unknown*.

Browning treads a fine line between the compelling and the ridiculous, but the film, like Hitchcock's *Vertigo*, overcomes its implausibilities by creating its own alternate world of obsession. In effect, the film succeeds in making the audience as focused and compulsive as its characters by eliminating any distracting subplots and unconvincing last-minute repentances. Each character follows his or her single goal to its end, thus making the story seem believable. Browning stated, "The thing you have to be most careful of in a mystery story is not to let it verge on the comic. If a thing is too gruesome and too horrible, it gets beyond the limits of the average imagination and the audience laughs. It may sound incongruous, but mystery must be made plausible." Browning succeeds in making it seem plausible, for the length of the movie at least.

Browning treads a fine line between the compelling and the ridiculous, but *The Unknown* overcomes its implausibilities by creating its own alternate world of obsession.

Many commentators at the time disagreed with Browning's contention that he had not made his film "too gruesome and too horrible." Writing in *The New York Herald Tribune*, Richard Watts Jr. felt that "the case of Mr. Tod Browning is rapidly approaching the pathological. After a series of minor horrors that featured such comparatively respectable creations as murderous midgets, crippled thieves and poisonous reptiles, all sinister and deadly in a murky atmosphere of blackness and unholy doom, the director presents us now with a melodrama that might have been made from a scenario dashed off by the Messrs. Leopold and Loeb in a quiet moment... What amazes me is that those careful custodians of public squeamishness, Mr. Hays and Mr. Thalberg, allowed the director to go on... compared to Tod Browning, the morose Erich von Stroheim is the original apostle of sweetness and light."

The Evening Post branded *The Unknown* "a remarkably unpleasant picture, which can hardly be recommended as even moderate entertainment. A visit to the dissecting room in a hospital would be quite as pleasant and at the same time more instructive." *The New York Sun* agreed completely, saying that "the suspicion that the picture might have been written by Nero, directed by Lucretia Borgia, constructed by the shade of Edgar Allan Poe and lighted by a well-known vivisectionist was absolutely groundless... *The Unknown* is merely one of the cute little bits of lace designed and executed by Tod Browning... (*The Unknown*) may be just what the public wants. If it is—well, the good old days of the Roman Empire are upon us." *The New York Post* wrote that "Mr. Chaney has been twisting joints and lacing himself into strait-jackets for a long time—so long, in fact, that there is almost nothing left

The Unknown **is a bizarre story of Alonzo's mad obsession.**

for him now but the Headless Horseman. No doubt that will come later." The New York *Daily Mirror* opined that "if you like to tear butterflies apart and see sausage made you may like the climax to *The Unknown*... typical Chaney fare spiced with cannibalism and flavored with the Spanish Inquisition."

Harrison's Report took up the cause of outrage against Chaney's pictures abandoned this time by *Variety*. They wrote, "One can imagine a moral pervert of the present day, or professional torturers of the times of the Spanish Inquisition that gloated over the miseries of their victims on the rack and over their roasting on hot iron bars enjoying screen details of the kind set forth in *The Unknown*, but it is difficult to fancy average men and women of a modern audience in this enlightened age being entertained by such a thoroughly fiendish mingling of bloodlust, cruelty and horrors... Of Mr. Chaney's acting it is enough to say it is excellent, of its kind. Similar praise might well be given the work of a skilled surgeon in ripping open the abdomen of a patient. But who wants to see him do it?"

There were those contemporary reviewers who appreciated Browning's work on its own terms. *Photoplay* recommended, "We think you will like it as an unadulterated shocker... Like other Chaney pictures directed by Tod Browning, this has a macabre atmosphere. If you wince at a touch or two of horror, don't go to *The Unknown*. If you like strong celluloid food, try it. It has the merit of possessing a finely sinister plot, some moments of real shock and Lon Chaney." And *Variety* finally lightened up about Chaney's efforts to thrill them. They wrote, "A good Chaney film that might have been great. Chaney and his characterizations invite stories that have power behind them... Another Chaney-Browning program

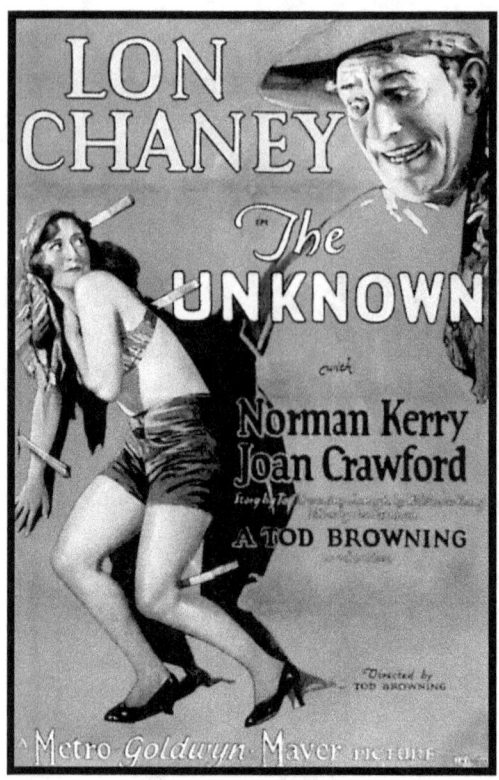

release that will reinforce the value of this combination. *The Unknown* is a paradox, in that it is not as great a picture as it might have been, but will undoubtedly have its compensation in the gross rentals."

In Europe, many cineastes, no longer influenced by the Puritanism that still pervaded much of America's popular tastes, were intrigued by Browning. French critic Jacque B. Brunius wrote in 1929 that Browning "is an unbridled romantic, and even when making box-office pictures for the average cinemagoer he does not conceal the fact that he is influenced by German romantic-expressionism — even when he uses, as in this case, a psychological situation as a springboard, he feels no compulsion to stay on this plane." Brunius described *The Unknown* as possessing "more than the usual ration of extravagance... fit with Tod Browning's relish for freaks, monsters and extravagant situations — enough for aesthetically minded people to be squeamish and patronizing about it. What does it matter for those who, like myself, discover in Tod Browning's films an undefinable poetry, an uncanny charm, probably irrelevant to the canons of Great Art, I confess, but nonetheless effective and disturbing."

In the end, *Variety* proved correct about the film's box-office potential. Despite the warning of critics eager to end the tide of horror before it really began, *The Unknown*, like all of Chaney's MGM films, earned a handsome return. On an investment of $217,000, the studio saw a profit of $362,000. Obviously, the public was neither as squeamish nor as influenced by their admonitions as many critics believed.

After the actor's death, *The New York Times* reported that "Chaney wanted to act Dracula and often discussed the part with Tod Browning... Both men believed the American public to be 90 per cent superstitious and ripe for horror films. Chaney had a full scenario and a secret makeup worked out even at that early date." Unfortunately, after the debacle of *Nosferatu*, Florence Stoker still jealously guarded the motion picture rights to her late husband's famous novel. In addition, the conventional wisdom in Hollywood said that modern audiences would not accept the supernatural in their stories. Executives felt that enlightened 20th-century Americans required a realistic explanation at the end of any film creating the atmosphere of other-worldly powers.

Hamilton Deane, who had secured the stage rights for *Dracula* from Mrs. Stoker, proved Hollywood wrong, at least on the boards. Beginning on February 14, 1927, his adaptation sold out the Little Theatre in West End, London. Later that year, Deane hired John L. Balderston, the London correspondent for *The New York Sun* and co-author with J.C. Squires of the supernatural play, *Berkeley Square*, to revise the London version of *Dracula* for its upcoming Broadway debut.

Therefore, if Thalberg or Browning did attempt to buy the American rights, they were undoubtedly refused them by Hamilton Deane. Undaunted, Browning devised a story he called "The Hypnotist," eventually to be called *London After Midnight*, which borrowed heavily from the stage version of *Dracula* while safely explaining away its vampires at the end as the trappings of an implausibly elaborate criminal investigation.

As Browning explained, "*London After Midnight* is an example of how to get people to accept ghosts and other supernatural spirits by letting them turn out to be the machination of a detective. Thereby the audience is not asked to believe the horrible impossible, but the horrible possible and plausibility increases, rather than lessens, the thrills and chills." Actually, vampires would have been more believable than the torturous plot mechanics used to inject them into Browning's story.

Chaney in *London After Midnight*

The film begins with the shooting of Roger Balfour, the distinguished patriarch of a wealthy London home. Chaney plays Inspector Burke of Scotland Yard, who arrives 15 minutes after the murder, then questions Balfour's friend and neighbor, Sir James Hamlin, played by Griffith actor Henry B. Walthall and his nephew, young Arthur Hibbs, played by Conrad Nagel. Burke has found a suicide note from Balfour addressed to his young daughter, Lucille, but Sir James insists that Balfour would never kill himself.

Five year later, the Balfour house stands vacant; "a place of weird noises and ghostlike shadows," says the intertitle. Thomas, the comic groom for Sir James and Miss Smithson, the comic maid, return by wagon from picking up luggage for Sir James' house guest. As they pass the bat- and cobweb-infested Balfour mansion, a strange man and woman descend the stairs.

Lon Chaney also plays this "Man in the Beaver Hat," as the script names him, and it is one of his most startling creations. The July 16th version of the script describes this character as being "as strange a creature as the eyes ever beheld. He wears a black beaver hat and a black Inverness coat and his face has on it the pallor of death. There is, indeed, something not of this earth in his appearance." The description is vague enough, not coming from an established literary source, to allow Chaney free rein in devising the look of a character who is soon established as the first vampire in an American feature.

Under his top hat, Chaney wore a straggly, shoulder-length gray wig. Along with pale base for the skin, he heavily shaded around his eyes, darkened his eyebrows and placed thin wire rings around the outside of his eyes, like a monocle, to keep them wide and staring. The upper and lower sharply pointed dentures were made from gutta-percha with small wires

Lon Chaney's "Man in the Beaver Hat," as the script names him, in *London After Midnight*, is one of his most startling creations.

placed in the upper plate to keep the corners of his mouth curled in a frozen grin. His slow, crouching walk resembled the stride of a living-dead Groucho Marx.

Inspector Burke, noticeably grayer than five years ago and wearing a pince-nez, arrives. Sir James has called the Inspector because of the activity next door and because Balfour's suicide note has turned up again despite being locked away in the Inspector's desk. In addition, young Hibbs shows Burke the new lease for the Balfour house signed by the late Roger Balfour in his own hand. Balfour's pretty daughter, Lucille, who lives at Sir James' home,

Inspector Burke (Chaney), between Hibbs (Conrad Nagel) and Sir James (Henry Walthall), investigates mysterious doings at Balfour Manor in *London After Midnight*.

claims that she hears her dead father's voice calling her at night. Burke and the nervous Sir James search Balfour's tomb and find that his body is missing.

The maid screams and tells the men that she has seen the vampire in the house. We view her story in flashback, even though it has just occurred. After locking herself in Lucille's bedroom, the maid sees a mist materialize into the vampire, who spreads his arms menacingly, revealing bat-like wings. The maid tells the men that when she screamed, the vampire flew out the window. The next day, Burke and Sir James search the Balfour house. They find five bats hanging from a rafter. Could they be the vampires hiding from the daylight?

Later, alone on the terrace, Burke secretly tells Lucille that he knows that her father did not commit suicide. He asks her to trust him and do as he commands without telling anyone. Hibbs does not trust Burke because he would not allow Sir James to call the police, but Lucille refuses to reveal to him Burke's secret request.

That night, Burke and Sir James spy through the window of the Balfour estate and see Roger Balfour himself sitting with the Man in the Beaver Hat and another male vampire. At that moment, Luna, the vampire girl, swoops down from the ceiling on giant bat wings to join the other undead beings.

Suspecting Hibbs, Burke hypnotizes him after everyone else has retired for the night. He takes Hibbs back to the time of the murder five year ago.

Later in the night, a hooded figure creeps into Hibbs' room. Instead of Hibbs, Burke rises from the bed and fires his pistol at the fleeing figure. In the hall, Burke finds a spot of blood on the carpet.

Upstairs, Burke enters his own room and finds Hibbs still in a trance. Burke awakens Hibbs and follows him as he walks down the hall. The young man senses something wrong and knocks on Lucille's door. When he, Burke and Sir James force the door open, they find the room empty and the furniture in disarray as if a struggle has taken place.

The vampire girl leads Lucille through the dead of night to the Balfour house. The Man in the Beaver Hat sweeps Lucille up in his arms and carries her into the house. He tells her, "Remember... Lucille... you... are... doing... this... for... your... father."

Burke commands Sir James to go to the Balfour house and ask for Roger Balfour. Meanwhile, Hibbs arrives at the old mansion with homemade wooden stakes to destroy the vampires. As he runs to Lucille's aid, he is grabbed by two vampires. Inspector Burke shows up and tells the vampires to lock Hibbs in a closet.

Luna brings Lucille a dress similar to the one she wore the night her father was murdered, and Burke orders her to put it on. A double wearing the costume of the Man in the Beaver Hat hands Burke a costume. The Inspector tells the double to make up as Roger Balfour again.

Two of Burke's assistants lead Sir James to the Balfour house and command him to do as Burke instructs. The Man in the Beaver Hat makes gestures in front of Sir James' eyes, hypnotizing him. The strange creature tells Sir James that it is five years ago, and he is at Roger Balfour's house.

In a trance, Sir James goes into Roger Balfour's study where he

Burke and Sir James search for the vampires in *London After Midnight*.

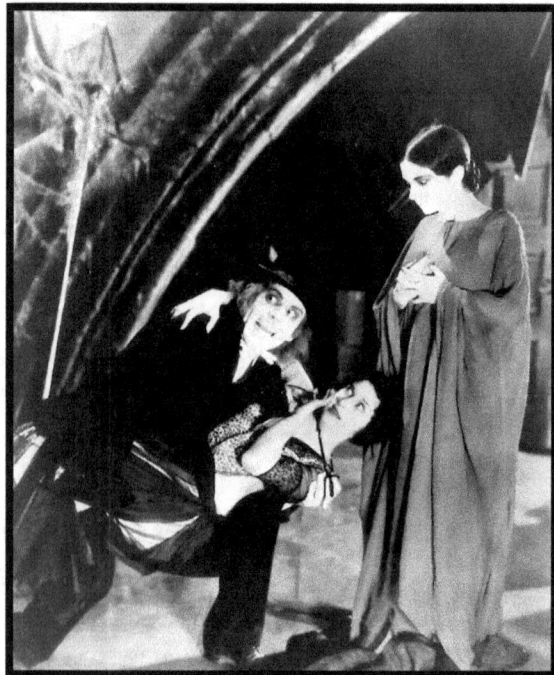

Lucille (Marceline Day) is threatened by Chaney and Luna (Edna Ticheno) in *London After Midnight*.

Luna, the vampire girl, swoops down from the ceiling on giant bat wings to join the other undead beings in *London After Midnight*.

finds Balfour with Lucille. The Man in the Beaver Hat takes off his hat, wig and cloak. It is Inspector Burke. He tells a detective that he is ready to prove that a criminal will re-enact his crime under hypnosis.

After Lucille has left the room to go to bed, the hypnotized Sir James reveals to the man playing Roger Balfour that he wishes to marry Lucille when she comes of age. Balfour refuses because Sir James is too old for her. Sir James angrily leaves, and Burke tells the detective that this eliminates him as a suspect.

But Sir James returns behind Balfour pointing a gun and forces Balfour to write the suicide note. When the note is finished, Sir James shoots Balfour, wipes the prints from the gun and puts it in Balfour's hand.

At that moment, the detectives enter the room and grab Sir James. He was the murderer of Roger Balfour five years ago. Burke brings Sir James out of his trance, pulls up his shirt sleeve and reveals the bandaged bullet wound where Burke shot him earlier in the evening. Sir James had entered Hibbs' bedroom wearing a hood, hoping to dispose of Hibbs, but instead, he had been confronted by Burke who was waiting for him. The actor playing Balfour is not dead because Sir James' gun held blanks.

Luna and the other vampires are actors who pack up their costumes, their performances finished. In gratitude, Lucille kisses Burke on the cheek, and the Inspector wistfully watches her go off with Hibbs.

Obviously, Browning concocted a remarkably far-fetched and confusing story in an effort to duplicate the atmosphere of *Dracula*. At one point, to protect Lucille in Sir James' home, Hibbs and the maid "place over the keyhole of the sleeping apartment a drawn sword

Sir James re-enacts the murder of Roger Balfour in *London After Midnight*.

of sharpest steel and a wreath of tube roses," as directed by a book on vampires. This strange piece of lore is obviously an effort by Browning to replace the use of garlic in *Dracula* without being accused of plagiarism.

The most pertinent question posed by the plot is why include the fake vampires at all? If Burke is trying to prove his theory that a perpetrator will repeat his crime under hypnosis, why not just put Sir James in a trance and re-enact the night of the murder at the beginning? How does the elaborate vampire masquerade, involving several actors and the expected gullibility of innocent characters, help solve the crime?

Symptomatic of Browning's casual attitude toward filling story holes, he never explains how or why Burke arrives at the scene of the crime within 15 minutes of its commission. In addition, the audience is asked to accept that Burke can stage an illusion such as the vampire forming out of mist right in front of the maid's eyes. That is, unless the maid is in on the hoax at this point. And if that is so, then why show her story in flashback as if it really happened?

The character of Burke often seems to be in two places at the same time, playing himself and the vampire simultaneously. That is, unless the vampire is sometimes enacted by the double. But if that is so, how can he look exactly like Chaney in the role? Browning succeeds in keeping the audience interested and mystified, and he even provides some chills with his intimations that Balfour has become the living dead, but his explanation at the end is woefully inadequate.

Another problem with the story is its removal of Chaney from any meaningful relationships with the characters. *Variety* noted this in its December 14, 1927 review: "Lack of interest in Burke (Chaney) may be attributed to the circumstances in which this character is placed in the story, having no interest in common either with the audience or the other characters in the production. If Burke had been linked with the girl there might have been a touch of sentiment.

"Burke is pictured as a detached character, mechanical and wooden. As such the only audience appeal is that of curiosity and that is not strong enough."

Other reviewers were more charitable, caught up, no doubt, in the baffling mystery, the gothic settings and the novelty of vampires in an American movie. *The New York Herald Tribune* noted that "the distinguished talents of Lon Chaney, Tod Browning and the late author of *Dracula* are shrewdly combined in the picture... the scenes are so imaginatively done and Mr. Chaney's passion for grotesque makeup is so effective, that you feel that shortly both director and star will be hard at work making the real Dracula—a 'movie' property if there ever was one." *Film Daily* agreed: "Thrills and weird doings in profusion. Fine entertainment for the mystery lover.

The audience is asked to accept that Burke can stage an illusion such as the vampire forming out of mist in *London After Midnight*.

Probably a trifle too spooky for the timid soul... Lon Chaney is right at home in one of his unusual characterizations. Will please his following." *Motion Picture World* also overlooked the implausibilities: "Lon Chaney is back, in a get-up which would make any sensitive girl quiver and quake on a dark night... This is a dark, foul mystery play, which has certain moments and certain elements as horrid as anyone could ask. But it's such a completely baffling mystery until almost the end, that you sit through it in a sort of creepy daze."

As with *The Unknown*, the critic for *Harrison's Report* was not amused: "Just like the last three or four pictures with this star—gruesome. Besides, it has the disadvantage of having a nonsensical plot... Mr. Chaney's makeup is at times hideous—enough to make one sick in the stomach. The picture succeeds in giving one a creepy feeling... It should please the morbid."

Apparently, there were many morbid to be pleased. The film went into production on July 25, 1927 and finished a mere 24 working days later, one week ahead of schedule, on August 20, at a cost of $152,000. Upon its release on December 17, 1927, two months after *Dracula* proved a hit on Broadway, *London After Midnight* became the most profitable film of the Browning-Chaney collaboration, grossing more than a million dollars in worldwide rentals and earning $540,000 for MGM.

For the first but not the last time, the question was raised whether entertainment of this sort could promote violence. On October 23, 1928, a 29-year-old Welsh carpenter named

London After Midnight remains a lost film and we may never know whether it would live up to the cult status it has achieved.

Robert Williams and a 22-year-old Irish housemaid named Julia Mangan were found in London's Hyde Park with their throats cut by a razor. The girl died before reaching St. George's Hospital, but the carpenter survived to be charged with her murder and his own attempted suicide.

The jury at his first trial could not arrive at a decision regarding Williams' sanity. During his second trial, his defense contended that the accused suffered a vision of Lon

Chaney as his vampire character from *London After Midnight* just before killing Miss Mangan. As reported by the *London Times*, "The prisoner, in the witness box, said that, while he was talking to the girl in the park noises came into his head, and it seemed as if steam was coming out of the sides of his head, and as if a red-hot iron were being pushed in behind his eyes. He thought he saw Lon Chaney, a film actor, in a corner, shouting and making faces at him. He did not remember taking a razor from his pocket, or using the razor on the girl or on himself. The next thing he remembered was a nurse washing his feet at the hospital."

Justice Travers Humphreys conceded that Chaney's makeup in *London After Midnight* was a "horrifying and terrible spectacle," and that members of the jury who had seen the film, or even its advertisements, might be horrified, but he felt that being frightened by a scary characterization and recalling it in a moment of emotional stress did not constitute insanity. The jury sentenced Williams to death on January 10, 1929, but three weeks later, the condemned was reprieved on medical grounds on advise of the Home Secretary.

Carroll Borland and Bela Lugosi in the *Mark of the Vampire*, the remake of *London After Midnight*.

After 1930, the negative and print of *London After Midnight* were stored away in vault 7 at MGM. The print, still in good shape, was viewed along with Browning's sound remake, called *Mark of the Vampire*, in 1935. The last known record of the film was in a note in the studio files in 1955. Twenty years later, a fire in vault 7, possibly caused by the ignition of improperly stored nitrate film, destroyed the last known print and original negative of *London After Midnight*.

On June 25, 1928, Browning and Chaney began shooting their ninth and, along with *The Unknown*, their best and most horrifying, collaboration. This time, Browning did not devise the story himself but instead, based his film on the lurid play, *Kongo*, by Charles de Vonde and Kilbourn Gordon which starred Walter Huston on Broadway. Eschewing their regular scenarist, Waldemar Young, Browning and Thalberg chose *The Phantom of the Opera* adapter Elliott Clawson to prepare the screenplay, called *West of Zanzibar*. As an indication of the success of his previous films with Chaney, this was Browning's first project under a new arrangement with MGM that increased his salary to $4,500 per picture with a contingent bonus of $5,000. Again, Chaney's role required him to be a vengeful cripple whose hatred escalates into a tragic insanity.

Phroso's (Chaney) wife Anna (Jane Daly) plans to leave him in *West of Zanzibar*.

Chaney plays Phroso, a Chaplinesque magician in an English music hall. Whether inspired by the famous comic himself or by the tradition that created him, Chaney does a marvelous imitation of Chaplin's double-take, dead-pan audience stare and backward,

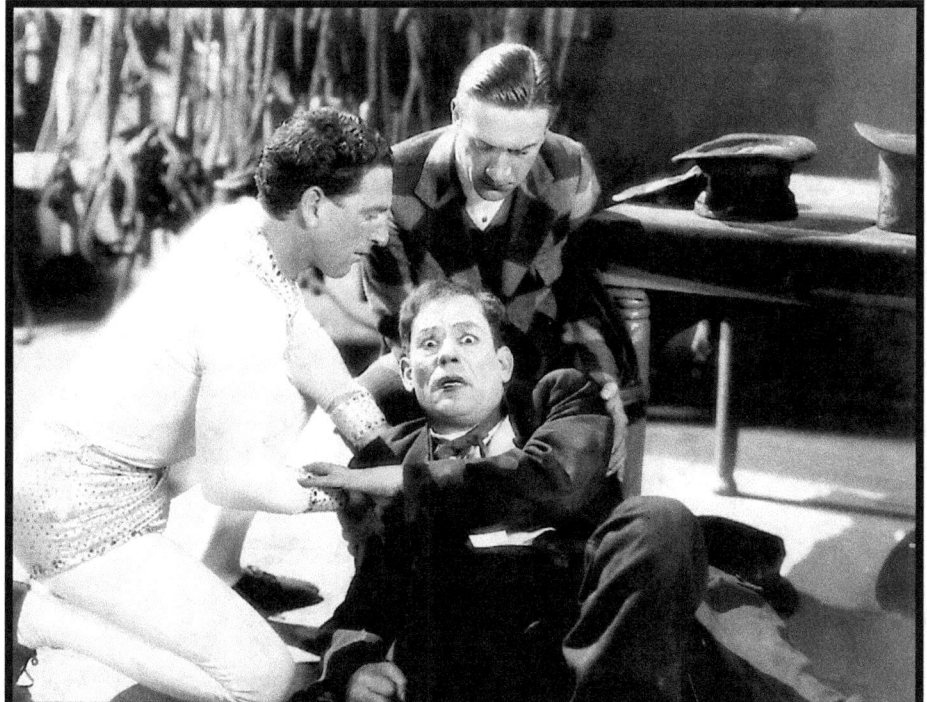

The horrendous fall leaves Phroso with both legs paralyzed in *West of Zanzibar*.

single-leg kick while performing the rather grim trick of turning a skeleton in a coffin into his beautiful wife, Anna.

Backstage, Phroso learns that his adored wife is leaving him for a man named Crane, played by Lionel Barrymore. The two men struggle, and Crane pushes Phroso over a balcony. The horrendous fall leaves Phroso with both legs paralyzed.

A year later, after receiving word of her return, Phroso pulls himself along the street on a wheeled platform to meet Anna in a church. Phroso finds Anna dead at the altar, and a baby girl sits on the floor next to her mother's body. In front of a statue of the Madonna and child, Phroso swears vengeance on Crane and "his brat" for destroying his life.

The location shifts to darkest Africa, west of Zanzibar, 18 years later. Phroso, now known as Dead Legs Flint, lives on a jungle compound with Doc, an alcoholic ex-physician played by Warner Baxter, and two criminal henchmen, Babe and Tiny. Dead Legs commands the loyalty of the primitive tribe that surrounds the compound by fooling them with his old magic tricks.

In the depth of his hatred for Crane, he arranges for Anna's daughter, Maizie, to be raised in the lowest brothel in Zanzibar.

In the original stage play, the daughter contracts syphilis, but Browning softened this by making the daughter into an alcoholic, thus circumventing the objections of the Hays Office.

Crane himself is also in Africa, and Dead Legs orders his henchmen to dress as a frightening Voodoo god to terrify the natives transporting Crane's valuable ivory. When the natives run away, Dead Legs steals the ivory, waiting for the day when Crane will trace the thefts to him.

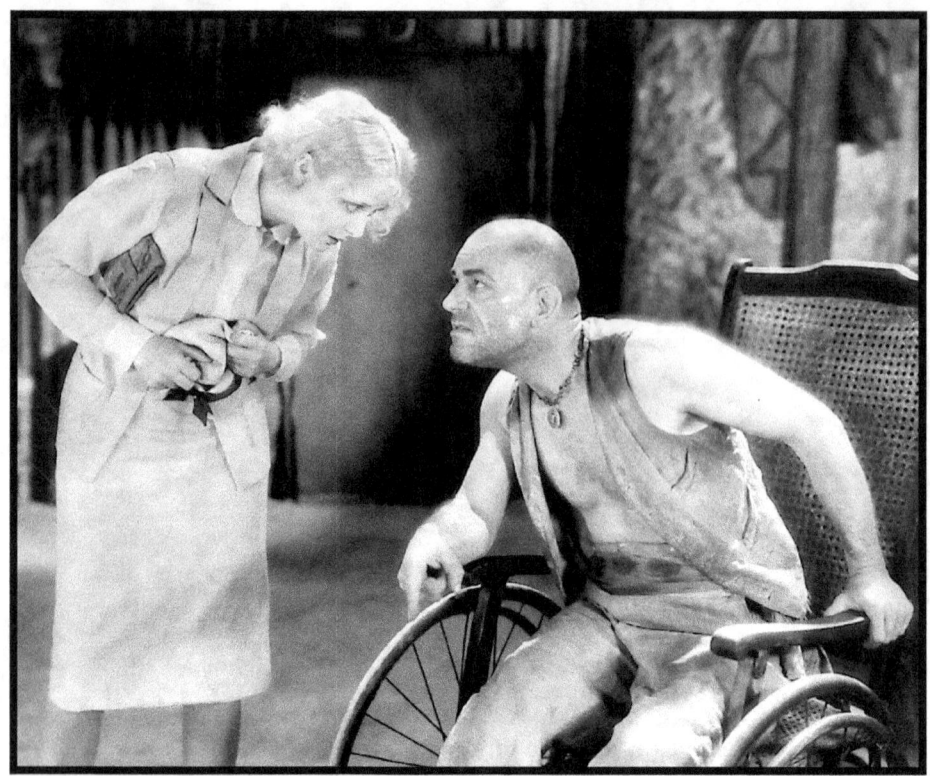

Dead Legs (Chaney) has Maizie (Mary Nolan) brought to him in *West of Zanzibar*.

On Dead Legs' orders, one of his henchmen brings the 18-year-old Maizie, played by the beautiful Mary Nolan, to the compound on the pretext of meeting her father. She is horrified to be confronted by Dead Legs, who treats her with open contempt. Soon, she is a physical and mental wreck, drinking heavily to deal with Dead Legs' continual abuse. Only Doc befriends her and even reforms his habits to try to protect her. Dead Legs delights in showing her the natives' custom of burning the first-born daughter alive on the pyre of any man who has died.

Following Dead Legs' command, the natives bring Crane to the compound. Dead Legs grins sadistically as he displays the dissipated Maizie to him, finally revealing that she is Crane's daughter by Anna. Crane is dumbstruck, collapsing into a chair and burying his face in his hands. His body convulses as if crying, only increasing Dead Legs' pleasure. But when Crane looks up, Dead Legs is confused to see that he is actually laughing. Crane says that Anna never ran off with him because of what he did to her husband. Dead Legs is horrified to learn that Maizie is actually his own daughter. Tears well up in Dead Legs' eyes as he realizes what he has done to his own innocent child.

He experiences an emotional collapse, preventing him from stopping the natives as they carry out the next step of his revenge and shoot Crane. Dead Legs desperately orders Doc to save Crane's life so that the natives, who are convinced that Maizie is Crane's daughter, will not burn her alive with his body. But Doc is too late: Crane dies.

When the natives come for the terrified Maizie, Dead Legs stalls them with his magic so that Doc can help her escape into the jungle. Dead Legs puts Maizie in his trick coffin with the rotating backboard. He shuts the lid on Maizie and opens it to reveal a skeleton.

Crane (Lionel Barrymore) tells Dead Legs that Maizie is actually his daughter as Doc (Warner Baxter) looks on in *West of Zanzibar*.

But the tribal chief, coveting Dead Legs' necklace medallion, refuses to believe the trick. On the chief's command, the tribe surrounds the helpless Dead Legs. The next scene shows the old chief pulling Dead Legs' necklace and medallion out of Crane's funeral pyre. Doc takes Maizie out of the jungle by boat, never revealing to her that Dead Legs was actually her father.

As in *The Unknown*, Browning overcomes the implausibilities of the story by concentrating on the intensity of his protagonist's obsession. Phroso is a complex character, like Alonzo, capable of extremes of love, hatred, evil and guilt. Chaney captures each of Phroso's changes in a bravura silent performance. The moral ambiguity of Phroso's actions keeps the audience fascinated and off guard in their response to him, even within a single scene. Never has a character in melodrama been more deserving of revenge than Phroso, but the nature of his scheme, involving the abuse of an innocent child, is so evil that it overshadows the crimes committed against him. When the truth about Maizie is finally revealed, Phroso is punished by his own plan, and this twist is one of the most ironic and devastating in the history of the movies.

The May 17th, 1928 draft of the script detailed a different fate for Phroso. After killing Crane, Dead Legs has his body hung by the feet with a goat's skull tied around his neck as an example for other "thieves." Dead Legs' henchmen become suspicious of his sudden kindness to Maizie and believe that he plans to leave them behind and take her for himself. As they load a canoe with supplies to run away, Maizie, in an emotional collapse after see-

In a deleted scene from *West of Zanzibar*, two tough guys (Rosco Ward and Kalla Pasha) taunt Phroso and finally, pick him up and throw him through a window into the street.

ing the death of the man she believes is her father, stabs Dead Legs while he sleeps in his room. He yells out that Crane was not her father and that her real father loves her. Doc takes Maizie away while Dead Legs crawls after them, still yelling hysterically that her father loves her. From his window, he watches their canoe disappear into the jungle as he dies.

The May 17 draft does not yet include the funeral pyre sequence, but it does feature a gruesome scene from the play that did not make the final revision. When Maizie arrives at the compound, Doc is intoxicated with liquor and hashish. Dead Legs commands two natives to restrain Doc while the magician makes small cuts on his upper body and legs. He then orders the natives to take Doc into the swamp and "let the leeches suck out the poison in him."

A sequence that did survive into the final June 7 draft that was actually shot but was ultimately cut from the film depicts Phroso's travels to Africa in search of Crane and Phroso's first attempts to earn money there. The camera, from Phroso's point of view, shows various faces of French, Italian, Turkish, Arabic and finally, African people pass by, indicating the many countries through which he travels. A dissolve takes us to a dive bar where Phroso wheels in on his cart, begging for a handout. Two tough guys taunt him and finally, pick him up and throw him through a window into the street. Doc pleads pity for the cripple and passes his hat around the saloon for charity. This dissolves to Doc, Phroso and the two men who threw him through the window dividing the money from the hat between them. The two men turn out to be Phroso's fat henchmen, Babe and Tiny.

Although cut from *West of Zanzibar*, this image of a human-duck monstrosity would be featured in the chilling climax of Browning's 1932 masterpiece, *Freaks*.

We next see Phroso smiling sadistically as he leaves the child Maizie with the local Madam. This dissolves to numerous carnival acts in Zanzibar, ending with Doc acting as barker for an attraction called the "human duck." People peer into a pit and start laughing at what they see. One of the people watching is Crane. This cuts to the interior of the pit in which we see Phroso, apparently legless, the bottom part of his torso feathered and shaped like the body of a white duck, including the tail. Phroso quacks and laughs hysterically, especially when he spots Crane and realizes that his old enemy does not recognize him. Doc notices Phroso's growing frenzy and tells the patrons, "See it while it lasts—the duck's gone crazy!" Although cut from *West of Zanzibar*, this image of a human-duck monstrosity would be featured in the chilling climax of Browning's 1932 masterpiece, *Freaks*. With these sequences deleted, Joseph Farnham, MGM's leading title writer, bridged the scene of Phroso finding his wife's body in the church and the scene of his reappearance in Africa as Dead Legs with a card reading, "Eighteen years later—West of Zanzibar."

The June 7 draft still fails to work out the final climax. The last scene ends with Dead Legs saying goodbye to Maizie as the native drums beat louder. A note on the final page indicates the action to be scripted: "There will be 20 additional scenes in which, in his efforts to save the girl, Chaney sacrifices his life and is burned upon the funeral pyre with the body of Johnson and following which, the girl, Moore and Kalla Pasha are seen gliding over the lagoon in a boat filled with provisions."

West of Zanzibar was an **unqualified** success at the box-office.

As this excerpt indicates, thoughout both the May 17 and June 7 drafts, the characters were referred to by the actors' last names. Although ultimately played by Warner Baxter, the role of Doc was written for Owen Moore, and it was his name that appeared in the scripts.

Browning shot the entire production on the MGM lot in Culver City, including the exteriors of the African compound which were constructed around the studio water tank on Lot Two and dressed to resemble a jungle lagoon. Numerous steam pipes running through this exterior kept the tropical plants from wilting in the hot, dry California sun. As he would in his sound films, *Dracula* and *Mark of the Vampire*, Browning shot numerous inserts of slimy animals, in this case, lizards, snakes, spiders and crocodiles, to establish the creepy, hostile environment in which the story took place. He also had a special filter put over the lens, as he did in the love scenes with Nanon and Malabar in *The Unknown*, that gave the intimate moments between Doc and Maizie the subtle texture of a painting on canvas.

West of Zanzibar finished shooting on July 31, 1928 after 31 days of production, one day over schedule. The final cost was $249,000. It was released on December 24, both silent and with a synchronized musical score and sound effects, and immediately incurred the wrath of

Harrison's Report. Not only did this paper pan the picture, but it ran a lead editorial entitled, "An Outpouring of the Cesspools of Hollywood!" detailing its outrage. The review said, "This piece of filth is the stage play *Kongo*. And upon this play the Metro-Goldwyn-Mayer picture *West of Zanzibar* has been founded. How any normal person could have thought this horrible syphilitic play could have made an entertaining picture, even with Lon Chaney, who appears in gruesome and repulsive stories, is beyond comprehension. But here it is, a Metro-Goldwyn-Mayer picture, which you will be compelled to show to the people of the United States as entertainment."

Expanding on this, the editorial called for theater owners to refuse to show the film because of its lurid subject: "If business is bad, don't attribute it to any business depression—people will, as a rule, deprive themselves of food rather than entertainment; what makes it bad is the quality of the pictures. What mother will allow her young daughter to set foot into your theatre again after learning that she saw a picture of the *West of Zanzibar* type?

"The stupidity of producers seems to be unbounded. They know that ninety-five per cent of the people of the United States do not want such trash as they have been putting out. And yet they insist on putting it out. In no other industry do the manufacturers insist on producing an article that the consumers do not want. Only in the moving picture industry does this thing happen.

"If you run *West of Zanzibar*, you will run it at the peril of alienating many of your regular customers. Demand that it be taken off your contract."

Of course, those reviewers whose morality was not offended by the mere existence of the picture were more impressed. *The New York Herald Tribune* felt that, "Not since that memorable screen melodrama *The Unholy Three*, have Messrs. Lon Chaney and Tod Browning, those eminent apostles of the macabre, been as successful in the demonstration

Chaney in the railroad drama *Thunder*

of cinema terror as in *West of Zanzibar*... It is only fair to say that the film is a perfect vehicle for the unholy two." *The New York Times* agreed: "It is a well concocted narrative and Mr. Chaney gives one of his most able and effective portrayals as he drags himself through scene after scene without using his legs."

In the end, the picture was another unqualified success at the box-office for Browning and Chaney with a worldwide gross of $921,000, returning a profit to MGM of $337,000. After *West of Zanzibar*, there would be three more Lon Chaney pictures, only one of which, *Where East is East*, was directed by Tod Browning. On location in Wisconsin for his last silent, the railroad drama *Thunder*, Chaney developed a nagging respiratory infection. The underlying cause of his illness was lung cancer due to heavy smoking. On July 25, 1929, his MGM contract was suspended on grounds of incapacity. Chaney remained in seclusion for most of the summer and fall of 1929, keeping his illness a secret from the press. He finally returned to films in March and April of 1930, giving a fascinating talking performance doing several voices in a sound remake of Browning's *The Unholy Three*, directed this time by Jack Conway. The film was a box-office success, but just one month after its release, Chaney died of bronchial cancer at the age of 47. His unique artistry in movies has never be duplicated.

CHAPTER 7
THE SILENT ROAR

Arthur Conan Doyle was born at No. 11 Picardy Place, Edinburgh, Scotland on May 22, 1859 to Mary Foley and Charles Doyle. Arthur's father ignored the talent as a painter that he inherited from his own father, the celebrated caricaturist known as H.B. Instead, he became a civil servant who paid little attention to his job, his art, or his family, leaving the raising of the children to his wife. Perhaps from their resentment, both Arthur and his sister Annette preferred the surname Conan Doyle. The name derived from their father's uncle, Michael Conan, who was also Arthur's godfather.

At school, romantic, idealistic young Arthur Conan Doyle read adventure writers of his day such as R.M. Ballantine and Mayne Reid. He also adopted the heroic attitudes of his favorite fiction protagonists by championing and defending younger and weaker boys who were victimized by bullies. Conan Doyle studied at Jesuit institutions before qualifying for a bachelor of medicine degree in 1881 and receiving a medical degree in 1885 from the University of Edinburgh. Two of his professors there would inspire him to create major characters in his fiction. Dr. Joseph Bell, a surgeon, became Sherlock Holmes in Conan Doyle's first detective novel, *A Study in Scarlet* in 1887 and Professor Rutherford, an anatomist, became irascible Professor Challenger in Conan Doyle's science fiction novel about prehistoric beasts in modern times, *The Lost World*, in 1912.

In the early 1880s, to earn money to support his family after his father entered a convalescent home, Conan Doyle spent four months as a highly paid medical officer on an African steamer. An advocate of sports and outdoor life, he introduced skis to Switzerland and helped popularize prizefighting with his novel, *Rodney Stone*, in 1896. He returned to Africa in 1900, eager to witness the Boer War as both a doctor and an unofficial attaché. The resultant book, *The Great Boer War*, is still the standard reference work on the subject. He was knighted in 1902 for a self-financed pamphlet in which he attempted to help alter Europe's anti-British sentiment about the war. In 1903, he unsuccessfully ran for Parliament as a Liberal Unionist. He proved his dedication to justice for the underdog by devoting his skills as a detective to overturning the verdicts in two different cases for men he felt were mistakenly convicted of crimes.

In World War I, Conan Doyle's son Kingsley was badly wounded on the Somme and later died in London of pneumonia. Conan Doyle's grief completed his conversion to Spiritualism, to which he devoted the remainder of his life. He fanatically toured Great Britain, Australia and North

Their first sight of a monster pterodactyl.

America seeking converts and even made arrangements to communicate with his second wife after his own death.

In *The Lost World*, Conan Doyle introduced his character of Professor Challenger. The novel begins as the Professor stubbornly insists that there exists on top of a high plateau in South America a land in which creatures from all periods of time coexist, even extinct species such as dinosaurs, ape-men and primitive Indians. Despite the hostile disbelief of the press and scientific establishment of London, Professor Challenger mounts an expedition to his Lost World, taking along a young reporter, a knighted adventurer and another scientist. They encounter every type of danger, including attacks by prehistoric monsters, before escaping after a destructive volcanic eruption. Challenger manages to capture a small Pterodactyl which escapes in London and flies home.

In 1919, Conan Doyle sold a five-year option for £500 to London producer J.G. Wainwright of Cineproductions, Ltd. to make a film of *The Lost World*. Chicago promoter Watterson R. Rothacker bought out Wainwright's option in September 1922, making a new eight-year arrangement with Conan Doyle. Rothacker owned film laboratories and produced advertising films. His interest in making a movie of *The Lost World* resulted from his four-year partnership with pioneer stop motion animator Willis O'Brien.

Stop motion animation had been used to bring inanimate objects and models to life on film before the turn of the century by the French producer, Georges Méliès. A subject was placed in position and a single frame was shot of that placement. The subject was then moved slightly and another frame exposed. The strip of still frames, when projected as a movie, was blended by "persistence of vision" into the illusion of movement. The speed of the subject was determined by the distance between the positions photographed. Fast-

Willis O'Brien's dinosaurs from *The Lost World*

moving subjects required less footage. Therefore, the placements were farther apart than would be necessary for slow-moving subjects. In 1906, the American filmmaker Edwin S. Porter used this method to create the illusion of a bed dancing and leaping all over a room in *The Dream of a Rarebit Fiend*.

Willis Harold O'Brien, who refined and developed this technique into near perfection, was born in 1886 in Oakland, California. He had been a cowboy, prizefighter, newspaper cartoonist for the *San Francisco Daily News* and commercial sculptor for the San Francisco World's Fair in 1913. While O'Brien was making clay models of boxers for an exhibit, his brother began manipulating the arms of one of the figures, saying, "My fighter can beat yours."

From this inspiration, O'Brien began experimenting with stop motion photography of pliable clay figures. Filming them with a borrowed newsreel camera, O'Brien made the models seem to move on their own, although they appeared jerky and too rapid. Late in 1914, he created a 75-foot film featuring a caveman and a comical Brontosaurus. An interested audience member at the screening of some of O'Brien's experiments was Watterson R. Rothacker.

O'Brien filmed a short comedy about a caveman, an ape-man and various prehistoric monsters called *The Dinosaur and the Missing Link* in 1915. The creatures were fashioned from clay over jointed wooden skeletons and photographed amid settings constructed from rocks and tree limbs set up in the basement of the Imperial Theatre in San Francisco. It took O'Brien two months to produce the film. The Thomas A. Edison Company of the Bronx, New York bought the short for $525—a dollar per foot—and distributed it theatrically.

Bessie Love hides from a Brontosaurus in *The Lost World*.

O'Brien set up on the roof of the Bank of Italy Building at Powell and Market Streets and filmed two more shorts, *Morpheus Mike* and *Birth of a Flivver*.

In New York in 1916, O'Brien made more dinosaur comedies for Edison's Conquest Film Programs. He formed Mannikin Films, Inc. with himself as president and produced *R.F.D., 10,000 B.C.*, *Prehistoric Poultry*, *In the Villain's Power*, *Curious Pets of Our Ancestors*, *Mickey and His Goat*, *Sam Lloyd's Famous Puzzles—The Puzzling Billboard* and *Nippy's Nightmare*. The last short intercut live actors with the animated shots, convincing O'Brien that a stop motion movie could only be good if the effects were combined with a human element.

When Edison discontinued the Conquest Program, O'Brien was asked to contribute to a weekly film series in which he was to present an educational segment depicting extinct animals. He consulted Dr. Barnum Brown, the distinguished vertebrate paleontologist at the American Museum of Natural History, to make sure that his reconstructions were scientifically correct. Before the weekly series commenced, Edison sold out to Lincoln and Parker, who decided to abandon O'Brien's segments.

Instead, O'Brien met Major Herbert M. Dawley, a film technician and cameraman who had made a flip book of a plastic dinosaur in which the model appeared to move. They agreed to make a dinosaur short together called *The Ghost of Slumber Mountain*. Using only a sheet of titles as a scenario, O'Brien constructed five prehistoric monsters under the guidance of Dr. Brown, making them as accurate as possible. For each creature, he prepared a wooden skeleton, covered it in clay sculpted to express muscles and flesh, and sealed it with skin-like cloth painted a dark brown color. Dr. Brown suggested much of the movement of the creatures. Unlike in O'Brien's previous shorts, there was no slapstick, and the dinosaurs were not caricatured. The camera itself was animated twice, panning across the landscape to reveal a Triceratops and moving slowly up the body of an Allosaurus to his toothy head.

Uncle Jack, a writer, tells his two young nephews of his adventures in a hidden valley. In flashback, we see his encounters with a Brontosaurus, a Triceratops and a vicious, flesh-eating Allosaurus. "His fevered breath was in my face," says Uncle Jack. "I could almost feel his fangs tearing my flesh!" But Uncle Jack manages to escape from the valley to tell the tale.

Costing only $3,000 to produce, the 520-foot short grossed more than $100,000. The April 18, 1919 *Variety* wrote, "The idea is a big one, capable of infinite extension and, even as achieved in the initial attempt, embodied in the present sketch, of strange and shuddering interest... these dinosaurs that suggest impossible lengths and heights, as well as the horned hobgoblins of the period... walk, twist, gaze and eat, as we imagine they must have in the long, long ago."

When the film premiered at the New York Strand, O'Brien received full credit for its production. But his name was removed from the 1919 release prints circulated by Paul M. Cromelin's World Cinema Distributing Company of Fort Lee, New Jersey. Producer Herbert M. Dawley took sole credit on screen and even told the reporter from the popular magazine, *Illustrated World*, that he had constructed and animated the dinosaurs in the film himself.

Watterson Rothacker was impressed with the film and horrified by Dawley's blatant attempt to steal credit from O'Brien. He quickly placed O'Brien under contract to make similar novelty films. Both men lost interest in shorts when they realized that Conan Doyle's novel, *The Lost World*, was the perfect vehicle to present O'Brien's work in a feature-length context.

On the night of June 2, 1922, at a dinner of the American Society of Magicians at the Hotel McAlpin in New York, Conan Doyle took the dais from Chairman Harry Houdini around one o'clock in the morning following magical demonstrations from such greats as Goldin, Heller and Houdini himself. Having come to America to give a series of lectures on Spiritualism, Sir Arthur had been invited by his skeptical friend Houdini to attend the annual meeting.

As a movie projector and screen were set up in the banquet room, Conan Doyle addressed the group: "If I brought here in real existence what I show in these pictures, it would be a great catastrophe. These pictures are not occult. This is psychic because everything that emanates from the human spirit or human brain is psychic. It is not supernatural. It is the effect of the joining, on the one hand, of imagination and on the other hand, of some power of materialization. The imagination, I may say, comes from me. The materializing power comes from elsewhere." Sir Arthur warned the professional magicians that he would answer no questions, and the film began.

The next morning, the front page of *The New York Times* announced: "DINOSAURS CAVORT IN FILM FOR DOYLE, Spiritist Mystifies World-Famed Magicians With Pictures

Willis O'Brien and Marcel Delgado brought Doyle's novel to life in *The Lost World*.

of Prehistoric Beasts." The reporter from the *Times* was impressed, to say the least: "Monsters of several million years ago, mostly of the dinosaur species, made love and killed each other in Sir Arthur's pictures," he reported in the article. "His monsters of the ancient world or of the new world which he has discovered in the ether, were extraordinarily lifelike. If fakes, they were masterpieces."

The same day, Conan Doyle sent a letter to Houdini explaining that what he had shown the Society was O'Brien's test footage from an upcoming motion picture adaptation of his novel, *The Lost World*. "The dinosaurs and other monsters have been constructed by pure cinema, but of the highest kind," he wrote, adding that his goal in showing the film was "to provide a little mystification to those who have so often and so successfully mystified others... And now, Mr. Chairman, confidence begets confidence, and I want to know how you got out of that trunk."

Alerted by Conan Doyle's very public demonstration of his project, Catherine Curtis, who called herself "the only woman producer," sued Rothacker claiming that he had sold her the film rights to *The Lost World* in July 1920, that she had already spent $35,000 on preproduction and that Rothacker had hired O'Brien and Herbert Dawley to animate the model dinosaurs on film. Dawley promptly denied any association with Rothacker and sued Conan Doyle and Rothacker for $100,000 apiece for violating his patent on O'Brien's process of frame-by-frame animation of models. He had filed the patent in February 1920, two years after producing O'Brien's *The Ghost of Slumber Mountain*. Dawley was presented with notarized statements attesting to O'Brien's early development of stop motion animation, and he decided to settle out of court. Another lawsuit against an unnamed major studio was dismissed, and Rothacker was finally able to sign an agreement with Associated First National Pictures on December 14, 1923 to produce the movie.

At the Burbank studios of First National, the project was put under the supervision of Earl Hudson with a scenario written by Marion Fairfax. In his contract, Conan Doyle had final right of approval of any adaptation. He did not object when Fairfax added female characters to Conan Doyle's original all-male cast. Her new character of Paula White formed a love triangle with the courtly elder sportsman and hunter Sir John Roxton and the exuberant young reporter Ed Malone. The character of Marquette, a flirtatious half-caste girl encountered by the adventurers at a South American trading post, provided more sex appeal to the film.

First National also envisioned a spectacular ending. In Conan Doyle's novel, Professor Challenger smuggles a young Pterodactyl back to London which escapes with minor incident from Queens Hall before flying back to the Lost World. In the new scenario, Professor Challenger returns to London with a fully grown Brontosaurus which breaks loose, wrecking the city in its confusion before swimming home by way of the Thames.

O'Brien, who usually did all of his animation alone, realized that he would need some assistance to complete this massive project. Fred W. Jackman, the head of First National's special effects department, collaborated with O'Brien, providing the expertise needed for shots combining live actors with model sets and stop motion dinosaurs. Ralph Hammeras operated his own motion picture special effects company on the First National lot when Earl Hudson persuaded him to join the staff. Hammeras impressed O'Brien with his development of the glass painting which he patented in 1925. Elaborate vistas could be painted on glass and combined with live photography and animation, allowing the exotic locales needed for *The Lost World* to be created affordably at the studio. O'Brien brought his own dinosaur models to the studio from New York, but Hammeras persuaded O'Brien that they were too small. New ones needed to be built. O'Brien also realized that creatures made of wood, clay and cloth would be inadequate for so ambitious a film.

At a class he attended at night at the Otis Art Institute, O'Brien met a talented 20-year-old sculptor named Marcel Delgado. The young Mexican worked as a grocery clerk and student assistant to finance his studies. During the Mexican Revolution, his large, impoverished family had moved from the village of La Parrita to California and found work in the bean fields and walnut orchards around Saticoy. Delgado did not speak English until he was 17, but he had been sculpting and even creating his own mechanical toys since he was six.

Delgado remembered his first meeting with O'Brien: "Mr. O'Brien took an interest in my work and one night, he asked me, 'Would you like to work in motion pictures?' I told him I would not because I wanted to be an artist and didn't want to lose any time. Every time he saw me, he asked again and offered me $75 a week to come to work for him. I always said no, and I don't really know why; I was only making $18 a week, but I guess I felt secure. One Friday, he asked me to lay off work and visit the motion picture studio. OBie left a pass at the gate and when I went in, OBie met me and took me to his little shop. There was a phone, some cameras and pictures all around. 'How do you like your studio?' he asked. 'It's yours if you want it.' It was a 20-year-old boy's dream! So I signed up and worked for the next couple of years building dinosaurs for *The Lost World*. I made 49 or 50 of them, and it was all done under cover with no visitors allowed—although some of the studio big shots came in anyhow."

Improving on O'Brien's wooden frames, Delgado fashioned the skeletons for his models from tempered dural with articulated backbones and ball-and-socket joints for all the moveable digits and appendages. The muscles were no longer clay but sponge rubber which could flex and stretch like real muscles. The skins were made of latex and rubber sheeting which reacted more naturally to movement than painted cloth. All plates, spines, warts and other protuberances were made separately and glued to the textured skins. Some of the featured dinosaurs even included a bladder under the skin which could be animated with an air compressor to make the animals appear to breathe. Each dinosaur averaged 18 inches, with the giant Brontosaurus who starred in the film's climax being considerably larger.

Delgado consulted the celebrated paintings of Charles R. Knight from the Field Museum of Natural History and the American Museum of Natural History to make the appearances of the creatures as believable as possible. Knight's reconstructions were not only lifelike, but they gave the extinct monsters personalities. Delgado captured this quality in his sculptures, and O'Brien extended it in his animation.

Ralph Hammeras and his crew of 125 technicians created the miniature sets for O'Brien's creatures. They typically measured six feet wide by four feet deep, elevated on platforms three feet off the floor. The sequence of the fire and dinosaur stampede required a special 75 by 150 foot stage depicting a huge scaled-down jungle. Miniature trees featured leaves and fronds made from cut sheet metal to avoid movement between exposed frames. Special backgrounds included rods for the positioning of dinosaurs that would be animated to leap off the ground to attack or fly. Seven cameras mounted on dollies recorded the animation with shutters operated simultaneously from a single control.

The sets were lit with flickerless Cooper-Hewitt mercury vapor lamps, and O'Brien shut himself up with the miniatures so nothing could disturb his concentration. Except for the complex stampede sequence, O'Brien performed all of the animation himself. A typical day for O'Brien yielded 35 feet of film, which was less than 30 seconds of screen time. After a year of this, First National relocated to New York where O'Brien completed the project at the old Biograph studio in the Bronx.

The Lost World was O'Brien's first film to include actors and stop motion animals in the same shot. Portions of the negative of static animated scenes were masked off, and actors photographed against matching backdrops were printed into the masked-off areas. In the London climax, hordes of extras run through the streets from the Brontosaurus in a single shot. These scenes employed an early traveling matte process. The dinosaur was animated against a stark white background, and the resulting film was made up two ways: as a negative with the animal appearing against a black background and as a high-contrast positive with the figure in silhouette against clear film. The high-contrast positive was used as a mask through which to print the street scene, producing a copy in which the contours of the animal were left unexposed. The negative then was employed to print the Brontosaurus into the masked areas. It was marred only by occasional matte bleeds caused by variable shrinkage of the different emulsions. This process was made obsolete by the more dependable ones invented by C. Dodge Dunning and Frank Williams and by the development of optical printing.

In addition to the spectacular ending, the film's major set piece is the stampede of monsters during a volcanic eruption on the lost plateau. Dozens of dinosaurs flee through the burning forest, sometimes in the same frame with live actors, the exploding volcano, flames and smoke. During all this, the Allosaurs prey on the smaller animals which fight them off as they run. In one shot, an entire family of Allosaurs feed on a large fallen herbivore. In complexity and visual detail, the sequence still ranks as one of the most spectacular stop motion scenes of all time.

Meanwhile, shooting of the live action progressed with Harry O. Hoyt directing. Hoyt, a graduate of Columbia and Yale, had been a lawyer before becoming a scriptwriter for D.W.

In the London climax of *The Lost World*, hordes of extras run through the streets from the Brontosaurus in a single shot. [Photofest]

Griffith among others, as well as an editor and finally, a director. Studio supervisor Earl Hudson established a second unit when it became evident that shooting would require a year without one. William Dowling directed this second company which eventually merged with Hoyt's main unit during the final weeks of production.

Burly character actor Wallace Beery played Professor Challenger. The accompanying cast included venerable Lewis Stone as the dignified skeptic Sir John Roxton, Bessie Love as lovely Paula White, Lloyd Hughes as the ambitious young reporter Ed Malone and Bull Montana, in a startling disguise by pioneer makeup artist Cecil Holland, as a ferocious ape-man the party encounters in the Lost World.

Like Lon Chaney, Holland relied heavily on cotton wool and collodion to alter actor Montana's face. With this technique, Holland built up Montana's forehead, giving him the projected brows of a simian. He also created heavy bags under the eyes and filled Montana's mouth with sharp, protruding teeth. The actor's body was covered in a shaggy suit of stiff yak's hair that made him look like man's missing link to the gorilla.

In July 1924, First National announced that more than $1,000,000 would be spent on production of *The Lost World*. A set representing two downtown London streets was one-eighth of a mile long. Two thousand extras, 200 automobiles and six omnibuses were illuminated at night on the set by the maximum lighting capacity of the studio. Twenty-five assistant directors and 18 cameramen under the direction of Arthur Edeson who had photographed Douglas Fairbanks' epics, *Robin Hood* and *The Thief of Baghdad*, recorded the scene. Equally impressive were exterior and interior sets of the Royal Museum in which Professor Challenger confronts the scoffing audiences with his discovery of the Lost World. South American jungles, a trading post, caverns and the precipice that must be scaled to reach the Lost World were constructed along the concrete Los Angeles River.

Enough footage was shot for two movies. Much to O'Brien's annoyance, screenwriter Marion Fairfax assured him that she had constructed the script in such a way that the dinosaurs could easily be cut out if the animation did not work. Of course, the monsters turned out to be the show's strength. So instead of cutting O'Brien's work, editors removed live-action scenes amounting to nearly half an hour before the film's premiere. A whole section before the party reaches the Lost World was easily jettisoned. It involved a scheme by Challenger to prove he is the leader of the group, a visit to a primitive trading post, the entire character of Marquette who flirts with reporter Malone at the post, a close call with a tribe of cannibals and a mutiny led by the sinister guide Gomez, who, like the ape-man, was played by Bull Montana. Along with Marquette, the character of Gomez disappeared from the film completely.

In February 1925, the 10-reel *The Lost World* premiered at Broadway's Astor Theatre in New York on a limited twice-a-day engagement. The spectacularly publicized opening followed a clever Boston preview run. This pre-release showing was so monumentally successful that New York journalists shipped reporters ahead to Massachusetts for advance reviews. During the silent era, the press usually restricted such reverential coverage to theatrical productions.

The film was an immensely popular success, and contemporary critics appeared as convinced of the genuineness of the monsters as did the crowds. Wallace Beery's robust performance as Professor Challenger also met with approval. One 1925 critic enthusiastically described *The Lost World* as "the most marvelous film of all time." The reporter for *The Boston Herald* queried, "How was it done? We have seen seas open and shut... We have seen flying carpets and horses... but how a naturally moving animal as big as a ship could chase real people down a real street and apparently break through a real bridge is too much for us. We'd better just believe it happened."

Even after the advances in special effects that have rendered O'Brien's work antiquated, *The Lost World* is a charming, exciting and sometimes shocking experience. The dinosaur fights contain a large quantity of torn flesh and glistening blood, and the choreography of the animals give them a reality and personality that overcomes the jerky stop motion animation. Beery makes an amusingly stubborn, arrogant and intimidating Challenger. Cecil Holland's makeup for the ape-man remains startling, and the character himself makes an original and unpredictable menace. The final destruction of London by the Brontosaurus, while perhaps tame by the standards of later imitators, including the great *King Kong*, moves swiftly. It is full of great ideas such as the monster's head suddenly poking through the window of an upper-story apartment and the collapse of Tower Bridge under the beast's enormous weight.

The dinosaurs were the real stars of *The Lost World*.

On the other hand, the characters are superficial and the romantic triangle is sketched in briefly as befits an adventure designed for adolescent boys. The love story never delays or intrudes on the action more than is necessary to allow the audience to know something about the people involved. Of course, the film has none of the resonances of the relationship between Ann Darrow and Kong, and one of the weaknesses of the original novel is the lack of interaction between the explorers and the monsters they encounter. *The Lost World* is no masterpiece, but it is full of technical innovations and is still an entertaining first draft for later, fuller treatments of its themes.

The picture went into general release in early summer. It made a huge amount of money for both First National and Rothacker. In addition to profits as owner of the property, his Rothacker Film Manufacturing Co. had the exclusive contractual rights for making all domestic release prints, in addition to those for Canada, Mexico, South and Central America and Asia.

Ultimately, the expensive production was so successful that production manager Earl Hudson quickly announced that O'Brien and Hoyt would collaborate on a sequel "entirely different" from the original. As late as February 1928, negotiations were still being made with Rothacker to begin production despite several changes of studio ownership and policy. Finally, a new management decided to abandon the costly project. O'Brien tried to interest studios in an adaptation of *Frankenstein* using stop motion animation for the monster in addition to a film version of H.G. Wells' giant animal epic, *Food of the Gods*, both without success.

As O'Brien's fortunes fell, so did those of his talented collaborator, young Marcel Delgado. Later, Delgado recalled, "While *The Lost World* was in work, I got to be well known at the studio. Big stars like Milton Sills, Colleen Moore and Wally Beery were my friends. But after I was demoted to the prop shop, they treated me like I had the mange. A couple of years later, Warner Bros. bought out First National, and I was laid off, but I was quickly hired to build miniatures and special props at the old William Fox Studio. I stayed there until OBie called again."

CHAPTER 8
OLD DARK HOUSES

The American mystery writer Mary Roberts Rinehart was born to a poor family in Pittsburgh in 1876. Her father, Thomas Beverly Roberts, was a dreamer and unsuccessful inventor who committed suicide just as Mary finished nursing school. During her studies, she met Dr. Stanley Marshall Rinehart, married him in 1896 and had three sons within five years. In 1903, when the Rineharts found themselves in debt due to some bad stock market investments, she began to write, and she eventually sold 45 stories during her first year. She earned the considerable sum of $1,842.50 that year, and the editors of *Munsey's Magazine* suggested she write a crime serial. *The Man in Lower Ten* was quickly followed by *The Circular Staircase*, which was her first to be published as a book in 1908.

After a string of best sellers in a similar vein, Mrs. Rinehart decided to convert *The Circular Staircase* into a play in 1917. With the help of playwright Avery Hopwood, she compacted the long, rambling book into a single night of terror in a spooky house. The plot revolved around a large sum of money concealed in a once-vacant dwelling whose new tenants are terrified by a fiend intent on reclaiming the cash. In transferring the story to the stage, Rinehart and Hopwood changed the murderer from the woman housekeeper to a master criminal known simply as "The Bat." In 1920, *The Bat*, as the play was ultimately named, debuted on Broadway at the Morosco Theatre. It was a tremendous hit, running for 867 performances and spawning innumerable road-company tours.

Because of the success of *The Bat*, a flood of similarly atmospheric mystery-comedy plays followed. John Willard wrote and starred in *The Cat and the Canary* in 1922, which inspired D.W. Griffith to film *One Exciting Night* the same year. *The Charlatan*, *The Night Call*, *Drums of Jeopardy*, *The Return of Peter Grimm* and a revival of *Trilby* all opened on Broadway that season, followed later in the year by *The Last Warning* and *The Monster*. Every one of these plays eventually became films.

The first to reach the screen was director Roland West's version of playwright Crane Wilbur's *The Monster* starring Lon Chaney. For much of its length, more of a rural comedy than a mystery, it still managed enough sinister and perverse atmosphere because of its origins as an uncredited adaptation of Poe's "The System of Dr. Tarr and Professor Feather" to be regarded as a horror movie.

Its author, Crane Wilbur, was born November 17, 1889 in Athens, New York. As an actor, he played in stock and repertory beginning in 1904. He entered films in 1910, co-starring in many of Pearl White's early silents and playing her leading man in the famous serial, *The Perils of Pauline*. Audiences considered him one of the most handsome screen personalities of that period. *The Monster* was his first work as a writer to be filmed, but it was far from his last. He became a prolific screenwriter and director for the rest of his career, penning the scripts for later genre efforts such as *House of Wax* in 1953, *The Mad Magician* in 1954, *Mysterious Island* in 1961 and a sound version of Rinehart's *The Bat*, which he also directed in 1959. The actual scenario for his first effort, *The Monster*, was adapted from his play by Willard Mack and Albert Kenyon.

Director Roland West was born Roland Van Ziemer in Cleveland, Ohio, in 1887, the son of noted theater actress Margaret Van Tassel. His aunt was a local theater producer, and when Roland was 12, she cast him in her 1899 production of *The Volunteers*. By 1904, the youth had changed his name to Roland West and had become a seasoned stage performer. At 19, West co-wrote and starred in a vaudeville sketch called *The Criminal*, later retitled

The lunatics are running the asylum in *The Monster* with Lon Chaney, Johnny Arthur, Edward McWade, George Austin, Knute Erickson and Walter James.

The Under World, in which he played five parts. *Variety* called the sketch "a tale of murder, robbery and police inquisitions (in which) five distinct characters are drawn... with a remarkably short time elapsing for (costume) changes... Voice, action, manner and method are completely changed with each." The act was a precursor of things to come from West: his later films would be preoccupied with the criminal mind and melodramatic plot twists.

West decided to turn from acting to film directing. During his early years as a performer on the Loew's circuit, he befriended Joseph M. Schenck, Loew's general manager in charge of bookings. Fortunately for West, Schenck also had ambitions to go into motion pictures. In 1915, they partnered. Schenck would produce movies written and directed by West. On a budget of $27,000, they made *Lost Souls* which, though amateurish, was bought by Fox and released as *A Woman's Honor*. Their next effort, *De Luxe Annie* in 1918, starred Schenck's wife, the popular Norma Talmadge and was a hit. Also in 1918, West wrote and produced a successful play, *The Unknown Purple*, about a scientist who discovers the secret of invisibility. In 1921, he wrote and directed two films, *The Silver Lining* and *Nobody*, starring his own wife, Jewel Carmen. His 1923 film of *The Unknown Purple* featured a hand-tinted purple glow to indicate the presence of the vengeful scientist.

In 1925, his company, Roland West Productions, produced *The Monster* with Tec-Art Studios on Melrose Avenue on the stages that eventually became Raleigh Studios. Despite his top billing, Lon Chaney is in relatively little of *The Monster* compared to actor Johnny Arthur who plays Johnny, the under clerk of Watson's General Store.

Correspondence school detective Johnny (Johnny Arthur) meets his match in Dr. Ziska (Chaney) and his henchmen (George Austin and Walter James) in *The Monster*.

In the first scene of the picture, strikingly photographed at night by Hal Mohr, a gaunt, ghoulish-looking man lowers a mirror ringed with foliage onto a rural dirt road from his perch in a tree. Luke Watson, the middle-aged owner of the local general store, approaches the mirror in his car. He swerves to avoid the reflection of his own oncoming headlights, and his car turns over in a ditch. Another dark figure in a hat and long coat emerges from underground, and the two men approach Watson's unconscious body.

When Watson turns up missing, the ineffectual local police cannot solve the case and seem disinclined to try. A small, weak-looking but determined young man, Johnny has recently received his diploma from a detective correspondence school. Although neither bright nor respected by the locals, he intends to put his training to use in finding his boss.

After a comic party scene in which Johnny is mocked behind his back for his false bravado, the handsome and oily Head Clerk of Watson's store takes Betty, the girl Johnny loves, out for a night drive. Of course, they encounter the mirror trap and smash their car.

Johnny has a hunch that Watson may be in the nearby sanitarium so he finds his way inside. Betty and the Head Clerk also end up at the sanitarium and meet Chaney as Dr. Ziska.

The Monster only really comes alive when Chaney is on screen. He plays Dr. Ziska as Boris Karloff would later enact his civilized villains: grinning, unctuously courteous, with more than a hint of insanity and sinister purpose behind his smile. Chaney's simple makeup consists of a gray wig parted in the middle and a slight darkening under his eyes. He constantly manipulates a long cigarette holder and wears an elegant dressing gown. At one point, just before exiting a room, he twitches his shoulder and face, hinting at his real identity.

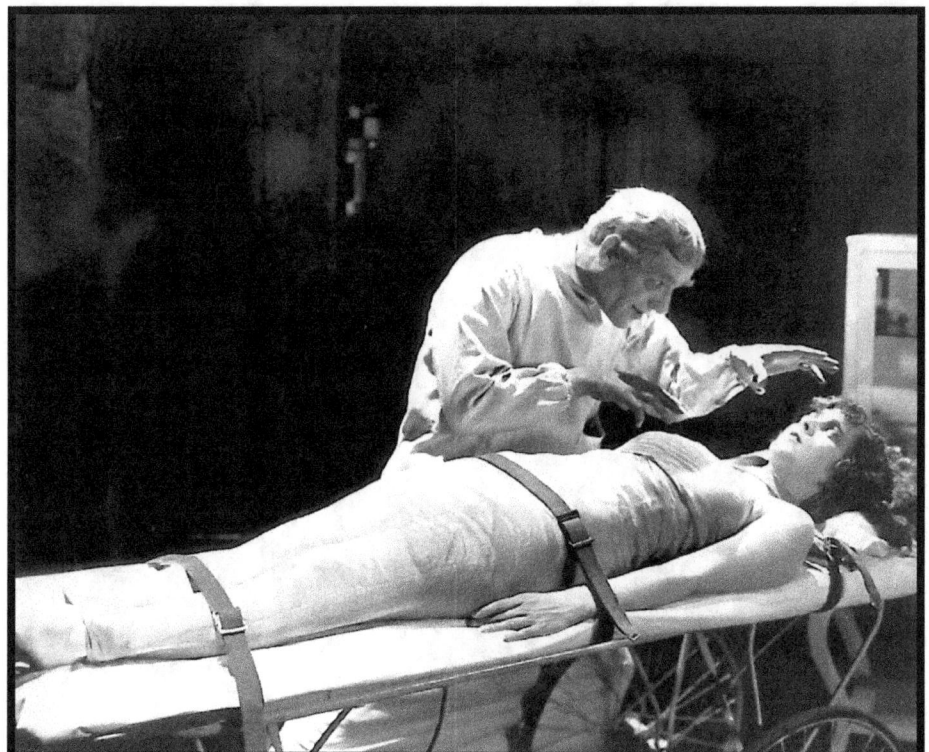

Dr. Ziska insanely plans to transfer Betty's (Gertrude Olmsted) soul into the Head Clerk's body in *The Monster*.

After a series of strange characters and events assault Johnny, Betty and the Head Clerk in the mysterious house, the truth finally emerges. Dr. Ziska and his helpers are actually the inmates of the sanitarium who have imprisoned the doctors in a pit under the cellar. Once a great surgeon, Dr. Ziska insanely plans to transfer Betty's soul into the Head Clerk's body and straps the Head Clerk into an electric chair.

Johnny overpowers the ghoulish-looking inmate Rigo in a beautifully photographed slapstick fight in a rainstorm that involves Johnny balancing on telephone lines like a tightrope walker, falling though a window and sliding down a banister. Wearing Rigo's cloak and hood, Johnny sneaks into Dr. Ziska's basement lab and frees the Head Clerk. They strap Dr. Ziska to the electric chair, gag him and turn out the lights.

When another of Ziska's helpers, the brutish Caliban, enters the basement, he switches on the chair which kills Ziska. Finally, Johnny cuffs Caliban's ankles to the chain of the winch that uncovers the pit in which the doctors are imprisoned. He turns on the winch, which pulls Caliban up by the heals and frees the doctors. The police arrive, Johnny is a hero, and he gets the girl.

In the February 14, 1925 issue of *Moving Picture World*, MGM announced that it would distribute the film. It opened the movie on February 22 and eventually bought the full rights from Roland West in 1927.

The reviews were mostly kind. *Film Daily* said, "Spook story that mingles laughs and thrills in rapid succession and includes a quantity of hair-raising stunts... Johnny Arthur's part seems more important than Chaney's." *Photoplay* agreed: "B-r-r-r, this one will give you delicious creeps... A real thriller." *Harrison's Reports* offered more of the same: "An

Despite the low comedy of Johnny and the rural stereotypes, *The Monster* is entertaining for the undemanding.

entertaining comedy and mystery play... There are situations which make one laugh and which at the same time hold him in breathless suspense... *The Monster* should also please. But it will prove too grewsome [sic] for tender-hearted people."

The most extraordinarily positive review came from *Movie Weekly*: "*The Monster* seems to us Lon Chaney's best part of recent years, because his art comes from within and not from without. Let a man be an adept at putting on a paper mache [sic] torso, a putty nose and protruding teeth and everyone is ready to proclaim him a great actor. In *The Monster*, he appears as himself, with no disfiguring makeup... *The Monster* is a thrilling picture."

The New York Times may have caught the lasting impression of the picture when it wrote, "The starch seems to have been taken out of the pictorial conception of *The Monster* by the inclusion of too much light comedy. The result is that, although this film possesses a degree of queer entertainment, it is neither fish, fowl nor good red herring... The ludicrous situations and comical antics of the players are all the more surprising, as one does not expect much fun in a film featuring Lon Chaney... Mr. Chaney does not have very much to do, but his various appearances are effective... Mr. Chaney looks as if he could have enjoyed a more serious portrayal of the theme." *Variety* was even more blunt: "Lon Chaney does not make the crazed surgeon as terrifying a picture as he might have and, in that, the film lets down to a certain extent."

Despite the low comedy of Johnny and the rural stereotypes, the movie is entertaining for the undemanding. It announces itself as a comedy as soon as Johnny and the locals are introduced and later, much later, punctuates the lightness with a few perverse thrills involving Chaney and the other lunatics. West directs competently but without the beautiful design and art direction of his adaptation of *The Bat* the following year or Paul Leni's brilliant camerawork in his version of *The Cat and the Canary* in 1927.

Much of the problem with the film involves the character of Johnny. He is determined and well intentioned, but he is too naive and self deluded to be an attractive identification figure. Of course, some of the great silent comics such as Buster Keaton share many of Johnny's deficiencies, but Keaton has the saving grace of being funny. Keaton is also one of the most beautiful looking men in silent films, and Johnny Arthur appears more like a minor character actor than a romantic lead.

Johnny prevails mostly through luck except in the end when he bravely captures Caliban. The Head Clerk is brighter, but he appears foolish in his mail-order tails at the rural house party and insincere in his pursuit of the girl. Betty is merely pretty and young, her affections seemingly easy to manipulate.

In order to accept the clichés of the haunted house mystery, such as secret chutes that transport bodies to the basement, a couch that lowers into the cellar while hands grab its victim from underneath, plaques that slide away to reveal peering faces and the like, the viewer is asked to believe that the raving lunatics have constructed them in the time they have imprisoned the doctors. Not only is this too much to swallow, but these implausibilities merely serve to introduce devices that have already become overly familiar through repetition in similar plays. In fact, even at the time of the movie's release, *The New York Post* bemoaned, "The only thing against the show is that it is becoming well worn out."

Roland West's partner, Joseph M. Schenck, became chairman of United Artists, the independent company formed by D.W. Griffith, Charlie Chaplin, Douglas Fairbanks and Mary Pickford to give them autonomy. Schenck signed West as a producer at United Artists and, following the policy of the founders of the company, gave him complete freedom to pick his projects. West still had a fondness for the mystery-comedy thrillers that were in vogue on Broadway so he chose the first and most popular for his premiere film under his new contract: Mary Roberts Rinehart's *The Bat*.

The Bat is a master criminal who disguises himself in a mask and arrogantly announces to the police that he will commit a daring heist. Despite police guards, he manages to murder Gideon Bell, the owner of the Favre Emeralds and make off with them. His next job is the looting of the Oakdale Bank. But a rival crook foils the Bat by getting to the bank first and stealing the cash right under the Bat's nose.

The Bat follows the robber to the old dark country house of Courtley Fleming, the Oakdale Bank president, who supposedly died while on vacation. The house is being leased by a wealthy spinster, Miss Cornelia Van Gorder. This quietly clever woman lives there with her comical maid, Lizzie. The plot is complicated by the disappearance of Brook Bailey, the meek bespectacled young cashier of the robbed bank, who loves the spinster's lovely niece, Dale. The entire cast of characters, including an ugly Japanese manservant named Billy, suspicious Dr. Wells and bumbling private detective Anderson, converge on the spooky mansion while the sinister Bat sneaks about in the shadows trying to locate the loot.

A police detective named Moletti is present, while Brook Bailey poses as a gardener in the hope of clearing himself of suspicion. In reality, the creeping monster has knocked out the real detective Moletti and poses as the law officer in order to search the house. He kills the robber who turns out to be Courtley Fleming, the not-dead bank president, and runs off with the satchel of money. As the Bat escapes, he is caught in an animal trap devised by Lizzie at the beginning of the story and forgotten by the audience.

The twist of the detective turning out to be the killer did not originate with Mary Roberts Rinehart. In Gaston Leroux's 1907 novel, *The Mystery of the Yellow Room*, the investigator turns out to be the perpetrator. Agatha Christie later credited Leroux's locked door mystery with inspiring her interest in crime fiction. Like Rinehart with *The Bat*, she even featured a fake detective who turns out to be the murderer in her famous 1952 play, *The Mousetrap*.

For the 1920 stage version of *The Bat*, producers Lincoln A. Wagenhals and Colin Kemper cast Harrison Hunter as the detective but withheld from him and the rest of the company that his character was actually the Bat in disguise. Hunter believed himself to be the hero until just before dress rehearsal when the final scene was released. The actor angrily called the stunt "a low joke," but his performance as the phony detective so convinced audiences that they were as shocked as he at the final revelation.

What distinguished West's film version of *The Bat* above its mystery-comedy stage roots and raised it to a level of cinematic achievement were the extraordinary designs of the visuals by William Cameron Menzies, the stunning miniatures and effects by Ned Herbert Mann and the atmospherically lit photography of *The Lost World*'s Arthur Edeson. A very young Gregg Toland, who would go on to film such deep-focus masterpieces as *The Grapes of Wrath*, *Citizen Kane* and *The Best Years of Our Lives*, assisted Edeson.

By the time of his collaboration with West, William Cameron Menzies was already becoming one of the most gifted visual stylists of the American cinema. He was born on July 29, 1896 in New Haven, Connecticut and graduated from Yale University. He served with the American Expeditionary Forces in Europe during World War I, attended New York's Art Student League after demobilization and took a job with Famous Players as an art director. Bringing to the screen his own audacious personal visual style, he immediately began to dominate Hollywood's movie design scene. He created the extraordinary Arabian Nights sets for Douglas Fairbanks' film of *The Thief of Baghdad* as well as the exotic locals for the Rudolph Valentino vehicles, *The Eagle*, *Cobra* and *Son of the Sheik*.

His work and that of effects designer Ned Herbert Mann dominate the opening of *The Bat*. After the credits, which are etched on metallic plates, the first image is a black screen with two small glowing circles. Slowly, the figure of a bat fades in around the lights, revealing them to be the creature's shining eyes. This dissolves to Herbert Mann's elaborately detailed model of tall buildings at night against a bright full moon. The model of a bat circles the buildings and lands on a roof. West dissolves to a long lighted window against a black background and then wipes the screen slowly to reveal the stylized set of an office with the thin, high window overlooking the city. Two huge silver candleholders frame the back of Gideon Bell, wearing a high black collar and sitting at a small table in front of the window.

After a well shot and edited scene of Bell strangled and robbed by the Bat, the film returns to the work of Menzies and Mann. The silhouette of the murderer climbing down a rope in front of the long lighted window is followed by another beautifully designed model, this time of the Oakdale Bank against the full moon. Again, the bat circles the sky and lands on the roof.

The most impressive shot in the movie is a high angle of the Bat looking down through an enormous skylight that is framed in smaller squares like a chessboard. Far below him in the shadowy bank, another criminal packs his satchel with stolen cash. The visual metaphor

of the game board created by the squared skylight is apt since the Bat is being checked by another player in this secret game of larceny.

West flawlessly combines models and sets in this opening. He is able to cut long shots of a model car racing from the bank with closer views of an actual car on the road. Menzie's full-sized sets are so stylized that they match the slightly unreal look of Mann's models. For example, a stunning long shot of the tiny figure of the Bat sliding down a rope against a huge blank wall would appear to be a model if it were not for the movements of the actor in costume.

A model of the lonely mock-Tudor mansion against the full moon introduces Miss Van Gorder. By first showing her through another window squared like a chessboard, West tells the audience that she is a new player in this game of crime and detection. Menzies' interior Art Nouveau sets emphasize height with long windows and drapes, 18-foot doors, columns, double-deck staircases and even vertically lined wallpaper in Lizzie's bedroom. West masks the screen lengthwise when the bank robber climbs up a ladder in the laundry chute, a lighted tunnel created by blacking out the frame on both sides of the ladder. West also masks the space above a stairway making it appear to be a hidden passageway.

Edeson consistently creates the spectral quality of lunar light pouring through windows into the immense rooms. For the night exteriors, Edeson sidelights or backlights the massive trees and garden wall as if the full moon's glow were filtering through the branches.

The Bat himself does not wear the black hood that had become the conventional disguise for stage mystery villains. Even in the hit Broadway play, the Bat merely wore a black handkerchief around his face. In West's film, the Bat's mask reproduces the hideous fanged mouth, bristly ears and turned-up snout of the actual creature, edging this offering closer to a horror film. The Bat scurries through the sets, climbs ropes, walls and branches and attacks his victims as if possessed with the unbridled energy of a demon. West emphasizes The Bat's frightening mask by introducing it slowly, first in long shots, then in close silhouette

against a grimy window and finally, approaching the terrified heroine's point of view in the manner of Chaney's first appearance as the unmasked Phantom of the Opera.

This scene ranks as one of the high points of American silent screen terror. Dale, played by West's wife, Jewel Carmen, chances upon an entrance to a hidden room behind a fireplace. We have already seen the Bat enter the secret chamber and try to open the safe inside. When Dale steps into the room with only a lighted candle, the Bat hides in a dark corner. The door swings shut, trapping Dale in with the killer. Until this point, the heroine has been shown only in long shots as she moves through the darkness. When she turns and spots the hideous creature staring at her, West cuts to a close shot of her terrified reaction. As the Bat slowly approaches her, his fanged mouth opens as if to bite. He steps so close to the camera that all we can see are his cold, staring eyes behind the mask.

Unfortunately, although Arthur Edeson's atmospheric lighting is impressive throughout the movie, the shots that follow the bravura opening mostly consist of groups of characters going in and out of the cavernous rooms of the spooky mansion. Because this is a silent film based on a stage play, the pace slackens once the theatrical scenes must be rendered for the camera, and much of the storytelling is accomplished by intertitles. Unlike Paul Leni's later *The Cat and the Canary*, there is not a single camera move in the entire film.

Nevertheless, there are some scenes of action. The group tracks Courtley Fleming, the supposedly dead bank president, across the roof, ending with Lizzie and Anderson both comically hanging from the same rope on either side of the house. The set piece in which Dale is trapped in the secret room with the Bat climaxes in a fight between the Bat and Fleming, ending with Dale witnessing Fleming's murder. Also, the deft construction of the play ensures that the mystery rarely loses interest.

In terms of performances, Emily Fitzroy stands out, skillfully underplaying Mrs. Von Gorder as she works on her embroidery while cleverly deducing who is who and what is what. Louise Fazenda is suitably frantic as Lizzie, enthusiastically delivering the requisite cowardice and slapstick comedy. Unfortunately, the least impressive performance comes from stage singer Tullio Carminati, a Dalmatian count, who portrays the ersatz detective and the Bat. Carminati is so bland and straight-faced, even after he is unmasked, that it is hard to believe his detective capable of the evil and skill required to be a master criminal.

The reviews for the film were mostly positive. The March 17, 1926 *Variety* enthused: "This picture ran 91 minutes—a long time for anybody's film, but it was interesting every minute of the way... an excellent picture... the exhibitor buying it can depend on real value." Two days earlier, *The New York Times* said, "Doubtless the film conception of *The Bat* will prove both entertaining and exciting despite the mechanical twists employed... People in the theater yesterday were distinctly affected by the spine-chilling episodes, and they were relieved by the comedy interludes." P.S. Harrison, publisher of the film guide, *Harrison's Report*, wrote: "Few pictures have been released lately that hold the spectator as breathless as does *The Bat*, and not only does it hold him breathless but it thrills him and at the same time makes him laugh to his heart's content."

On the strength of his direction of the German Expressionist anthology, *Waxworks*, Paul Leni was lured to Universal Pictures in 1927 by Carl Laemmle. His first assignment in America was to turn John Willard's 1922 stage hit, *The Cat and the Canary*, into a film. Laemmle hired Robert F. Hill and Alfred A. Cohen to adapt the popular play. Hill, who was born on April 14, 1886 in Port Rohen, Ontario, Canada, entered films as an actor and writer. In addition to penning several scenarios, he had directed low-budget features and serials starting in 1916, including Elmo Lincoln as Tarzan in the 1921 chapter play, *The Adventures of Tarzan*.

Although Leni had designed the sets for many of his German films, including *Waxworks*, Laemmle assigned *The Cat and the Canary* to English art director Charles D. Hall who had worked on the sets for *The Phantom of the Opera* as well as Chaplin's *The Gold Rush*. But the studio head wisely allowed Leni free rein in his use of director of photography Gilbert Warrenton's camera.

The story of *The Cat and the Canary* concerns the demise of eccentric millionaire Cyrus West and his order that the last will be read at midnight 20 years after his death in his supposedly haunted old mansion. The sinister housekeeper who has lived alone there admits the family lawyer, Roger Crosly, to announce the inheritor. He is followed by Harry Blythe and his cousin, Charlie Wilder, nervous old Aunt Susan and her stylish young niece, Cecily, a timid, bespectacled young man named Paul Jones and finally, Paul's beloved distant cousin, the beautiful and sweet Annabelle West.

As the wind howls outside, the ancient clock, which has not struck since the night the old man died 20 years ago, manages to sound the hour of midnight. Lawyer Crosly reads the document which says that, "My relatives have watched me as if they were the cat and I the canary. Therefore my wealth goes to the most distant relative bearing the name of West: Annabelle."

A codicil to the will states that Annabelle's sanity must be established by a doctor. Should the physician judge Annabelle to be mad, West's fortune is to go to another relative. That person's name is in an envelope in lawyer Crosly's pocket. The codicil also mentions a bejeweled necklace of great value hidden by West somewhere in his bedroom.

A uniformed guard from the local madhouse appears after midnight to announce that a homicidal lunatic has escaped. "He's a maniac who thinks he's a cat," the guard warns, "and he tears his victims as if they were canaries."

Meanwhile, the old lawyer asks to see Annabelle alone. Before Crosly can tell Annabelle the name of the other heir, a claw-like hand emerges from a secret panel behind him and drags him through it by the throat. Annabelle has her back turned to the attack, but she alerts the others that the lawyer has mysteriously vanished. When the panel slides open again, Crosly's dead body falls out. Acting on his growing love for Annabelle, Paul goes to search for the letter in the dead man's pocket and finds that the body has disappeared.

A sinister Caligari-like doctor arrives to determine Annabelle's sanity. Acting a bit mad himself, the doctor intimidates Annabelle with questions and even looks into one of her eyes as if he could see through to her brain.

Later in the evening, Annabelle discovers the West jewels behind a secret panel in the bedroom. When she retires for the night wearing the valuable necklace, another panel opens behind the bed, and the clawed hand emerges to snatch the jewels from her throat. She bolts up from bed, screaming in terror.

Meanwhile, Paul searches a passageway behind the walls. A hideous, stooped figure with one eye bulging, a pointed nose and tusk-like fangs attacks the young man. Knocking Paul unconscious, the monster emerges from the wall behind Annabelle, creeps up behind her and pounces. Paul emerges from the passageway to grab the creature and pull off his disguise.

It is Charlie Wilder, who turns out to be West's heir in the case of Annabelle's insanity. He had broken into the safe before lawyer Crosly's arrival, read the will, murdered the lawyer, stolen the letter with his name in it and even hired the asylum guard to help drive Annabelle crazy with fright. His eyes staring with madness himself, Charlie is led away along with the phony guard. Annabelle and Paul reveal their mutual love, and the other relatives smile approvingly.

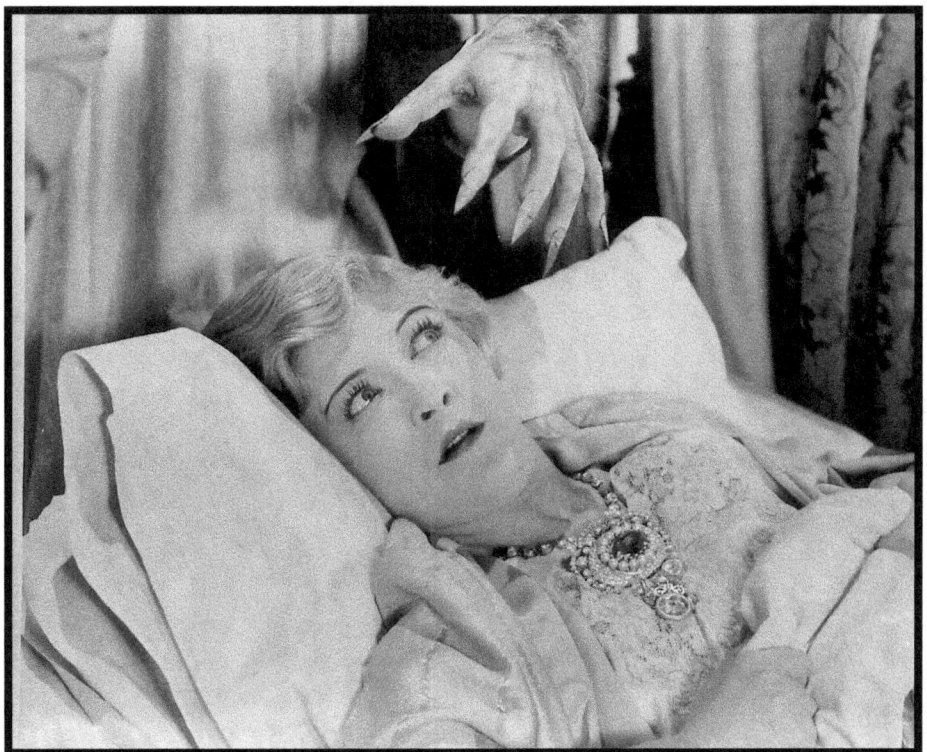

When Annabelle (Laura La Plante) retires for the night wearing the valuable necklace, a panel opens behind the bed and a clawed hand emerges to snatch the jewels from her throat in *The Cat and the Canary*. [Photofest]

Obviously, this by-now-familiar material would have to be presented with a great deal of style to work on an audience already jaded by such thrills. By hiring Paul Leni, Laemmle was assured of a director with a gift for visual elegance and creativity. Even the opening credits show cinematic imagination: gloved hands clear dusty cobwebs away to reveal the title card, *The Cat and the Canary*.

Leni's presentation of the back story of the lonely death of Cyrus West is brilliantly cinematic and brief. An Expressionistic rendering of the exterior of West's mansion, all geometric towers and strange light sources, becomes West's prison as Leni superimposes the old invalid's tiny, aging form in the middle of the house. Then the outer walls of the house dissolve into giant medicine bottles surrounding West's frail body. From behind the bottles come the superimposed flashes of giant cats, representing West's greedy relatives waiting for him to die. West recoils from them as they snarl and swat at him. It is a stunning, abstract opening, worthy of the best of German Expressionism but with a dash of brash, irreverent American humor.

Leni introduces the interior of the supposedly haunted manor by tracking down a long hallway, alive with curtains billowing from the tall windows. This forward dolly shot becomes the point of view of an unseen intruder as it dissolves to a push-in on the safe hidden in West's bedroom wall. Gloved hands emerge from behind the camera to pull two envelopes from the safe and shine the beam of a flashlight on them.

Leni moves the camera with the confidence of a master, whether in these eerie opening tracking shots or when simply following a character across the dark and cavernous rooms.

Paul Leni and Laura La Plante on the set of *The Cat and the Canary*

His framing is often eccentric, especially in close-ups of the dour housekeeper who is mostly seen from low angles.

Annabelle's examination by the sinister doctor is a symphony of expressive close shots. She is seen from the physician's point of view as he sits right in front of her, his twitching hands emerging from behind camera and moving threateningly toward her face. Her eye is seen in extreme close-up as he holds the lids open. These shots alternate with Annabelle's points of view of the doctor peering directly into the camera from behind his pebble glasses with an inscrutable but chilling glare.

Leni made *The Cat and the Canary* the same year that sound finally became wedded to the movies. But the director devised visual techniques for suggesting sound in this silent film that were more effective than the noises themselves would have been. He superimposes the ghostly image of a knocker over the faces of those hearing it so that the audience sees the source and the reaction of the listeners simultaneously. In the same way, when the rusty old clock announces the hour of 12 for the first time in 20 years, Leni superimposes the image of its hammer striking the chimes over a shot of the startled relatives. The ghostly dissolve continues over an insert of the lawyer's hands opening the will. This transparent image of the no longer dormant clock acts as a visual correlative for the iron will of the long-dead Cyrus West directing the actions of the living from his grave.

Leni's handling of the comedy elements is equally deft. He cast baby-faced Creighton Hale as the clumsy, timid Paul Jones. Born Patrick Fitzgerald on May 14, 1882 in Cork, Ireland and arriving in America on tour with an Irish theater troupe in 1913, Hale had been used as comedy relief in the Griffith films *Way Down East* and *Orphans of the Storm*. In *The Cat and the Canary*, he is able to suggest both Harold Lloyd's unlikely heroic qualities and Harry Langdon's childlike sweetness.

When Hale enters the old house for the first time, the door slams behind him, frightening him into dashing down the long, windswept hall. Leni cuts to a brief waist shot of Hale from behind, speeding down the corridor without moving his legs. The actor pedaled an unseen bicycle to achieve this effect, giving his flight a cartoon-like quality perfectly in keeping with his exaggerated cowardice. He is engagingly unashamed of his early reactions, smiling when caught hiding under the bed of Aunt Susan and Cecily and writing on an envelope, "Paul Jones, Millionaire," before hearing that he is not the heir. Even though we are told in the titles that Paul was dropped on his head as a child, he is the character who eventually acts as hero, attempting to protect Annabelle, exploring the dark passages alone and beating the killer in a fierce fight.

Laura La Plante as Annabelle does what she can with a rather colorless role. She is pretty and sweet, but neither funny nor heroic. She is mostly called upon to be mystified and threatened. Gertrude Astor as the brash and stylish Cecily is more potentially interesting but is given little to do but be a foil for the cowardice of middle-aged character actress Flora Finch's Aunt Susan.

Leni's cinematic artistry paid off: *The Cat and the Canary* was a critical and commercial success. The *Variety* of September 14, 1927 stated, "What distinguishes Universal's film version of the play... is Paul Leni's intelligent handling of a weird theme." *The New York Times* announced that the story "has been turned into one of the finest examples of motion picture art. Mr. Leni has not lost a single chance... to show what can be done with the camera. He creates excitement by pitching his camera high and low, or rolling it along. He makes you feel that you are one of the characters in the haunted house of the story. There are scenes in this piece of work that are amazing, especially those in which Mr. Leni photographs his characters through the backs of chairs and first gives one an impression that the books on a shelf are long, narrow, deep-sunken windows... while the lines of the furniture bring to mind the interior of a cathedral. This is the first time that a mystery melodrama has been lifted into the realms of art, for this feature is something that those who rave about cinematics will find delightful and those who are only anxious for a movie probably will find almost blood-curdling."

After the triumph of *The Cat and the Canary*, Paul Leni became Universal's resident specialist in the dark and the macabre. Laemmle revived plans to produce Victor Hugo's *The Man Who Laughs* on the same lavish scale as *The Hunchback of Notre Dame* with Leni at the helm and Gilbert Warrenton again as his director of photography. Unfortunately, Lon Chaney was no longer available to Laemmle, having signed an exclusive contract with Irving

Before Crosly (Tully Marshall) can tell Annabelle the name of the other heir, a claw-like hand emerges from a secret panel behind him and drags him through it by the throat in *The Cat and the Canary*. [Photofest]

Thalberg at MGM. Studio makeup man Jack Pierce created a fearsome grinning visage by using over-sized false teeth for Conrad Veidt who took over the role of Gwynplaine, the nobleman whose mouth was carved into a perpetual smile by evil Gypsies.

The resulting film was not intended as a horror movie despite the hero's disfigurement, but as a poignant and occasionally perverse period romance. Nevertheless, under Leni's Germanic direction, many of the evil supporting characters are photographed from bizarre angles with low-key lighting emphasizing their horrific traits. In the prologue, wicked King James II and his Mephistophelean jester, Barkilphedro, merrily prance down a secret passageway from the King's bedroom to a torture chamber photographed in a long, low-angle tracking shot that makes them appear as giggling demons from Hell. The moment recalls a similar scene in Leni's *Waxworks* in which Conrad Veidt as Ivan walks with his astrologer from his bedroom to the torture chamber through a hidden passage.

In *The Man Who Laughs*, there follows a grim scene in which Veidt, playing Gwynplaine's Scottish noble father, is killed in the iron maiden, much to the delight of the King and his jester. In the next scene, the nobleman's young son, his face already carved and hidden behind a scarf, is abandoned by the Gypsies in a studio created blizzard as the ship bearing the fleeing Gypsies pulls away from the dock covered in ice. As the boy wanders alone through the storm, he passes the silhouettes of bodies swaying on the gibbets. Leni creates an unforgettable frozen Hell for Gwynplaine before the story becomes more romantic and sentimental.

Most of the movie involves Gwynplaine's love for a beautiful blind girl played by Mary Philbin and their efforts to live a normal life. But a fascinating subplot features sexy Olga Baclanova as Duchess Josianna and her perverse seduction of Gwynplaine. Attracted by his ugliness, she pulls off the scarf around his deformed mouth and kisses it passionately, sexually stimulated by the aberrance of her lust. Despite offering Gwynplaine and the audience abundant glimpses of her flesh as she lolls on her bed, the Duchess fails in her attempt at corruption, and Gwynplaine flees back to his loving blind girl. The seduction scene is one of the most nakedly sensual in all silent films, doubly remarkable for appearing in an American movie from a major studio.

Conrad Veidt in *The Man Who Laughs*

Despite being better directed and equally elaborately produced, *The Man Who Laughs* did not duplicate the success of *The Hunchback of Notre Dame*. Veidt's performance lacked Chaney's warmth and especially his menace. It was passionate but too stylized for American audiences and failed to capture the popular imagination. Despite Leni's visual elegance, the film seemed long and slow. Universal attempted to liven up the proceedings by adding a Dumas-inspired swashbuckling chase and a happy ending not present in Hugo's downbeat novel, but these elements merely increased the confusion. The result was an expensive flop for Universal and reinforced the value of Lon Chaney, no matter how morbid his tastes seemed to Laemmle.

At the end of 1928, obviously attempting to duplicate the impact of *The Cat and the Canary*, Laemmle reunited director Leni, screenwriters Alfred A. Cohen and Robert F. Hill and lovely actress Laura La Plante in another adaptation of a Broadway comedy mystery hit, *The Last Warning*, from the play by Thomas F. Fallon and the source novel by Wadsworth Camp. This time, the script was further refined by J.G. Hawks who had written *A Blind Bargain* for Chaney. Hal Mohr, who had photographed *The Monster*, replaced Leni favorite Gilbert Warrenton behind the camera.

Instead of an old dark house, the spoof thrills are set in a theater which had been dark for five years since the leading man was murdered during a performance and his body vanished. A producer attempts the same play again with most of the original cast, but rehearsals are plagued by the usual arsenal of trapdoors, falling scenery and prowling menaces. The company ignores a final warning from the unseen villain not to reopen. At the first performance, the stage is plunged into darkness, and the new leading man is nearly killed at

The tragic lover Gwynplaine (Conrad Veidt) and Dea (Mary Philbin) in *The Man Who Laughs*

exactly the same moment in the play. The masked villain attempts to escape by scampering up the catwalks and swinging on a rope above the stage, but he is finally apprehended and unmasked. He turns out to be the stage manager killing on behalf of one of the owners to devalue the property for a real estate scheme.

Only the theatrical setting and Leni's skill with the camera and editing prevented *The Last Warning* from being a tepid rehash of previous mystery comedies. Leni opens the film Expressionistically as he had done with *The Cat and the Canary* with a brilliant montage of Broadway nightlife featuring superimpositions of flashing signs, dancing chorus girls and the close-up of a jazz singer in blackface. Emerging from the montage, two glowing orbs speed toward the audience, and they become the headlights of a police car racing to the front of the theater.

The impressive *Phantom of the Opera* auditorium is used again, but Leni's camera moves boldly and playfully through it as Rupert Julian's never did. A tracking shot closes in on one of the boxes when the police charge in to learn that the audience has witnessed the death of the leading man. As the show's director walks downstage to address the crowd, Leni's camera follows him from behind. The curtain falls in front of the camera, and Leni swoops under the curtain to emerge on the other side facing the audience before our view can be blocked.

In *The Last Warning*, Paul Leni takes Montagu Love, John Boles and Roy D'Arcy backstage at a theater to solve a mystery. [Photofest]

In a flashback of the murder, Leni cuts from the body lying on stage to an extreme low angle of the tiers of boxes and the audience's faces looking down in shock. The shot seems like the point of view of the corpse or perhaps his last sight before he expires.

In a long scene without intertitles, Leni's camera follows a detective as he prowls around the dressing room of the leading lady. He notices that despite the many bouquets of roses from the actress' male admirers, she has put a tiny flower onto the photograph of her director. As the detective carries one of the small blooms out of the dressing room, Leni has him walk straight toward the camera until the flower fills the screen. The detective sees that the actress wears a bloom from the same arrangement in her dress, close to her heart. This type of cinematic storytelling delights Leni, and his enjoyment is communicated to the viewer.

Years after the murder, the theater remains dark. The facade of the building becomes a sinister, staring face with round windows resembling eyes, and the empty marquee looking like a huge mouth. When Leni takes us inside, he again reveals himself to be the master of atmosphere with cobwebs in every corner, birds flying around the auditorium and paper and debris blowing through the deserted corridors.

A spider swings on a strand away from the camera, and Leni changes focus to an aging actress ascending the stairs backstage to join the company who have not seen her in five

Director Leni reveals himself to be the master of atmosphere with cobwebs in every corner in *The Last Warning*. [Photofest]

years. In close-up, she walks right into the sticky spider's web which wraps itself around her screaming face. In long shot, she steps up the stairs to the waiting crew. They turn to see a close shot of her stunned and wrinkled visage dripping with webs. Leni cuts to the startled actors from her point of view, careful to obscure the camera's lens with spider's webs.

Another expressive use of the subjective camera occurs when the same old actress emerges from under the stage on a hidden lift. Leni shows her viewpoint as the camera moves from below the boards to the huge auditorium. The sequence continues as another spider swings toward her face and ours in a point-of-view shot. The actress' eyes follow the insect as it scampers up its thread to reveal a tottering piece of heavy scenery about to fall on the leading lady. Leni puts us in the middle of the action by showing it from one character's viewpoint, and we become involved in the melodrama despite its familiarity.

As in *The Bat* and *The Cat and the Canary*, this mystery comedy edges into the terrain of the horror film when the villain is first glimpsed. After a close view of feet walking toward the camera, we move up the cape-shrouded body to reveal a hideous, decomposing face with dead, staring eyes and wild gray hair. Despite the fact that the countenance is obviously a mask, its stiffness reminds us of the corpse of the murdered actor whose ghost the cast fears is still haunting the theater.

Leni again uses superimposition to simulate sound effects as in *The Cat and the Canary*. This time he dissolves clawing hands over a scene of the terrified theater crew while they listen to mysterious scratching and moaning from the dressing room of the murdered actor which has been sealed for five years.

Appropriately for a story with a theatrical background, Leni is not afraid to use shifts in lighting which one might expect more from a stage production than a motion picture. During the revival of the play, the leading man backs toward a candlestick that proved lethal to the last actor in the part. As he reaches back for it, Leni brings down the lights on the characters in the background and intensifies the light on the candlestick, causing it to glow ominously in the foreground.

At the film's climax, Leni cuts to the escaping phantom's dizzying viewpoint as he leaps from balcony to balcony, swinging the camera on ropes to simulate the effect. Despite these efforts on Leni's part, the ending remains a disappointment with the murderer revealed as one of the least interesting supporting characters and the motive being a prosaic scheme for money by one of the theater's owners. The result barely qualifies as a horror movie, the final impression almost as tame as other mystery comedies like *The Gorilla* and *One Exciting Night*.

The Last Warning premiered the last week of 1928 and went into general release in 1929 with some added sound scenes. The film had actually been produced by Carl Laemmle, Jr., not his famous father. In 1928, as a 21st birthday present, Carl, Sr. had given over control of Universal Studios to his son. Born Julius Laemmle, the young man had reciprocated his father's generosity by changing his name to Carl Laemmle, Jr.

Shortly after Laemmle, Jr. became head of production, an erroneous story appeared in newspapers announcing that Universal had bought the rights to Stoker's *Dracula*, which they actually had not and that "the part of Count Dracula, the vampire, is stated to be admirable for Conrad Veidt." If discussions of a film of *Dracula* were taking place at Universal at this time with Veidt as the probable star, no doubt the only director on the lot to be considered for the project was Paul Leni. Unfortunately, Leni became ill with blood poisoning in the summer of 1929 and died on September 2 at the age of 44. At the time, he was working on an experimental sound short subject called *Puzzles*.

The international reputation of *Haxan* gained Benjamin Christensen an invitation to work for UFA in Berlin. There, he directed three films as well as playing the lead in Carl Dreyer's *Mikael* in 1924. Impressed with Christensen's work, Irving Thalberg lured the European director to MGM in California. At the Culver City studios, Christensen directed Norma Shearer, soon to be Thalberg's wife, in the 1926 romantic melodrama, *The Devil's Circus* and Lon Chaney in a Quasimodo-like role as a simple-minded peasant in love with a Russian noblewoman during the Revolution in 1927's *Mockery*. Although both were based on stories by Christensen, neither film allowed him to display his talent for the sinister. Both, however, were critical and commercial successes, and First National hired Christensen away from MGM to make three horror comedies inspired by the success of *The Bat* and *The Cat and the Canary*.

The first project was based on Owen Davis' play, *The Haunted House: An American Comedy in Three Acts*, but as adapted by screenwriters Richard Bee and Lajos Biro, the subtitle was mercifully dropped. Suspense writer William Irish, who would eventually create such classics as *Rear Window*, *Black Alibi*, *The Bride Wore Black* and *I Married a Dead Man* under both his own name and his pseudonym, Cornell Woolrich, provided the intertitles.

Borrowing many elements from *The Cat and the Canary*, the story of *The Haunted House* tells of an eccentric millionaire who attempts to discover which of his four heirs is the most deserving of his fortune. They each receive a sealed letter with orders not to open it until after the millionaire's demise. Of course, every one of them ignores his instructions. The letters tell of hidden money in the old man's supposedly haunted estate. Each relative descends on the location, either to find the treasure or prevent the others from doing so. Naturally, they are confronted with noises, ghosts, lunatics and other familiar ingredients of the genre. In a not-very-surprising twist ending, the monsters and madmen turn out to be actors hired by the millionaire to frighten his relatives into revealing their true characters. The handsome young man played by Larry Kent turns out to be the most honorable of the dishonorable bunch, and he is named the inheritor of the fortune.

The film now appears to be lost, but reviewers of the time were understandably impatient with its lack of originality. Mordaunt Hall called the picture, "a synthetic spook show" that was "as impossible as other stories of its kind." He did allow that the film possessed "the virtues of being mildly amusing during some of its stretches and judging by the demeanor of the audience [contained] sufficient suspense to hold the attention." Hall admired Christensen's cinematic technique but found it "more than slightly reminiscent" of Paul Leni's work on *The Cat and the Canary* the year before. Despite the dismissal of the critics, audiences still

found the mixture of comedy and horror clichés sufficiently entertaining to make *The Haunted House* a significant popular success.

For their next old dark house thriller, First National and Christensen did not turn to a popular Broadway play. In fact, the proceedings of *Seven Footprints to Satan* do not even take place in an old dark house, but rather in a huge, brightly lit modern mansion full of New York sophisticates in tuxedos and evening gowns. Screen adapters Richard Bee and William Irish based their script on a five-part serial by Abraham Merrit from the July through November 1927 issues of *Argosy—All Story* magazine. First National had immediately bought the rights to the suspenseful tale upon its publication and arranged to have it presented in book form in February 1928 to promote the film's release.

The Haunted House tells of an eccentric millionaire who attempts to discover which of his four heirs is the most deserving of his fortune. [Photofest]

Merrit was born in 1889, became a full-time newspaper journalist at the age of 18 and continued at this occupation until his death in 1943. In his spare time, he wrote eight complete novels and two unfinished ones as well as a handful of short stories. Four of the novels were science fiction, one was pure fantasy and three involved the occult.

Seven Footprints to Satan, the first of the supernatural novels, deals with a modern cult of devil worshippers in a chateau on Long Island which is overseen by a criminal who calls himself Satan. The cultists lure victims to the mansion where Satan forces them to ascend seven steps to his throne. Each step can either add or subtract years of servitude to the Prince of Darkness. Satan orders a daredevil explorer named Jim Kirkham kidnapped to face the challenge. Along with Kirkham, the Devil's minions bring a plucky girl named Eve and a stalwart Englishman. Satan finally meets his match in Kirkham who outwits the fiend with the help of his two fellow victims. As the three escape, the chateau explodes, consuming Satan and his followers.

Unfortunately, First National felt that a straight adaptation of Merrit's novel would not meet with acceptance from an audience accustomed to having its terrors explained away. The complex super-villain, Satan, who in the novel initially seemed to be the dark lord himself and later expounded grandiose schemes for world domination worthy of Sax Rohmer's Fu

Thelma Todd is given little to do in *Seven Footprints to Satan* but panic and be victimized. [Photofest]

Manchu, was changed in the scenario into a mysterious, hooded figure worshipped by the various elegant minions at his mansion.

In the beginning of the screen version, Kirkham, bored between adventures, tells his Uncle Joe that he yearns for excitement. That evening, he meets his sweetheart, Eve, at a reception at her home. As in one of Hitchcock's later thrillers, chaos erupts into the order of the wealthy when guns are fired by some of the well-dressed party guests, and a valuable diamond is stolen.

Kirkham and Eve climb into a waiting limo to notify the police, but they find the doors locked and the windows blacked out. The car takes them to the mansion of Satan where they are immediately accosted by strange characters and given clues as to the location of the jewel. Guns are waved, shadows creep across walls, and secret panels slide open and shut.

Screenwriters Bee and Irish change the ending so that the entire kidnapping, including the beautiful girl, elegant cultists, dwarf, gorilla and demons are staged by Kirkham's Uncle Joe, who himself dons a hood to play Satan. After the climax, Kirkham finds all of the bizarre actors eating together in a huge, elegant dining room, congratulating themselves for giving him the ultimate thrill and toasting his courage.

First National further sought to identify the film with other popular mystery-comedies by casting Creighton Hale, the awkward hero of *The Cat and the Canary*, as the insatiable adventurer. Hale even wears the same round spectacles as he did in the previous role. Actually, the choice of Hale turns out to be an interesting one. Rather than projecting the virile masculinity one would assume, Hale comes across as intelligent and enthusiastic; a gentleman explorer in his tuxedo and glasses; curious and courageous, despite his physical limitations. As in *The Cat and the Canary*, he reminds the viewer of Harold Lloyd with an accessible vulnerability humanizing his heroics.

Hale is strongest in his first and last scenes. Before the excitement begins, he is shown at home, practicing his shooting on a row of candles flickering in a dark garage. At the climax of the picture, Hale angrily goes face to hood with Satan who sits above him in an elaborately designed throne, flanked by turbaned African slaves and sophisticated worshippers in evening dress. Despite his terror, our hero accepts the challenge of ascending the seven lighted and numbered steps to save the life of Eve. In between these scenes, Hale is required mostly to be frightened and dumbfounded by his confusing confrontations with a sinister Oriental, a sympathetic dwarf, a threatening gorilla, an exotically beautiful devil worshipper, a doctor who looks like a well-tailored monkey and a low-browed demon on crutches. Understandably, Hale's expression in these encounters freezes into wide-eyed, open-mouthed amazement.

As in *The Haunted House*, Christensen's leading lady is Thelma Todd, one of the most beautiful and talented blondes of the silents and early talkies. She was born July 29, 1905 in Lawrence, Massachusetts. A former schoolteacher and part-time model, she entered motion pictures in 1926 after winning a beauty contest. Equally adept at both comedy and drama, Todd was cast by Christensen in all three of his First National haunted house features.

Like most heroines in this type of picture, Todd is given little to do in *Seven Footprints to Satan* but panic and be victimized, but she performs these duties radiating such platinum loveliness that she makes the clichés interesting. At one point, she seduces one of the hooded devil worshippers up the winding marble stairs so that Hale can knock him out and steal his robe. Her flirting backward glance and coy finger wave is so sweet and inviting, one almost pities the minion of the Devil after he follows her and is stripped of his hooded gown.

Released in early 1929, *Seven Footprints to Satan* took advantage of the new technology by having talking sequences, sound effects and music on Vitaphone disc. *Variety* opined, "Another of those fright producers, wholly baffling from start to finish. Elucidation of mystery which encompasses the production reveals the salacious scenes a frame-up, which doubtless accounts for its not being censored. A midget, a gorilla and a demon in the guise of Satan, who is operating a secret society, comprise some of the terrors ... All hokum."

A few months later, in April 1929, yet another of Christensen's comedy thrillers for First National arrived in theaters, this one called, *The House of Horror*. Richard Bee churned out the script based on his own story, Tom Miranda wrote the intertitles, and William Irish contributed dialogue for a talking sequence which arrived on Vitaphone disc along with sound effects and a musical score. Like *The Haunted House*, this picture is also lost.

Another retread of *The Cat and the Canary*, the story concerns the familiar demented millionaire living in a foreboding mansion surrounded by weird characters who are waiting for him to die and leave them his wealth. James Ford and Thelma Todd play wisecracking reporters who pose as a married couple to get into the estate and find a valuable missing diamond. Comic actors Chester Conklin and Louisa Fazenda are the cowardly relatives who arrive to find out if their inheritance will save their struggling antique shop. Trap doors, secret rooms, spectral visions and sliding panels abound.

Thelma Todd and Creighton Hale seem unaware they have company (Charles Gemora) in *Seven Footprints to Satan*. [Photofest]

Variety deplored the results: "*The House of Horror* is one of the weakest and most boring afterbirths of pseudo-mystery-comedy ground out of Hollywood... If the thing ever had a script Christensen apparently never knew it, judging strictly from the finished product."

After completing this third haunted house comedy for First National, Christensen returned to MGM to direct an elaborate but hardly faithful version of Jules Verne's *The Mysterious Island* starring Lionel Barrymore as the Nemo-like character Count Dakkar. Christensen also had a part in the picture. But when the Danish director went over schedule during shooting, MGM dismissed him, afraid that the already expensive film would never recoup its costs. French director Maurice Tourneur replaced Christensen, but he, too, was fired and for the same reason. The film was finally completed by Lucien Hubbard.

Disappointed with Hollywood, Christensen returned to Denmark and worked on the stage until 1939 when he wrote and directed the film, *Children of Divorce*. In the next three years, he directed a final trio of movies, none of them in the horror genre, before retiring from the screen. He acquired a license to manage a cinema, a lucrative honor reserved for aging artists in Denmark. Christensen spent the last 15 years of his life running this theater

Lionel Barrymore, Jane Daly, Lloyd Hughes and director Lucian Hubbard on the set of *Mysterious Island*. [Photofest]

in a Copenhagen suburb. He died in Denmark at the age of 80 in 1959.

Christensen's American career became the victim of a trend of stories with little possibility for achievement. Even at its best, as in *The Cat and the Canary*, the old dark house mystery-comedy was a limiting step backwards for the horror film. Deliberately relying on devices that were already clichés, this subgenre mitigated against originality. Its appeal derived from the audience's familiarity with conventions, certainly not the best strategy for creating suspense and shock. The comedy resulted from its characters' exaggerated fear at events that the audience knew were not what they seemed. Only a master of atmosphere such as Paul Leni could wring any effect out of the familiar settings and situations.

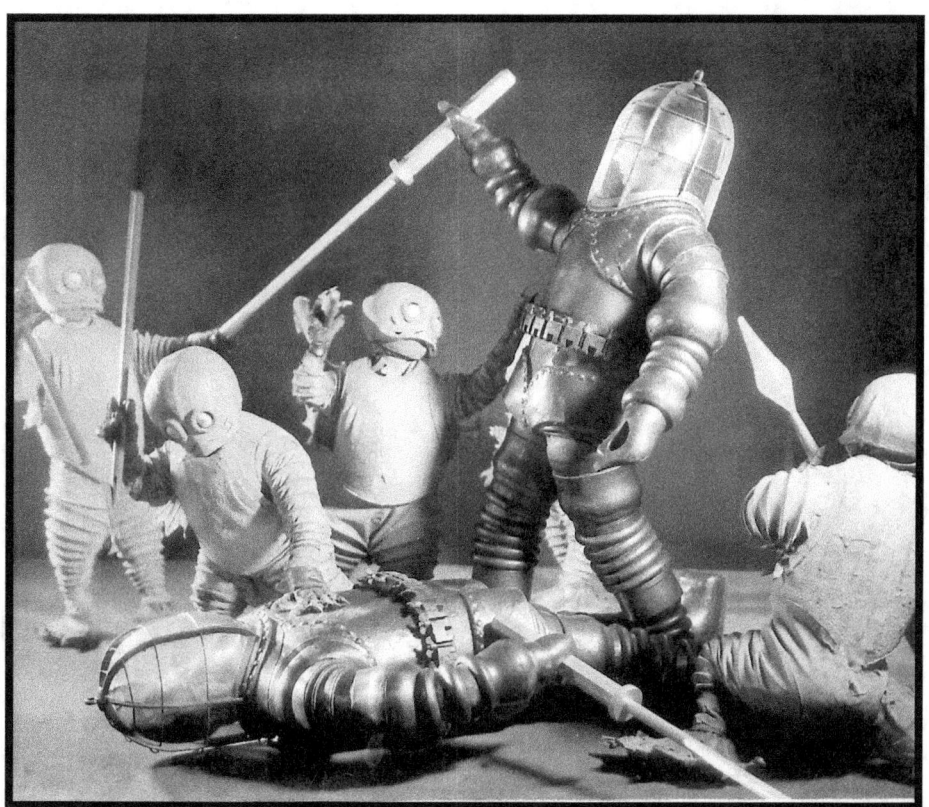

Director Christensen was fired from *Mysterious Island* for running over schedule. [Photofest]

Horror films are most potent when the audience distrusts the filmmaker not to present them with something too strong for them to handle emotionally. That element of walking on the edge of the precipice is missing from the old dark house comedy because the protagonists are less sophisticated than the audience. What frightens them seems tame and cozy to a spectator watching from the safety of his theater seat. As James Whale proved in his 1932 masterpiece, *The Old Dark House*, this genre can achieve a high degree of perversity by presenting truly disturbed and disturbing characters, but silent films never attempted such a stretch and, as a result, except for the works of Chaney and Browning, the American horror movie stagnated in the second half of the 1920s.

AFTERWORD

If this study of the horror film emphasizes the details of each individual movie over its place in an historical pattern, there is good reason. It is dangerous to try to apply, as many historians do, sweeping generalizations about an art form as unpredictable and uncontrollable as cinema. Anyone who has worked in a creative capacity in movies knows that each film has its own requirements, its own challenges, its own compromises and its own reliance on luck, even within the same genre or made by the same team.

For example, the Germans were obviously attracted to stories of the strange and supernatural, but beyond that, each German filmmaker approached the material differently and obtained different results. Except for the superficial similarities that they all lack a soundtrack and are in black and white, the look and feel of *The Cabinet of Dr. Caligari*, *The Golem*, *Nosferatu* and *Metropolis* are worlds apart. Both versions of *The Student of Prague* have the same story and events, but one is raw, primitive and relies on actual locations, while the other is cinematic, controlled and detailed. Both have their virtues, but because they are made by different people at different times in the development of the art and under different circumstances, they must be approached as separate achievements.

The films of Chaney and Browning share their creators' obsessions, talents and blind spots, but in different measures. Working at the peak of their form, the team could produce a one-of-a-kind masterpiece like *The Unknown* or a confusing misfire like *London After Midnight*. Only in retrospect do the virtues of the one and the mistakes of the other seem obvious. Both films were unconventional and attempted to sidestep some obvious requirements for easily acceptable stories, such as naturalistic plausibility. *The Unknown* manages to transcend its weaknesses by virtue of the hypnotic power of its obsessive characters and shocking events. On the other hand, *London After Midnight* becomes bogged down in complications, explanations and contrivances that never allow the characters to achieve compelling relationships with each other. Certainly, in both cases, Browning and Chaney believed that they could achieve work that was exceptional. Chaney's brilliant and painful makeup for *London After Midnight* attests to his dedication to the project. But the challenges set out by Browning were different in each case, and in *London After Midnight*, even this talented team could not overcome them.

As controlling a director as Alfred Hitchcock was also subject to the unpredictable forces confronting him while making *The Lodger*. In hindsight, the film seems like the first of a long list of Hitchcock movies presenting an innocent man accused of a crime he did not commit and chasing the actual culprit while being pursued by the police. Without knowing the facts of the film's production, one might assume that Hitchcock willingly manipulated the events in Marie Belloc Lowndes' story to present a situation he preferred. But this was not the case. At the time, Hitchcock wanted to make a more faithful adaptation of *The Lodger*, but he was forced to introduce the other elements because commercial pressures prevented his star from being guilty of the killings. Thus, chance and compromise played their part in the film's success as much as design and execution.

By the end of the 1920s, sound in films was firmly established as a commercial necessity. With the death of Lon Chaney in 1930, America's foremost apostle of the weird and morbid in cinema was gone. In Germany, financial collapse and frightening political upheavals drove filmmakers to abandon the supernatural for the grim realities of modern life. But the silent era had introduced most of the major themes of the horror film that would be revisited and explored for the remainder of the century. Manmade monsters, vampires, soulless robots,

The futuristic city of *Metropolis*

Satanists, witches, sex killers, deformed maniacs, mad scientists, giant dinosaurs, ghosts and the Devil himself had all been subjects in the medium's first two decades. The genre had even produced enduring masterpieces such as *The Cabinet of Dr. Caligari*, *The Golem*, Barrymore's *Dr. Jekyll and Mr. Hyde*, *Haxan*, *Nosferatu*, *The Phantom of the Opera*, *Metropolis*, Galeen's remake of *The Student of Prague*, *The Unknown* and *West of Zanzibar*.

The flourishing of the cinema of terror in the first decade of sound would come from an unlikely source. Carl Laemmle, Jr., whose father gave him Universal studios for his 21st birthday, loved tales of the dark and supernatural. The young mogul also admired European filmmakers and their cinematic techniques. He, more than anyone, would coalesce these ingredients at a modern American studio into "a new world of gods and monsters."

Lon Chaney in *West of Zanzibar*

SELECT BIBLIOGRAPHY

Introduction—The Conqueror Worm

Dixon, Wheeler Winston, *The Charm of Evil, The Films of Terence Fisher* (Scarecrow Press, 1991)
Matheson, Richard, *The Incredible Shrinking Man* screenplay (Universal International Pictures, 1957)
Poe, Edgar Allan, *Tales of Mystery and Imagination* (Brentano's, no date)

Chapter 1—Seeds of Terror

Eisner, Lotte H., *The Haunted Screen* (University of California Press, 1969)
Frayling, Christopher, *Nightmare, The Birth of Horror* (BBC Books, 1996)
Gifford, Dennis, *A Pictorial History of the Horror Movies* (Hamlyn Publishing Group, 1973)
Gordon, Mel, *The Grand Guignol, Theatre of Fear and Terror* (Da Capo Press, 1997)
Hardy, Phil, ed., *The Encyclopedia of Horror Movies* (Harper and Row, 1986)
Katz, Ephraim, *The Film Encyclopedia* (Harper Perennial, 1994)
Kinnard, Roy, *Horror in Silent Films, A Filmography 1886-1929* (McFarland and Co, Inc., 1995)
Luhr, William and Peter Lehman, *Authorship and Narrative in the Cinema* (G.P. Putnam's Sons, 1977)
Prawer, S.S. *Caligari's Children* (Da Capo Press, 1980)
Rhodes, Gary Don, "Bits and Pieces, American Cinema and Radio Representations of Shelley's Monster Before and During the Creation of Karloff," *Monsters from the Vault* (vol 5, no 9; Monsters from the Vault, 1999)
Rumbelow, Donald, *The Complete Jack the Ripper* (Penguin, 1988)
Stevenson, Robert Louis, (ed. Booth, B.A. and Mehew, E.), *The Letters*, volume five (July 1884-August 1887) and six (August 1887-September 1890) (Yale University Press, 1995)
Wilstach, Paul, *Richard Mansfield, the Man and the Actor* (Chapman and Hall, 1908)
Winter, William, *Life and Art of Richard Mansfield* (vol 1; Greenwood Press, Connecticut, 1910)

Chapter 2—The Dark German Soul

Aranda, Francisco, *Luis Bunuel, A Critical Biography* (Secker and Warburg, 1975)
Bogdanovich, Peter, *Fritz Lang in America* (Studio Vista, 1967)
Eisner, Lotte H. *Fritz Lang* (Oxford University Press, 1977)
Frohlich, Gustav, *Waren das Zeiten: Mein Film-Heldenleben* (Herbig, 1982)
Heiss, Lokke, *Nosferatu* laser disc commentary (Image Entertainment, 1991)
Herzog, Peter and Gene Vazzana, *Brigitte Helm: From Metropolis to Gold, Portrait of a Goddess* (Corvin, 1994)
Kracauer, Siegfried, *From Caligari to Hitler* (Princeton University Press, 1947)
McGilligan, Patrick, *Fritz Lang, Nature of the Beast* (St. Martin's Press, 1997)
Moller, Kai, ed., *Paul Wegener* (Rowohlt Verlag, 1954)

Ott, Frederick W. *The Films of Fritz Lang* (Citadel Press, 1979)
Pollock, Channing, *Harvest of My Years* (Bobbs-Merrill, 1943)
Pommer, Erich, "Carl Meyer's Debut," *A Tribute to Carl Meyer, 1894-1944* (Scala Theatre, 1947)
Rhodes, Gary Don, *Lugosi* (McFarland and Company, 1997)
Schreck, Nikolas, *The Satanic Screen* (Creation Books, 2001)
Skal, David J., *Hollywood Gothic* (W.W. Norton and Company, 1990)
Skal, David J., *The Monster Show* (W.W. Norton and Company, 1993)
Sullivan, Jack, ed., *The Penguin Encyclopedia of Horror and the Supernatural* (Viking Penguin Inc., 1986)
Veidt, Conrad, "Mein Leben," *Ufa Magazin* (vol II, no 3, Jan. 14-20, 1927)
Wells, H.G., "Mr. Wells Reviews a Current Film," *New York Times* (April 17, 1927)

Chapter 3—European Evil

Bogdanovich, Peter, *Who the Devil Made It* (Alfred A. Knopf, 1997)
Bunuel, Luis, *My Last Sigh* (Vintage Books, 1984)
DeRosa, Steven, *Writing with Hitchcock* (Faber and Faber, 2001)
McCarty, John, ed., *The Fearmakers* (St. Martin's Press, 1994)
Smith, Don G. *The Poe Cinema* (McFarland and Company, 1999)
Spoto, Donald, *The Dark Side of Genius, The Life of Alfred Hitchcock* (Little, Brown and Company, 1983)
Truffaut, Francois, *Hitchcock* (Simon and Schuster, 1967)
Tybjerg, Casper, *Haxan* DVD commentary (The Criterion Collection, 2001)

Chapter 4—America the Hideous

Cavendish, Richard, ed., *Man, Myth and Magic* vol 4, (BPC Publishing, 1970)
Glut, Donald F., *Classic Movie Monsters* (Scarecrow Press, 1978)
Kronenberger, Louis, ed., *Atlantic Brief Lives* (Little, Brown and Company, 1971)
Mank, Gregory William, *Hollywood Cauldron* (McFarland and Company, 1994)
Masello, Robert, *Raising Hell* (Berkley Publishing Group, 1996)
Nollen, Scott Allen, *Boris Karloff, A Gentleman's Life* (Midnight Marquee Press, 1999)

Chapter 5—Genius of the Grotesque

Blake, Michael F., *Lon Chaney, The Man Behind the Thousand Faces* (Vestal Press, 1990)
Blake, Michael F., *A Thousand Faces* (Vestal Press, 1995)
Blake, Michael F., *The Films of Lon Chaney* (Vestal Press, 1998)
Miller, Patsy Ruth, *My Hollywood, When Both of Us Were Young* (O'Raghailligh Ltd. Publishers, 1988)
Riley, Philip J., ed., *London After Midnight* (Cornwall Books, 1985)
Riley, Philip J., ed., *The Hunchback of Notre Dame* (Magic Image Filmbooks, 1988)
Riley, Philip J., ed., *A Blind Bargain* (Magic Image Books, 1988)
Riley, Philip J., ed., *The Phantom of the Opera* (Magic Image Books, 1999)

Chapter 6—The Weirdest Show on Earth

Fischer, Dennis, *Horror Film Directors: 1931-1990* (McFarland and Company Publishers, 1991)
Skal, David J., *Dark Carnival* (Anchor Books, 1995)

Chapter 7—The Silent Roar

Goldner, Orville and George Turner, *The Making of King Kong* (Ballantine Books, 1975)
Gottesman, Ronald and Harry Geduld, *The Girl in the Hairy Paw* (Avon Books, 1976)
Taylor, Al and Sue Roy, *Making A Monster* (Crown Publishers, 1980)

Chapter 8—Old Dark Houses

Clarens, Carlos, *Horror Movies* (Secker and Warburg, 1968)
Searles, Baird, Beth Meacham and Michael Franklin, *Reader's Guide to Fantasy* (Avon Books, 1982)
Steinbrunner, Chris and Otto Penzler, *Encyclopedia of Mystery and Detection* (McGraw-Hill, 1976)
Turner, George E., ed., *The Cinema of Adventure, Romance and Terror* (ASC Press, 1989)

Index

39 Steps, The 94
Ace of Hearts 122, 124
Adams, Claire 120, 123
Alaune (novel) 24, 78, 80-83
Alaune 26
Alien 11
Androschin, Hans 65
Ankerstjerne, Johan 85
Arbuckle, Fatty 130
Armitage, Frederick S. 18
Arnold, Jack 12
Arthur, Johnny 197, 198, 200, 201
Astor, Gertrude 209
Aukor, Adolf 108
Austin, George 197, 198, 200
Avenging Conscience, The 26-29
Baclanova, Olga 211
Baggot, King 101, 102
Balcon, Michael 92, 95-96
Balderston, John L. 167
Barrymore, Ethel 104
Barrymore, John 15, 21, 101-108, 226
Barrymore, Lionel 104, 108-111, 179, 222
Barrymore, Maurice 104, 106
Bartning, Otto 70
Bat, The 196, 201-205, 215, 216
Baxter, Warner 179, 182
Beast from 20,000 Fathoms 12
Beauty and the Beast 140
Bee, Richard 216, 217, 221
Beery, Wallace 193, 194, 195
Belajeff, Olga 63
Belling, Rudolf 33
Bells, The 108-111
Benham, Harry 100
Beranger, Clara S. 102, 103, 104
Bergner, Elisabeth 66
Bernheim, Julius 141, 152
Biebrach, Rudolf 38
Binet, Alfred 21
Birds, The 9, 96
Biro, Lajos 216
Birth of a Nation 27, 43

Black Cat, The 10
Black Orchids 114
Blackbird, The 159
Blackton, J. Stuart 109
Blind Bargin, A 125-130, 133, 212
Blom, August 84
Blyth, James 125
Boese, Carl 44-47
Bogdanovich, Peter 40, 94, 95, 96
Boilieau, Pierre 63
Boles, John 213
Bonomo, Joe 136
Booth, Elmer 156
Borzage, Frank 110, 132
Bride of Frankenstein, The 72, 117
Brides of Dracula 12
Bronson-Howard, George 141
Brood, The 11
Brooks, Louise 81
Brown, Clarence 141, 143
Brown, Harry D. 135
Browning, Alice 157, 158
Browning, Tod 46, 126, 130, 141, 142, 156-167, 172-184, 223, 225
Brunton, Robert 122
Bryson, James 155
Bunuel, Luis 76, 99
Burton, Tim 10
Cabinet of Dr. Calagari 9, 10, 34-44, 48, 51, 56, 61, 62, 63, 65, 66, 67, 78, 80, 225, 226
Camp, Wadsworth 212
Carmen, Jewel 197, 204
Carminati, Tullio 205
Carpenter, Grant 143
Carr, John Dickson 63
Carre, Ben 144, 155
Cat and the Canary, The 196, 201, 205-210, 212, 213, 215, 216, 217, 220, 222, 223
Cayatte, Jeanne 139
Chadwick, I.E. 108
Chaney, Creighton 118
Chaney, Lon 9, 17, 118-155, 156-184,

232

194, 196-201, 203, 211, 212, 216, 223, 225
Chatrian, Alexandre 108
Chautard, Emile 132
Christensen, Benjamin 84-90, 216, 217, 220, 221, 222, 223
Christy, Howard Chandler 119
City Girl 59
Clawson, Elliot 143, 144, 175
Coeur fidele 96
Cohen, Alfred A. 212
Collier, Willie 121
Comstock, Daniel 149
Conklin, Chester 152, 222
Conqueror Worm, The 9
Conway, Jack 184
Corman, Roger 11-12
Craft, The 10
Crawford, Joan 161, 165
Creighton, Cleva 118
Cronenberg, David 11
Crosland, Alan 130
Crowley, Aleister 111
Cruze, James 100, 108
Curse of the Demon 10
Curtis, Catherine 190
Curtiz, Michael 80
Cutts, Graham 95
D'Arcy, Roy 213
Dagover, Lil 35, 39, 41-42, 67
Daly, Jane 176, 222
Dangerous Flirt, The 158
Davis, Owen 216
Dawley, Herbert M. 188, 189, 190, 191
Dawley, James Searle 16, 18-19, 21
Day of Faith, The 157
Day of Wrath 90
Day, Marceline 170, 174
de Lorde, Andre 21-22
de Vonde, Charles 175
Dean, Priscilla 156, 157
Deane, Hamilton 58, 167
Delgado, Marcel 190, 191, 192, 195
Delluc, Louis 96
DeMille, Cecil B. 139

Der Mude Tod 67
Deveuve, Catherine 12
Devil Rides Out, The 10, 12
Die Nibelungen 68-71
Dieckmann, Enrico 49, 52, 57
Dieterle, William 59, 63, 139
Dinosaur and the Missing Link, The 187
Dismute, Paul 162
Dowling, William 193
Doyle, Arthur Conan 13, 185, 186, 189, 190, 191
Dr. Jekyll and Mr. Hyde (1908) 13, 16, 40
Dr. Jekyll and Mr. Hyde (1913) 101
Dr. Jekyll and Mr. Hyde (1920) 101-108, 226
Dr. Jekyll and Mr. Hyde (novel) 13-14, 100
Dr. Mabuse 68
Dr. Mabuse, The Gambler 68
Dracula (novel) 49, 57-58, 172, 175, 182, 216
Drew, Georgiana 104
Drew, John 109
Dreyer, Carl 90, 216
Dunning, C. Dodge 192
Dupont, Ewald André 99
Earles, Harry 158
Edeson, Arthur 194, 202, 203, 205
Eisenstein, Sergei 38, 62
Epstein, Jules 96-99
Erckmann, Emile 108
Erickson, Knute 197
Ewers, Hanns Heinz 23-24, 32, 45, 78, 80, 82, 83
Exorcist, The 12
Fairbanks, Douglas 143, 156, 194, 201, 202
Fairfax, Marion 191
Fall of the House of Usher, The (film) 98-99
"Fall of the House of Usher, The" (short story) 96-97
Fallon, Thomas F. 212
Farnham, Joseph 181

Faust 56, 59
Fazenda, Louisa 205, 222
Feuillade, Louis 84
Fish, George F. 14-15
Fisher, Terence 12
Fitzroy, Emily 205
Florey, Robert 46
Fly, The 11
Fontaine, Joan 93
Ford, James 222
Forepaugh, Luella 14-15
Four Devils 59
Frankenstein (1910) 16-21, 48
Frankenstein (novel) 13, 23, 29, 195
Frankenstein 9, 47, 49, 117
Freaks 181
Frenzy 94
Freund, Karl 46, 67, 70, 71
Frohlich, Gustav 72-74, 76
Frowlich, Finn 133
Galeen, Hanrik 26, 32, 49-50, 59, 61, 78-80, 82-83, 226
Gance, Abel 99
Gance, Margaret 98, 99
Garbo, Greta 104
Garnett, Tay 135
Gein, Ed 10
Gemora, Charles 221
George, John 163
Ghost of Slumber Mountain, The 188, 190
Gibbons, Cedric 162
Gillespie, A. Arnold 162
Godsol, F.J. 124
Godzilla 12
Goetzke, Bernhard 67
Goldbeck, Willis 114
Goldburg, Jesse J. 29
Goldwyn, Samuel 42-43, 119, 121, 124
Golem and the Dancing Girl, The 26, 32
Golem, The (1914) 25, 32
Golem, The (1920) 26, 44-49, 56, 62, 67, 78, 225, 226
Gordon, Kilbourn 175
Grant, Cary 93
Grasso, Alfred 130, 132, 137, 141

Grau, Albin 49-50, 52, 55, 57, 74
Grey Lady, The 15-16
Griffith, D.W. 13, 26-29, 38, 43, 65, 109, 139, 156, 167, 193, 196, 201, 209
Grune, Karl 66
Gulliver's Travels 70
Hale, Creighton 209, 220, 221
Hall, Charles D. 205
Halloween 10
Hammeras, Ralph 191, 192
Hands of Orlac 40, 64-66
Hastings, Hazel 118
Haunted House, The 216-217, 221
Hawks, J.G. 126, 212
Haxan 84-90, 216, 226
Hayden, Charles J. 108
Hays, Will 130, 164
He Who Gets Slapped 141, 142
Head of Janus, The 51
Hedren, Tippi 79
Helm, Brigitte 71-76, 78, 81-83
Hill, Robert F. 205, 212
Hitchcock, Alfred 12, 29, 65, 79, 91-96, 164, 225
Hoffmann, E.T.A. 23, 61
Holland, Cecil 194
Hopwood, Avery 196
Horror of Dracula 12
Houdini, Harry 189, 190
Hound of the Baskervilles (1909) 13, 15
House of Horror, The 221, 222
House of Wax 9
Howard, James L. 133
Hoyt, Harry O. 193, 195
Hubbard, Lucian 222
Hudson, Earl 191, 193, 195
Hughes, Lloyd 193, 222
Hugo, Victor 130, 138, 139, 143, 210, 212
Hunchback of Notre Dame, The 130-139, 141, 143, 155, 157, 210, 211
Hunte, Otto 70
Hunter, Harrison 202
Huppertz, Gottfried 75
Hurt, John 11
Huston, Walter 175

Iles, Francis 93
Incredible Shrinking Man, The 12
Ingram, Rex 26, 114, 116-117
Invasion of the Body Snatchers, The 12
Irish, William 216, 217, 221
Irving, H.B. 108
Irving, Henry 13, 108
Jackman, Fred W. 191
James, Walter 197, 198
Jannings, Emil 63, 66
Janowitz, Hans 33-34, 36-37, 40-41, 51
Jaws 11
Julian, Rupert 142, 143, 145, 147, 153, 154, 213
Kalmus, Herbert 149, 150
Karloff, Boris 9, 17, 39, 46, 110-111, 198
Kauffer, E. McKnight 96
Kemper, Colin 202
Kenyon, Albert 196
Kenyon, Charles 120
Klein-Rogge, Rudolf 68, 71-72, 74
Knight, Charles R. 192
Kongo 175
Kortner, Fritz 66
Krampf, Guenther 65, 78
Krauss, Werner 37, 39, 63, 78, 111
Kubin, Alfred 37
La Belle Nivemaise 96
La Plante, Laura 207, 208, 209, 212
Laemmle, Jr., Carl 142, 215, 216, 226
Laemmle, Sr., Carl 100, 101, 130, 131, 136, 141, 142, 143, 148, 150, 152, 154, 155, 205, 207, 210, 215
LaMarr, Barbara 114
Lang, Fritz 40, 46, 59, 66-78, 82-83, 92
Larsen, Viggo 15-16
Last Laugh, The 46. 58, 80, 99
Last Warning, The 212-216
Laughton, Charles 139
Lehr, Abe 119
Leni, Paul 61-62, 78, 83, 205, 207, 208, 209, 210, 211, 213, 214, 215, 216, 217, 223
Leopard Man, The 22
Leroux, Gaston 139, 140, 141, 143, 144, 146, 202
Lewis, Leopold 108
Lewis, Ralph 114
Lewis, Sheldon 108
Life Without Soul 29-31
Light in the Dark 136
Lloyd, Frank 132
Lodger, The 91-96, 225
London After Midnight 159, 167-175, 225
Lonergan, Philip 120
Lorre, Peter 46
Lost World, The 185-195, 202
Love, Bessie 188. 193
Love, Montagu 213
Lowe, Edward T. 131
Lowndes, Marie Belloc 91, 93, 94, 225
Lubitsch, Ernst 66
Lucas, Georges 98
Lucas, Jean 98
Lugosi, Bela 9
Lunatics in Power 22
Lunatics, The 23
Mack, Willard 196
Magician, The 26, 111-117
Man Who Laughs, The 141, 142, 210-212
Mann, Ned Herbert 202, 203
Mansfield, Richard 13-14, 106, 122
March, Fredric 15, 104
Mark of the Vampire 175, 182
Marnie 79
Marshall, Tully 210
Mathers, MacGregor 111, 112
Matheson, Richard 12
Mathis, June 114
Maugham, William Somerset 113
May, Joe 67
Mayer, Carl 33, 34, 36,37, 40,41, 58,59, 83
Mayer, Louis B. 107, 108, 114, 132
McConville, Bernard 141, 143
McKee, Raymond 126
McRae, Henry 101
McWade, Edward 197, 200
Meinert, Rudolf 37-38

Méliès, Georges 13, 186
Menzies, William Cameron 202, 203
Merrit, Abraham 217, 219
Metenier, Oscar 21
Metropolis 46, 68-78, 92, 225, 226
Milland, Ray 11
Miller, Patsy Ruth 133-135, 136, 147, 161
Miller, Virgil 135
Miracle Man, The 118, 119, 124
Miranda, Tom 221
Mockery 212
Mohr, Hal 198, 212
Monster, The 142, 196-201, 212
Montagu, Ivor 95-96
Montana. Bill 194
Moore, Owen 182
Morris, Governeur 119, 124
Mountain Eagle, The 92, 95
Mummy, The 9, 39, 46
Munch, Edvard 52
Murders in the Rue Morgue 46
Murnau, F.W. 50-59, 65-66, 78, 80, 83, 92, 97, 99
Mysterious Island 222-233
Mysterious X, The 84
Mystery of the Wax Museum, The 10
Mystery of the Yellow Room, The 139
Nagel, Conrad 167, 169
Narcejac, Thomas 63
Nerz, Ludwig 66
Newhard, Robert E. 135
Niblo, Fred 114, 132
Night of Vengeance 84
Nitzchmann, Erich 78
Nolan, Mary 178, 179, 182
North by Northwest 96
Nosferatu 50, 52-58, 67, 78, 80, 95, 97, 130, 167, 225, 226
Notorious 96
Novarro, Ramon 114
Novello, Ivor 93, 95
O'Brien, Willis 186, 187, 188, 189, 190, 191, 192, 194, 195
Ogle, Charles 17-20
Old Dark House, The 223

Olmsted, Gertrude 199, 200
Osborn, Thomas 84
Outside the Law 126, 155, 157
Overbaugh, Roy 102
Packard, Frank 118
Pain, Barry 125
Pasha, Kalla 180
Penalty, The 119-124
Perry, Harvey 136
Phantom of the Opera, The 9-10, 140-155, 175, 205, 213, 226
Philbin, Mary 145, 147, 148, 149, 151, 153, 155, 161, 211, 212
Phillips, Augustus 16, 18
Picture of Dorian Gray, The 102
Pierce, Jack 17, 33, 145, 210
Pit and the Pendulum, The 11-12
Pleasure Garden, The 92-93
Poe, Edgar Allan 9, 11, 13, 22-23, 26-30, 61, 83, 96-99, 100, 105, 139, 140, 165, 196
Poelzig, Hans 45, 62
Poelzig, Marlene 45
Polanski, Roman 12
Pollard, Harry A. 156
Pollock, Channing 76
Pommer, Erich 36-40, 42-43, 67-71, 74
Porten, Henny 38
Porter, Edwin S. 18, 187
Power, Sr., Tyrone 142
Premature Burial, The 11
Price, Vincent 9
Psycho 10-12, 94, 96
Rabid 11
Rasp, Fritz 76
Rat, The 95
Raven, The 9
Rear Window 96
Reimann, Walter 37
Reinhardt, Max 23, 39, 44-46, 50, 55, 61
Renard, Maurice 63, 66
Repulsion 12
Reville, Alma 95
Richter, Kurt 45
Riefenstahl, Leni 77
Rinehart, Mary Roberts 196, 201, 202

Rittau, Gunther 70, 73
Road to Manderlay, The 159
Robertson, Clifford 110, 119
Robertson, John Stuart 102, 104, 106, 107, 132
Rohrig, Walter 37
Rosenthal, Lisa 67-68, 70
Rothacker, Watterson, R. 186, 189, 190, 191, 195
Rye, Stellen 24, 25, 44, 78, 79
Saboteur 94
Salmonova, Lyda 25, 32, 44, 45
Scanners 11
Scheider, Roy 11
Schenck, Joseph M. 197, 201
Schreck, Max 53-55, 57-58
Schrock, Raymond L. 143, 152, 154
Schufftan, Eugen 70, 71
Scott, Ridley 11
Sedgwick, Ernest 152, 154
Seeber, Guido 46
Seigmann, George A. 156
Seitz, John F. 114
Selig, William N. 14, 15, 16, 100, 101
Seven 10
Seven Footprints to Satan 217-222
Shadow of a Doubt 96
Shea, Thomas E. 15
Shearer, Norma 131, 216
Sheehan, Poore 131
Sheeley, E.E. 144
Sheeley, Elmer E. 133
Shelley, Mary 13, 16, 19, 23, 29
Shivers 11
Shock, The 155
Shraeder, Paul 96
Siegel, Don 12
Silence of the Lambs 9
Silk Stocking Sal 158
Siodmak, Curt 75
Sleepy Hollow 10
Smalley, Philip 142
Smiley, Joseph W. 30, 31
Snow, Marguerite 100
Son of Dracula 75
Sondheim, Stephen 11
Sorina, Alexandra 66
Spearing, James 141, 143
Spellbound 94
Spiders, The 40, 67
Spielberg, Steven 11
Squires, J.C. 167
Stannard, Eliot 93
Stevenson, Garcia 59
Stevenson, Robert Louis 13-15, 51-52, 100, 102, 103, 104, 107,
Stoker, Bram 49-50, 57, 97, 216
Stoker, Florence 57-58, 95, 167
Stoker, Noel 57
Stone, Lewis 193
Stranger on a Train 94, 96
Student of Prague, The (1913) 24, 26, 28, 32, 44
Student of Prague, The (novel) 23, 78
Student of Prauge, The (1920) 40, 79-80, 82, 225, 226
Sullivan, Thomas Russell 13-14, 100, 104
Sunrise 56, 59
Suspicion 93, 94
Sweeney Todd 11
Talmadge, Norma 197
Taylor, Julia Marie 121
Terry, Alice 114
Terry, Ruth 116
Texas Chain Saw Masscare, The 10
Thalberg, Irving 130, 131, 132, 136, 137, 141, 142, 144, 158, 164, 167, 175, 210, 216
Thanhouser, Edwin 100
Them! 12
Thief of Baghdad 202
Thing, The 12
Thunder 184
Ticheno, Edna 170, 171, 174
Todd, Thelma 219, 220, 221, 222
Toland, Gregg 202
Torrance, Ernest 137
Tourneur, Jacques 22
Tourneur, Maruice 17, 22, 132, 144, 222
Tracy, Spencer 15, 104
Trap, The 135

Treasure Island (1920) 17, 144
Trifling Women 114
Tripp, June 93, 95
Truffaut, Francois 96
Tucker, George Loane 118
Turszinsky, Walter 38
Ullman, Sidney 133, 144
Ulmer, Edgar G. 10
Unholy Three, The 158, 159, 184
Unknown, The 159-167, 174, 175, 179, 183, 225, 226
Vale, Vola 153
Valentino, Rudolph 114, 202
Van Enger, Charles 147, 148, 150
Varieté 99
Veidt, Conrad 35-37, 39-42, 51, 60, 62-66, 78-80, 210, 211, 212, 216
Verne, Jules 61, 222
Vertigo 96, 164
Videodrome 11
Virgin of Stamboul, The 156
Voices of the City 122, 124, 128
von Harbou, Thea 67-69, 72, 77, 83
von Seyffertitz, Gustav 109
von Sternberg, Josef 59
von Stroheim, Erich 114, 130, 131, 132, 141, 142, 147, 164
Wagenhals, Lincoln A. 202
Wagner, Fritz Arno 52, 67
Wainwright, J.G. 186
Walsh, Raoul 132
Walthall, Henry B. 27-28, 167, 169, 170, 172
Ward, Rosco 180
Warm, Herman 37-38, 80
Warrenton, Gilbert 205, 210, 212
Waxworks 59-63, 78, 205, 211
Webber, Lois 154
Wegener, Paul 23-26, 32-34, 39-40, 44-49, 78-79, 81-83, 114-116
Wells, H.G. 75, 195
Werewolf, The 101
Wescott, W.A. 149
West of Zanzibar 175-184, 226
West, Roland 142, 196, 197, 201, 202, 203, 204
Whale, James 48, 72, 117, 223
Where East is East 184
Which Woman 156
White Tiger, The 157
Wicked Darling, The 156
Wiene, Robert 10, 38, 40-42, 44, 63, 66, 83
Wilbur, Crane 196
Wilde, Oscar 102, 103
Willard, John 196, 205
Williams, Frank 192
Williams, Grant 12
Witchcraft Through the Ages (see Haxan)
Withey, Chet 132
Wolf Man, The 12, 75
Wong, Anna May 157
Woolf, C.M. 92, 95
Worsley, Wallace 121-125, 128, 132-137
Wray, John 152
Young, James 108, 109, 111
Young, Waldemar 175

About the Author

Steve Haberman has written several screenplays including *Dracula: Dead and Loving It* (1995) and *Life Stinks* (1991) for Mel Brooks. He began his Hollywood career as a story board artist for *Midnight Blue* (1996) and *Return to Horror High* (1987) and pictorial consultant on *Girls Just Want to Have Fun* (1985). He is currently working on his directorial debut on *Not Human*, a horror thriller about scientists trapped in a sealed biodome with a dangerous, genetically created being in female form, from a script he wrote with Rudy DeLuca for Brooksfilm.

*If you enjoyed this book
please call, write or e-mail for a free catalog.
Midnight Marquee Press, Inc.
9721 Britinay Lane
Baltimore, MD 21234
410-665-1198
www.midmar.com*

www.ingramcontent.com/pod-product-compliance
Lightning Source LLC
Chambersburg PA
CBHW071318110526
44591CB00010B/934